SPEECH!

How Language Made Us Human

Simon Prentis

hogsaloft

ISBN: 978-1-9168935-4-2 (paperback)

Cover image: Brijith Vijayan
Cover design: Jamurai
Formatting: ebookpbook

Published by hogsaloft
www.hogsaloft.com

For Lisa, Julian, Oscar
and their generation.
May you make a better
job of it than we have...

...and to Tina and Tyler –
you know the reasons why!

(& with thanks to Andrew
for his eagle eyes)

石の上にも三十年

"All truth passes through three stages.
First, it is ridiculed. Second, it is violently opposed.
Third, it is accepted as being self-evident."

PRELUDE: The Question

"I was educated once – it took me years to get over it."

– Mark Twain

Sometimes, finding the right question is the hardest part. In his book *Guns, Germs and Steel*, Jared Diamond explains how he was inspired by a question put to him by Yali, a local politician in Papua New Guinea: *Why do the white people have all the cargo, and we brown people have none?* It took him 25 years to come up with a convincing answer. The question that drives this book took me 25 years to even arrive at: *Why are humans so different to all other animals?* Like the language we use to frame it, that can seem too obvious to ask. But the answer is rooted in words, and turns out to have been hiding in plain sight.

The winding road that led me to it goes back to my earliest experiences of interpreting Japanese. After nearly eight years spent living in Japan, learning the language and preparing myself for a professional role, what I discovered when I first began doing it for real was a surprise: I would frequently find myself in situations, especially in business settings, where both sides were privately being disdainful of each other – implying that the other side couldn't be trusted because they were 'foreign', and generally casting aspersions on their way of doing business, or other 'strange' customs.

It was a very odd sensation to be caught between two worlds (sometimes even in the same room!) where both parties would be talking to me in a language the other party couldn't understand, yet both were taking me into their confidence: not just because I could understand their language, but because my familiarity with their culture led them to feel I was one of 'them' – unlike the people they were paying me to talk to. It was particularly odd because neither party knew the others were doing exactly the same thing – and it wasn't really my place to tell them. I was just a hired hand.

It quickly became obvious that in most cases their mistrust and disparagement of 'the other side' was due to ignorance and/or lack of interest in the other culture – an inability or even just an unwillingness to put themselves in the shoes of anyone who'd grown up in a different environment. To some extent, that's forgivable: it can be hard to understand something you've never experienced. But the default reaction so often seemed to be that if they'd never heard of it, it didn't count. Rather remarkably (as I thought), this tendency was most noticeable amongst the more 'educated' of the people I was dealing with: perhaps because the more you focus on the sophistication of your own culture, the more you suspect its absence in another, as the potential gap seems even greater.

At first my work was mainly limited to interaction between Japan and the UK, both island nations with long and proudly independent cultures that tend to foster a sense of entitlement. But as I grew more experienced – and more in demand – I began being asked to interpret in countries where I would either be working with people from other cultures who spoke English, or through a second interpreter. In these situations too, I often saw the same thing happening. Unless individuals make the effort to get outside their cultural box, people from every background – from every unique group – seem to stay locked into their assumptions, unwilling to accept the 'other'.

So I started thinking about writing a book that would draw on my experiences to try and highlight these rather absurd attitudes. It was really quite ridiculous to see two (or more) groups of people all priding themselves on the superiority of their own culture without realising that they were being privately patronised by the very people they were looking down on – and for exactly the same reasons. My initial working title for the book was 'Far East, Far West' – that seemed a neat way of summarising the chasm in perception – and as I began to move in more exalted circles, I was tempted to add the phrase 'Far Out' into the mix: celebrity is by no means immune to cultural snobbism.

My main concern was to put the myth to rest. I wanted to show that we're all doing the same thing, just differently, and there's no reason why one way of doing it should be better than any other – apart from the fact that you're just used to it, which is a pretty poor excuse. Whether it's language, food, art, religion or sport, 'your' culture is only just another frozen accident of history careening down the hill of time, studded and scarred with random shards picked up along the way – and nothing to feel superior or proud about. As an Australian friend once put it when I ran my thesis by him: "Mate, we have a saying for that back home: '*Same sh*t, different bucket*'." That nearly became the title of the book.

Except that there's more to it than that. Much more. An experience I kept having, often (again) with people who fancied themselves a cut above, was for them to use a word they considered very specific to their own language (such as '*soothsayer*') and wonder how it was going to be possible to translate that. Not because they didn't think I would know the word, but because they genuinely thought there might not be a word for it in the other language, because, you know, there probably isn't. This would happen just as frequently in both languages; each culture has its own special words that it believes are uniquely theirs. Yet that's just making a virtue of ignorance: language is limited only by the intelligence of its speaker – all of us can say what we need to, in any language.

That started me thinking more deeply about words, where they come from, how we came to have them in the first place, and why we are the only animals that do – as our ability to speak is clearly our most valuable trait. But I soon discovered there was little in the literature to help me: its origin is still considered to be one of the deep mysteries of humanity, something that most academics seem to believe just happened along one day thanks to some fortunate yet equally unexplained 'cognitive revolution'. There's little discussion of what might have actually caused that – just a lot of neurobiological flailing in the dark, and endless speculation about the nature of grammar.

That's not so surprising: for most of history it's not really a question we've been asking ourselves much – like the air we breathe, language was just a gift from the gods and there was no more to be said. But the publication of *On the Origin of Species* threw a spanner into the works: like everything else, it was now clear that language must have evolved – but though Darwin realised it was the key to the puzzle of what he called our "god-like intellect", he was at a loss to explain it. Because if the secret of evolution was 'descent with modification' there didn't seem to be anything language could have descended or been modified from: there wasn't anything like it in the rest of the animal kingdom.

But perhaps we've been looking in the wrong place. In their obsession with unravelling the intricacies of grammar, the linguists have had the cart before the horse: Chomsky's convoluted syntactic structures have missed the trees for the wood. Grammar is of no use without words, as anyone who's struggled to learn a foreign language knows. The first step on the path from animal communication to language would not – and could not – have been the emergence of grammar. For the scaffolding of consciousness is built of words; and it's in the structure of words that we must look to find the crucial clue.

So that's where I decided the story had to begin. If language is what defines us, we need to focus on the nuts and bolts: how and why the trick of speech works so well for us. Because it's important to realise just how simple – and how arbitrary – the process really is, and remember that there's nothing magical about the actual sounds of the words we use – just modified grunts, after all. But the origin of speech is not the only aspect we need to consider, vital though that is. The really important thing is what we do with it, as the words of those we look up to – our leaders, whether cultural, religious or political – can determine the course and even the outcome of our lives. To really understand the effect language has on us, it's the origin of speeches we need to look to.

That too, nearly became the title of the book. *On the Origin of Speeches.* The pun was almost irresistible. But the picture is bigger still. For language is not just something that's more useful in the way that a longer neck or a webbed foot is to the individual who happens to inherit it. Being able to talk is not just an incremental advantage, like an extra toe, or even colour vision. The ability to communicate in endless, unlimited detail with other individuals is an utterly transformative change: it's a complete paradigm shift, a singularity in the evolution of life. Truly, language is what makes us human.

And so that is the story of the book. How we come to have language in the first place, why it gives us such an advantage, what it's done to us, how we've used it, and where it takes us from here – for our journey is not yet done. Language may be what makes us human, but the world is still divided by our misplaced faith in the superiority of certain cultures, religions and identities, especially our own: we have yet to escape from the illusions of exceptionalism that prevent us from realising that in the end, we're all in this together.

The first half of the book looks at what language is and how it works (Chapter 1), and the inevitable consequences of adopting it: the emergence of social culture (Chapter 2), religion (Chapter 3) and a sense of identity (Chapter 4). At the half-way point, Chapter 5 counts the ways we've found to reconnect with our pre-verbal selves: antidotes to the seductive traps of language. The final three chapters then focus on the more tangible benefits of our journey with words: how science has led us to a securer understanding of the nature of the universe and our place within it (Chapter 6), why the power of knowledge drives the spread of more effective media (Chapter 7), and where we must now go if we are to use that knowledge to save ourselves from ourselves (Chapter 8).

For in fact, we have no choice. Language is all about communication – and as our remarkable roller-coaster ride from hunter-gatherer to urban hipster races to a critical mass of interconnection, its logic will eventually become compelling.

Enjoy the book.

Simon Prentis, London, 2021

CONTENTS

WHO: The Trap of Identity

ESCAPE: Sex, Drugs & Music

INFORMATION: The Appliance of Science

WHAT: The Trick of Speech

"A mind enclosed in language is in prison."

– Simone Weil

Our mysterious magic

Have you ever lost your voice? If so, you'll know how frustrating it is not being able to tell people what you want, to express your feelings, or to communicate anything beyond what's possible with simple gestures. We take language so much for granted that we don't normally notice how completely we rely on it; but try not saying anything for an hour next time you're with friends. It's a hard thing to do. Not being able to speak means you begin to get left out of the loop, simply because you can't join in the conversation. Without a voice, your presence just slowly starts to fade away.

But at least you can still understand what's being said. Imagine you couldn't understand, either. That's what it's like to find yourself living in a culture whose language you don't speak. You're stuck in your own world, cut off from the very thing that makes us human. Without language we are back to our animal origins, able only to show our most basic feelings. We start out like that, after all. As any parent knows, until they learn to talk, a child is no more than a rather cute, very helpless pet. Whatever it may have been wrong about, the Bible was certainly right about this: *in the beginning was the Word*.

It all begins with words because without them we would simply be what our genes alone would make us – a vulnerable, largely hairless species of ape trapped with our own sensations, left guessing at what everyone else is feeling. No wonder most animals are so jumpy. With no language, you're on your own, unprotected from the worst fears of your imagination, limited to creature comforts and animal cunning. Without words to define and discuss them, there can be no beginnings, no ends, and no way of measuring the spaces in between – and so no culture, no technology, no civilization. Genetically, all that seems to separate us from our primate cousins is a tiny sliver of goo, a mere percentage point of a genome that we largely share with most of the other creatures on our planet – yet the difference between a chimpanzee and a cosmonaut is literally astronomical. DNA doesn't even begin to explain that difference.

Language, however, does.

That's because language is the killer app that trumps everything else. It's the killer app because it allows us to share ideas and pool our awareness as a species. To adapt a famous image, if I have an apple and you have an orange and we exchange them, we still have just one fruit each. But if I have an idea and you have another idea and we exchange them, then we each have two ideas. It's the magic of words that makes that possible. Multiply that process across a whole community, and you suddenly have an exponential growth in consciousness. Being born into a world with language means we are no longer limited to our own individual ideas and perceptions, but have potential access to all the ideas of our community – effectively creating a group brain. It's ideas that make the difference, and language is what allows us to transmit them.

As tricks go, it's pretty impressive. Just by making a few noises with my mouth, I can transfer a thought from the inside of my head to yours without having to do anything else. I don't have to make any gestures, helpful though they might be. I don't need any special equipment. You don't even have to be able to see me. In fact, you don't even have to know who I am. That's powerful magic, and it doesn't stop there. Through the extended magic of writing, with language I can travel in time, communicating ideas to you – as I am now – long after I originally thought them, wrote them down, or had them published. I may already be dead by the time you read them; it doesn't affect the communication. You don't even need to be able to speak the language I wrote in – you could be reading this in translation, and still be able to understand what I mean.

Like all magic, its power to amaze relies on the fact that we're not really aware of how the trick works. The trouble with language is that it comes so easily to us. Whatever country or culture we are born into, we have mastered our mother tongue by the time we start school, have picked up a perfect native accent along the way – and yet have absolutely no idea how we managed to do it. Like learning to walk, it just comes naturally to us. But as we discover as soon as we run into another one, language isn't as natural as we think. Language may be the one thing that distinguishes us from other animals, but it's really not like walking at all. We all walk in the same way, more or less. But the way we talk can be very different.

At least, it can seem like that. Our first exposure to another language, especially if it's unrelated to our own, can be quite a shock: suddenly the noises coming out of other people's mouths make no sense at all. But in fact, we are all doing the same thing, just in different ways. We're all using simple combinations of sound to express and transmit meaning – though the sounds we use will not all be the same, and the ways in which we organise them may be very different. In essence, though, the trick of speech is identical wherever it is found. We're just tagging our awareness with a digital suite of noises, and using that as a tool to share it with others. A digital suite of noises? Really?

What's surprising is that this seems surprising to us. But then most of the time, we don't think about language or how it works, any more than we think about how our body works – or even know very much about it. Though it's so central to everything we do, language remains largely invisible to us. We use it constantly and depend completely on the power it gives us to express the subtlest nuances of thought and feeling, but we still use it almost unconsciously, with little awareness of the ridiculously precise tongue dance going on inside our mouths. We take it totally for granted, and if we do think of it, it's generally with a sense of wonder at the fact that it exists at all. So where did language come from? When did it start? Why are we the only animals that can speak? Remarkably, there are still no certain answers to these questions.

Like many things that humans have wondered about through history, the traditional explanation has been that language is a god-given gift. The Christian world is familiar with the stories in the Bible, but this is not just a Christian story. Almost every culture around the world has some tale of how humans were granted the gift of speech by a supernatural being. To modern ears, that can seem a less-than-satisfactory explanation – but the current thinking about language and how it evolved is hardly any better. The leading theories still follow an idea made popular by Noam Chomsky in the 1960s, that some unknown genetic mutation must have endowed our species with what Chomsky called a "Language Acquisition Device" – a mechanism that allows us to speak.

But in the ongoing absence of any firm evidence, that doesn't really help us any more than the religious 'explanation'. True, we may now know that there are specific areas in the brain that handle speech, and have discovered a gene that is apparently associated with certain aspects of language production, but that's still a long way from explaining how language started, and how it developed. This astonishing ability of ours cannot have sprung fully-formed into existence. There must have been a process.

But the origins of this process are hard to discern. When we start to think about it, language seems so complex, so full of bizarre rules of grammar which we can struggle to understand, that it seems almost impossible that it could have just emerged naturally. Anyone who has felt the frustration of trying to speak a foreign language without making mistakes knows how difficult it is to follow the obscure patterns behind subject-verb agreement in French and Spanish, or the seemingly random use of onomatopoeic words in Japanese. It doesn't help that the mathematical acrobatics so typical of the generative grammars in Chomsky's work are likely to leave the average person's head going *gan-gan* (a neat Japanese expression that means 'pounding', amongst other things). How could such complexity have just evolved slowly from simple origins?

Well, we already know that life itself has done exactly that. Like every other species alive on our planet today, human beings are the result of a mind-boggling 3.5 billion years of natural evolution, nearly 3 billion years of which were spent reproducing as little more than single-celled organisms. The extraordinarily complex structure of the human brain is the result of countless generations of slow change: so in trying to puzzle out the abstract structures of language from its current level of development, we may find that we've been looking at it from the wrong end of the telescope.

Just as our complex early ideas about the nature of the universe gave way to the simplicity and elegance of the Copernican model once we realised that the sun was at the centre of the solar system, not the earth, it's quite possible that the development of language was a much simpler affair than we have imagined. The almost infinite palette of colours that we are able to see derives from just three basic types of colour receptor in our eyes; our rich sense of taste and smell also emerges from a very limited range of primary flavours. That's because our brain is fantastically adept at conjuring complexity from simplicity; much the same may be true for our ability to speak.

From analog to digital

To understand how that might be so, we'll have to take a closer look at how language actually works. Take a moment to notice what happens when you speak. When you think of it as a stream of noise, speech is really just a long, carefully choreographed groan. In effect, anything we say is nothing more than an overly-extended sigh, a sigh that's divided into bites of sound that are shaped and controlled by a range of simple mouth movements which act as road-blocks for the flow of air. Try it for yourself: make a groaning sound and continue to let it run until your breath runs out – *aaaaaahhhhhh*. As you do this, notice that you can change the pitch as you go, and that this alters the feeling with which you're expressing the sound – the emotional tone.

That's the core of all speech, the raw vocalization. This is the animal essence, the mooing, cooing, cawing, lowing expression of feeling that we share with all our fellow animals. Now do the same thing, but this time bring your lips together to stop the flow of air and then release them again, repeating it over a few times. *Aaaahh—ma-ma-ma-ma.* Now, instead of just putting your lips together, purse them slightly as you do it, putting a little pressure into your lips. *Aaaahh—ba-ba-ba-ba.*

Sound familiar? Well, you probably started out yourself that way. In many languages around the world, the first words children learn to refer to the people who look after them are some variation of *mama* or *baba* – they are the easiest sounds of all to make. All language begins with babble.

Now feel how your mouth has to move to create other sounds: a 'd' sound, for example, is made by placing the tip of your tongue against the roof of your mouth, a 'g' sound by closing your throat instead of your lips. Once you've got the hang of those, try changing the vowel sound from 'a' to 'o' and see how the shape of the inside of your mouth has to change to make it. Then take a look at how the position of your mouth and tongue changes as you combine these sounds into words. Try saying *hullabaloo*. Or *A squirrel called Rory*. It's quite a performance when you take all the movements apart and observe them consciously, but as adults we do it effortlessly thousands of times a day.

At the simplest level, language is just an agreement that certain noises mean certain things, and other animals can do this too. Some monkeys, for example, have different alarm calls to distinguish between predators like snakes and eagles, and use them to warn others in their group to take the appropriate evasive action. Chimpanzees use gestures and hoots to communicate their feelings. We humans are by no means unique in using unrelated signs and noises as a way of conveying meaning to others.

But it's what we've done with these noises that matters. It's a small thing in itself, but it's the crucial key to the difference between human language and how all other animals communicate. What we've done is to isolate some of the noises, and use them as units of sound that we combine together to make words. What that means is that unlike other species we don't just make a different single noise for each thing, a unique one-to-one analog representation of objects with sounds. You'd soon run out of noises that way. What we do instead is to put small numbers of noises together in a digital sequence, using them in combination. That makes new sounds easier to create and remember.

That's the essential trick of speech, and despite being so simple, it's extremely powerful. So for example, instead of just saying *Aah!* for snake or *Eeh!* for bird, we've realized that you can put the two sounds together to make new noises which mean something else, without having to use or think of a different new sound. You could say *Aah-eeh* for elephant and *Eeh-aah* for tiger. Or even *Aah-aah* for sex and *Eeh-eeh* for food. Combinations of just two distinct sounds, *Aah* and *Eeh,* can suddenly be used to create up to four words with different meanings. That's easy enough to grasp, but add just one more sound and as many as $3 \times 3 \times 3 = 27$ combinations are available, and four gives you up to $4^4 = 256$ words: the numbers increase exponentially. In essence all we've done is to digitize noise – and once you grasp this, you've opened the door to language.

The noises can be any sound that the human mouth can produce – clicks, clucks, pops, poops, parps, hoots and hisses. The International Phonetic Alphabet uses over 150 symbols to represent all the known sounds used by humans in their languages, but no language uses them all, or even most of them. All a language requires is that you have a range of them that can be used in combination. This is the raw material of speech. It's the same for every language. We all do it, even if the sounds we make when speaking French can be very different to those of German, Swahili, or Chinese. It's the same trick in every case. A small number of sounds are combined to make a large number of words. In linguistics, each of these distinct and different sounds is called a phoneme. Though it's not quite this simple, you can think of them as different vowel and consonant sounds, a closed set of noises that is the signature of that language.

The fact that each language has its own particular and unique group of noises means that other languages can sometimes sound very strange. English speakers often feel uncomfortable with the harsh, throaty sounds used in German and Arabic, for example, and the more diverse African click languages and tone-based Oriental languages can sound quite alien if you're not used to hearing them. But here's the thing: not only do these sounds sound quite natural to their own speakers, many of the normal sounds of English can seem very odd to people who have not grown up using them. Japanese and Chinese speakers often find it difficult to distinguish between R and L (Japanese speakers have to learn more than 20 new phonemes before they can speak natural-sounding English). That's because their language doesn't use those sounds – and along with most other non-native speakers of English, they also struggle with that strangely lisping 'th' sound, one of the most characteristic of the English phonemes.

But for language to work it doesn't matter what the sounds are – only that there is a limited number of them, and that they are used consistently and exclusively: the big secret of human language is its ability to generate a huge number of different words from a small number of sounds. Of course, language is not just about words – without grammar to organise them, it's difficult to make yourself understood with any precision: – anyone who's wrestled with another language will have learnt that the hard way. But words are still the indispensable first step, for without them there can be no grammar. So it should be no surprise to find that our animal cousins show so little sign of being able to use grammar – they don't have the words to make it necessary.

It can seem incredible that as many as a million words exist in English, but with a fixed system of phonemes in place, creating them is just the simple magic of maths. We would soon struggle to remember the names of numbers, for example, if there was a completely different word for each number after ten (like *eleven* and *twelve*) – but because we use a system that relies on combinations of ten basic digits, it's easy to create and remember new ones. There's no difficulty in saying or remembering even a relatively large number like 178,346 because we understand it as a systematic combination of digits, whereas it would be impossible to remember every new individual number as a unique analog noise, unrelated to any other.

With spoken language, the basic unit is the syllable, which in its simplest form is a combination of a consonant and a vowel – like *la*, *di* and *da*. English has a relatively large number of phonemes (around 44, depending on the dialect), and some of the oldest known languages, such as Khoisan group of so-called 'click' languages, use as many as 24 vowels and 117 consonants. But even languages with very few phonemes can manage just fine. As a crude rule of thumb, the potential number of syllables available to a language is the number of vowels multiplied by the number of consonants – and even though in practice phonemes often combine in ways that are complicated by various rules and exceptions, the basic maths is compelling.

Take the Pirahã language spoken in the rain-forests of Brazil – it may have only eight consonants and three vowels, but its speakers have little difficulty in fully expressing themselves. That's because even with the simplest of combinations, at least 8 x 3 = 24 different syllables can be made using this tiny range of vowels and consonants. That in turn means that with two-syllable words there are 24 x 24 = 576 combinations possible, and by adding just one more syllable the language can have as many as 24 x 24 x 24 = 13,824 different words. So with even just three syllables made by combining as few as eleven sounds, the number of potential words available is already close to the number of words the average adult is familiar with – in any language. Add in another syllable (not very difficult – even a relatively common word like 'astonishing' has four syllables) and the number rises to well over a quarter of a million. That's all it takes.

With that idea in mind, we can begin to see how language could have evolved through a process of gradually reducing the number of analog calls we were using, and using them in digital clusters instead – and there is increasing evidence that other species have already begun the process of combining sounds in this way. That doesn't mean that they're about to burst into speech, however. We have to remember that all such processes, like evolution itself, are extremely gradual. We are used to the pace of change and development that our language-enhanced society is able to deliver, but changes in the distant past happened much more slowly. The archaeological record shows that early humans started using simple stone tools as long as two million years ago – but we also know that another million years passed before any significant change was made to the shape and sophistication of these tools. Things take time to develop.

But understanding the essential simplicity of the trick that lets us create and use such large numbers of words can help us unmask the mystery of language. Once the idea of putting noises together in this way has taken hold, it's just a question of slowly agreeing which combinations of sound refer to the things we are interested in. The key thing is that it doesn't matter what the sounds are. There's no reason why the molecule H_2O, the essential building block of life, should be called water rather than *eau, acqua,* νερό, पानी or 水, or why cheese should be called *fromage* rather than *sajt,* сыр or 치즈. These are just the names different languages have come up with to refer to them. There's nothing about the sound of a word that makes it more like 'cheese' or 'water' in one language than another. It's essentially an accidental and random process, limited only by the range of noises we can make with our mouths. For despite any sentimental or patriotic attachment to them, there's nothing special about the actual words we use.

Grammar school

But the ability to slowly create and use different words still leaves us a long way from the complexity of the languages we use today. Young children learning to speak and adults picking up a foreign language may start out with single words, but it's just the beginning – the next step on the road from babble to Babel is grammar. The fact that grammar exists at all, and that children seem to grasp it so easily, is often cited as evidence of an innate language instinct, but here too, there is another way to think of it. What is grammar, in the end? In essence, it's just a way of ordering information to express relationships between ideas. Is the boy on the bus, or the bus on the boy? The words themselves may be the same, but there is a huge difference in meaning – a difference expressed through grammar (or 'syntax', to use the word that linguists prefer.) Once the idea of using words has taken root, the next logical step is to find a way to use combinations of words to express more complicated ideas. All languages do that. But once you start to do it, you soon need to have an agreement about word order.

To give a very simple example, if we already have the three words *man eat dog*, the meaning of the sentence will depend on what we've decided about the order of words. If we've decided that the person doing something should be mentioned before the thing that's having something done to it, then *man eat dog* tells us that the man is the one getting a meal. But if we've decided that the rule in our language is that the thing should come first, then the exact same sentence, *man eat dog*, means that the dog is the one getting the meal. Speakers of English may consider that strange, but languages do exist that naturally use that order. We tend to think the way sentences are ordered in the language we speak is normal – but it turns out there are many ways of doing it.

The key parts of any sentence in any language are the 'subject' (the person or thing doing something), the 'verb' (the action word) and the 'object (the thing that the action affects). If you think about it, you'll see that there are only six possible ways to arrange subject (S), verb (V) and object (O) in a sentence. They are SVO (the order we use in English), SOV, OSV, OVS, VSO and VOS – all of which exist in human languages, although the last three are quite rare. And though it may seem just common sense to native speakers of English that the order of a sentence should be subject-verb-object, SVO is not in fact the most common order in use worldwide. Nearly half the languages we know about use the order SOV, with the verb coming at the end of the sentence. This means *man dog eat* is the most common way of expressing a good result for the human. But it doesn't really matter which arrangement is used, as long as it's consistent. SVO works perfectly well for English, despite being a minority choice.

Linguists have long debated whether the core syntax or 'universal grammar' of human languages is determined by our genes (the view maintained by Noam Chomsky), or whether the patterns found in our speech emerge more from necessity (an approach pioneered by Joseph Greenberg). However, as our knowledge of rarer and less well documented languages improves, it's increasingly clear that there are very few universal tendencies. Beyond the similarities found in related language families, the evolution of the sentence order used in any one language seems to be largely random, just like the noises we use to make our words. Rather than there being any innate factors that control our choices, we appear to have just fumbled our way to something that works. As with our phonemes, the key to mutual understanding is consistency – sticking to what's been decided. And there are many such decisions to make.

That's because whatever order you pick, *man dog eat* still doesn't give you very much information. When did or will this event happen? We can't know from these three words alone. So if timing is important (which it will be if you're hungry), there has to be some way to express it. Is the eating something that has already happened, is happening now, or something you hope is going to happen soon? It's not difficult to see how the need to express relationships of time would emerge quite naturally, even if different languages have very different ways of expressing them. The next thing we need is words that can show the relative positions of things. *Man dog table eat* doesn't tell us whether the man ate (or is eating, or going to eat) the dog *on* or *under* the table, for example. You need a preposition – or rather, in the case of SOV word order, a postposition marker. So it has to become *man dog table under eat will* (for example). Then if you want to explain what kind of dog or man, you're going to need adjectives. And so on.

The development of grammar in this way (a process linguists call grammaticalization) probably occurred quite slowly. Like the switch from analog to digital in the creation of words, grammar is unlikely to have burst fully-fledged onto the scene – even if each new generation may well have picked it up faster, as with any new trick or technology. We may never know when anything close to the sophistication of modern grammar first appeared, but there is likely to have been a quite natural development in the progress from using words to directly reference the things and actions of most of importance to us, to using them to show the relationships between these things. There may even be a fractal component to the way syntax evolves, like the complex branching patterns we see in nature, with grammar emerging in gradual stages from a critical mass of words.

How could that happen, though? Actually, we don't need to go back very far in time to find examples in the historical record. Consider the expression 'going to' in the phrase *I'm going to eat that dog*. We know that even as recently as Shakespeare's time 'going to' meant what it literally says, that you were physically going somewhere to do something. But during the 18th century the meaning began to change to mean simply the intention to do something. In much the same way, the use of the word 'will' as a marker of intent (as in "I will eat the dog") has slipped from its old meaning of 'willing' something to happen, to become a more neutral marker of the future – a process that linguists call 'semantic bleaching'. In the case of 'will', its loss of semantic power is also shown by the way the form of the word is often just abbreviated to 'll (as in "I'll eat the dog") – just as 'going to' is now gradually being replaced with the contraction 'gonna'.

There are examples in all languages. In Japanese the verb meaning 'to see' (*miru*) is also used to mean 'try' – so 'see eating the dog' has come to mean 'try eating the dog', with the character reduced to a phonetic symbol. In French, the word *puisque* which means 'since' (in the sense of 'consequently') in modern French, has evolved from *puis que* which means 'after that'. Or consider the word 'goodbye', which evolved in historical times from the phrase *God be with thee*. As 'goodbye' it's just a remnant of its old self – a noise we make as a greeting when parting from someone, that no longer confers divine blessings on the traveller. The same is true for the Spanish '*adiós*' – which as 'a Diós' once commended the departee 'to God', although it no longer has that meaning for most people. In Japanese, with its very different heritage, the word for goodbye ('sayonara') literally means "If it must be so" – though no one thinks of that, either.

The evolution of grammar is also reflected in the types and frequency of the words we use when we speak. Linguists make a distinction between so-called 'content' words – nouns, verbs, adjectives and adverbs like *dog, eat, dirty* and *slowly*, which tag physical objects and qualities in the real world – and 'function' words which map the connection between them, like *in, on, under* and *through*. You can often draw a picture of a content word, but function words are much harder to represent, as they express a relationship between objects or actions rather than the things themselves. Yet function words are really at the heart of what we generally mean by 'grammar' – and it is the ability to use them correctly and effectively that distinguishes the speech of an adult native speaker from a young child or non-native speaker of a language.

What's interesting is that content words make up the vast majority of our vocabulary: as many as two-thirds of all the words we know are nouns, around 20% are verbs, with adjectives and adverbs together accounting for most of the rest. That's because there are only a very small number of function words in any language: English has only about 300 – and even Chinese, an uninflected language which depends more on function words, has only about 500. Despite that, between one half to two-thirds of all the words we use when we speak are function words (think how many times we need to use *a, the, of, on, in, at, or, and* and *but*, to mention just a few) – a fact that is less surprising when you realise they are the glue holding the structure of a sentence together. If you took the function words out of a sentence you might still be able to grasp the meaning, but you'd have much more difficulty understanding it. For example, that last sentence would become *'Took function words sentence grasp meaning difficulty understanding'*.

If the first step to human language was the creation of words through the digitisation of analog sounds, then we would expect the earliest stages of the development of human speech to have been as clumsy as we can often feel when we first start to learn a foreign language as adults – trying to make ourselves understood with just a handful of nouns, verbs and gestures. It can hardly be a coincidence that this is largely the way children learn their first language too – using first one word at a time, then two, and only later learning how to use the function words that express the relationships between the words they know. It is tempting to see in this process of acquisition a parallel with the way a growing embryo in the womb mirrors the evolutionary history of the animal it will become. And there is another, much clearer hint that this may be so.

The writing on the wall

While our understanding of the early evolution of language has to rely on inference (although the ongoing process of grammaticalization can still be observed in language today), the next important stage in its development – the invention of writing – allows us to see this process of digitization, simplification and abstraction at work from the ground up. Writing may only have been invented in the last few thousand years, but unlike speech it leaves a real-time record of how the process unfolded, and the stages it has gone through are likely to be similar to what must have happened as we learnt to talk. As we know it today, writing is also a digital system which can efficiently represent every word we say using a small number of symbols. But it didn't start out that way: writing also began as an analog system, with pictures representing words. And just as we must surely have done with the spoken language, we seem to have slowly worked out that a digital system is an infinitely more flexible way to communicate.

Though there may still be some disagreement about when true 'writing' began (as opposed to simple markings that represented things or allowed people to keep track of numbers) it is generally agreed that it first appeared in the Middle East: both Mesopotamia and Ancient Egypt developed their own systems around 5000 years ago. As with speech itself, the different systems may have emerged independently, or – as is perhaps more likely – once someone had the idea of using marks to represent speech, word quickly spread to the neighbouring centre of civilisation, where they worked out their own way of doing it. Other distinct writing systems emerge through time (China came on board some 2000 years later), but whether genuinely independent or inspired by hearsay, what matters is that the earliest scripts were all analog, not digital. In much the same way that animal calls are holistic noises, the first writing was pictorial – a representation of an object in the form of a unique drawing, or glyph. We see the exact same process at work in Ancient Egypt, Mesopotamia, China and Mesoamerica.

But whichever tradition we look at, the changes that followed show it didn't take us long to realise that pictures alone weren't going to work, any more than animal calls can function as language. Without some kind of system, the number of unrelated pictures required soon reaches the limits of human memory. So sooner or later these first writing systems all gave way to the idea of writing words using pictures of things that sound like other things, a process known technically as a *rebus*. Rebus is used in those word quizzes where words are made up using pictures that sound like the word being referred to, like drawing an eye to represent 'I', for example – and a similar principle is used in text messaging, where 'great' is written as gr8 to save time. But this too is an unwieldy and memory-heavy system, and although it served the Egyptian elites well enough for thousands of years, the rebus method gradually gave way to a system of writing that represented sound digitally, first as syllables, and eventually as individual phonemes. (The advantage of writing using letters rather than syllables is clear from the numbers: an 'average' language with 20 consonants and 20 vowels would need at least 20 x 20 = 400 symbols to write all the possible syllables, but if only the phonemes are represented, the number drops to 20 + 20 = 40 – a much more manageable number.)

Before the discovery of the Rosetta Stone it was widely assumed that the ancient Egyptian writing system must work by using pictures to represent concepts, in the same way that Chinese characters were thought to do. With this in mind, the leading thinkers of Renaissance Europe tried hard to develop a universal written language that could represent thought using idealised abstract 'characters' which could be read by anyone regardless of what language they spoke – but they had misunderstood (because they did not know) the history of writing. Leaving aside the question of how the key building blocks of thought could ever be isolated from language, the biggest problem is always one of memory. It's hard to hold a large series of unrelated images in your mind, even if you remember them when you see them – and drawing them from memory is even more difficult. No matter how many paintings you might recognise in an art gallery, for example, it's hard to bring them all to mind – let alone draw them – when you get home.

So it's no surprise that Chinese characters are much more systematic than they first appear to people who cannot read them. While each character does have a unique meaning, and they are not primarily phonetic (although there is a phonetic element, and they can be used to spell out unfamiliar words, much like a rebus), each Chinese character is essentially a combination of a relatively small number of graphic elements, called radicals. And when you realise that the 214 standard radicals are also mostly combinations of even simpler elements (think of the commonly used groups of letters found in English affixes like *mis–*, *–ible*, *–tion* and so on), that's really not much different to an English word, which is a unique digital combination of a limited number of shapes we call letters. In that sense the only real difference between Chinese characters and English words is that the shapes we use to form words are written out in a straight line, whereas those used to form characters are written inside conceptual squares.

English words are all written using a selection of the 26 letters of its alphabet, but although each letter has a sound associated with it, that doesn't mean you can read a word straight away. Just think of the words *tough, through, cough* and *dough*, all of which use the same *–ough* cluster but are pronounced quite differently. In fact, there are only 36 words in English which feature *–ough*, but there are as many as nine different ways of pronouncing it. Then there's *right, wright, write* and *rite*, for example, which are pronounced the same but spelt quite differently. As George Bernard Shaw pointed out, English spelling is so inconsistent that the word 'fish' could theoretically be spelt 'ghoti' – with *gh* for 'f' as in enou**gh**, *o* for 'i' as in w**o**men, and *ti* for 'sh' as in na**ti**on. According to the UK Spelling Society, nearly half of all English words contain unpredictable elements, and on average English children have to learn around 3500 irregular spellings to achieve adult standards of literacy. That's really not that different to the number of characters you have to learn to be able to read Chinese.

But the key thing about writing, just as with speech, is that the only really efficient and effective way of representing a large number of meanings is to use a small number of signs that can be combined to make any word. This is not just because they represent speech. Many writing systems – like Chinese – have a very complex relationship with the spoken language they represent, and can be understood without knowing exactly how they are supposed to be read (as with Egyptian hieroglyphs). But whether they represent syllables, phonemes or just patterns, letters allow you to easily create and remember words. That's because they are digital. Analog images like emoji may be useful when it comes to expressing your mood, or the feeling you want to convey, but they are not much help when it comes to saying anything complicated.

The glyphs used by the Mayan civilisation in central America, probably first developed about 2000 years ago, are another ancient early writing system which mirrors the same progression from analog to digital. Most of the books written using this beautiful and enigmatic 'logographic' script were destroyed by the Spanish during their relentless conquest of the region in the 16th century, and it remained largely undecipherable until about 50 years ago. But eventually it was realised that – just like the hieroglyphs of Ancient Egypt – Mayan glyphs were mostly phonetic, spelling out syllables that were intended to be read as sound, rather than being unique symbols with specific meanings. Though we still can't read all of the inscriptions that remain, we know that the language was written using as few as 500 logographic symbols with around 250 syllable glyphs.

Compared to this, the standard western alphabet may seem a model of simplicity, but things are not what they seem, even so. English has to manage with just 26 symbols to represent the 44 phonemes we use when we speak (which goes a long way to explain the unsystematic nature of English spelling). And although it may seem crazy to think that Japanese uses two separate sets of syllabic scripts to spell out identical sounds, we often fail to realise that we do much the same thing. The number of symbols we use may be less, but English also uses two alphabets to represent the exact same sounds: we just call them upper- and lower-case letters. We don't normally think of them that way, but that is what they are – some letters look similar in both upper and lower case (like c/C, o/O, s/S and v/V), but the majority look entirely different (*a* does not look like *A*, nor *b* like *B*, *d* like *D*, *e* like *E* and so on.)

Each writing system has its own little tricks and quirks, but in the end what we're all doing is using a limited number of visual 'digits' to represent words in the language, with varying degrees of correspondence with the sonic 'digits' – the phonemes – we use when speaking. Some languages may seem more well-aligned than others, but even a language like Spanish, often thought to use the alphabet very 'phonetically', has its issues: 'g's in words like *gringo*, *agua* and *gente* are pronounced differently, for example. There have been many proposals to reform the spelling of different languages over the years, but apart from the economic and emotional cost of changing the writing system of a whole society, we don't really seem to have too much difficulty managing with the ones we have. It's not perfect – but then it doesn't have to be. Our brains 'get' it anyway, just as they cope with grammatical peculiarities and weird phonemes. What matters is consistency, whether or not the patterns always make 'sense'.

We are not alone

So rather than relying on a lucky throw of the genetic dice to explain how language came to be the complex system of nested dependencies and recursive sub-clauses that scholars know it as today, it is equally possible that – just like any other evolutionary trait – human language could have developed slowly and gradually from what we were already doing before we learnt to speak. The gradual digitization of existing analog calls and the subsequent slow transformation of the resulting words into the abstract functions that enable grammar are quite sufficient to account for it. But if that's the big secret of language, why haven't any other animals learnt to do it? Why is it only humans who seem to be able to communicate so naturally in this way?

Well firstly, it doesn't come naturally to us. Though there are very few recorded cases – fortunately so – the rare examples of children brought up without language show that they struggle to learn to speak later on, almost as if there were a cut-off point beyond which it is no longer possible. Language appears to be something we have to actively learn while still young – mainly by example – and it is not something that we can do on our own, by instinct alone. To be able to speak, we have to learn to map the patterns of our perceptions onto the patterns of speech we hear being used, and to do that we need to have people using language intensively around us, from birth onwards.

Like speaking, reading and writing are also much easier to acquire at a younger age, and require more intensive exposure than speech – and in many parts of the world, writing did not develop until quite late in our cultural evolution. In England, the earliest texts only date back to the 7th century: Roman historians may have described what life in Britain was like, but the people themselves left no written records. Which means we have no idea who built the many hundreds of stone circles and hill forts they left behind, for example – or, more importantly, why they did it – just as we have no records of most pre-literate societies around the world. No matter how long we have been speaking, without being able to record speech we can never know what was being said. Writing really is ground zero in the history of mankind, but even though we've been doing it for several thousand years, global literacy is not yet at 100%, and in some countries is still less than 50%. Language and literacy take time to spread, and require nurturing. It's a skill that's intensively taught.

Secondly, we are not the only animals with the ability to communicate. As already noted, other species use analog noises to convey unrelated symbolic meanings, and these have to be learnt. Whales and dolphins teach their calves the distinctive noises used by their group, and birdsong too is largely learnt behaviour, with clear regional variations. We don't yet know enough about the sophistication of such forms of communication, but even granting the capacity to transmit information about danger or the location of food sources for example, there is clearly a limit to what our animal cousins can tell each other. There is no suggestion that two individuals of any non-human species can communicate anything as simple as *'Hide behind that tree until I give you the signal'* – let alone discuss the meaning of life or debate the merits of quantum theory.

But that doesn't mean that they lack the capacity to learn. Dog owners will happily tell you that their beloved pets eventually come to understand quite a lot of what is said to them, and experiments have shown that some dogs have a passive vocabulary of over 200 words (and if they are hearing these as analog noises, that's probably at the outer limit of what humans could remember, as well). Alex the famous parrot was credited with an active vocabulary of 100 words, which he was able to use creatively, and could even ask questions. Systematic efforts have been made to teach apes to learn human languages, though the results have been mixed. But that may be because we don't understand enough about how language works, or how we learn it ourselves.

The most significant result has been with a bonobo called Kanzi, who has learnt to understand quite sophisticated sentences spoken at normal speed (you can watch film of him on YouTube that will make the hairs on the back of your neck stand up). It's clear that real communication is taking place with Kanzi through the medium of human language alone (his trainer is masked to minimise the chances of him picking up on non-verbal cues, the so-called 'Clever Hans' effect). Asked to perform a series of quite random tasks (*"Could you put some salt on the ball?"*, *"Could you carry the television outdoors, please?"*) he does so with little or no hesitation. This is no longer a bonobo – by virtue of the fact that we can communicate with him, this makes him one of 'us'. Kanzi provides us with evidence that language acquisition need not be anything more involved than a process of pattern recognition, of mapping sensual perceptions onto statistical clusters in the noises that the people around them are making – just as learning to walk is no more than a process of learning the much simpler grammar of gravity as it acts on the joints of the human body.

Kanzi's achievement is all the more remarkable because he was never formally taught. His exposure to language came after he was allowed to remain with his mother from a very young age while efforts (largely unsuccessful) were being made to teach her the basics of human language when she was already an adult – something that seems to be beyond the capacity even of humans. Anyone who has spent frustrating years being taught a foreign language in the classroom to no avail will readily understand the plight his mother was in – but by the same token, if you've ever had the experience of picking up another language by just living in a country where it's spoken, you'll have a good feel for how Kanzi was able to do it. It should teach us some humility to realise that he learnt simply by observing what was going on around him, not by being taught.

Kanzi is still an exception – other experiments with chimps and gorillas have been less successful, but then it's difficult to expect anyone to give a member of another species the amount of time and attention a human child needs to learn to speak. Nor can we reasonably expect a chimpanzee, with a brain one third the size of a modern human, to be able to use language the way we do – especially if we consider that the growth of the human brain may well have been driven by specific adaptions to language. But that doesn't mean that the trick of language can never be learnt by other species. The 'dumb' animals are only dumb because they can't speak, and the fact that they cannot yet do so may just be down to the luck of the draw. As far as life on this planet is concerned, it seems we just happen to have got there first – and once the ability to speak is established, the difference between those who can and those who can't rapidly becomes exponential: for language links up our minds.

The jump from an analog to a digital system may seem a huge change – one that nothing short of divine intervention or a radical genetic mutation could be expected to have caused. But if we accept that other animals can associate random analog sounds with meaning in their use of distinct alarm calls, for example (which is really the harder thing to explain), the switch from one to the other is just a matter of efficiency and time – especially as it's likely to have occurred over hundreds or thousands of generations. It wouldn't have to have been a conscious process, any more than the digital organisation of data in DNA and its expression in proteins would have been conscious. The complex coding for the tens of thousands of different proteins that make up our bodies is ultimately signalled by combinations of just four bases, with the famous A, C, G and T pairings. DNA did not require a special 'faculty' to evolve its digital structure. If a digital solution is a more effective way of doing things, evolution will eventually take care of it.

The birth of Babel

But once it happened, it would have been a decisive and radical break. Being able to share ideas through language is not just a help for the individual, like the evolution of eyes, or wings – it's a virtual phase change that leaves species without language far behind. And it happened relatively recently: mammals may have been around for 200 million years, but we are unlikely to have been able to speak for much more than a tiny fraction of that time. Because it does not leave any physical fossils, we may never know exactly when and where language started, but there are some indirect clues, nonetheless. The first of these are behavioural. It seems clear from the archaeological record that there was a relatively rapid increase in cultural activity around 50-60,000 years ago, suggesting a dramatic change in our ability to communicate with each other. That's unlikely to have been when we first started talking, at least for the reasons given below, but it may perhaps point to the emergence of more sophisticated grammar.

Another intriguing baseline is the first appearance of burial practice. Like defecation, death is something that few animals bother to make any arrangements for – other animals do not bury each other, even if there is evidence that some species do tend to gather in a certain spot when they sense that they are near death, and are mourned by their fellows. Humans, however, have been burying themselves for at least 100,000 years – graves exist from around that time which show clear evidence of ritual practice, with grave goods and body painting. That still doesn't mean we weren't talking to each other before that, but it's difficult to see how the practice of burial could have begun without the ability to persuade others to help – certainly with the rituals that so often accompany it, if not with the actual burial itself. You wouldn't go to the trouble of burying someone, let alone in a widely-imitated style, unless you thought there was a reason – and without language, there is no means of supplying one.

One other method that's been much used to search for a starting line for language is to trace its evolution backwards through the changes we see over time, to tease out and reconstruct earlier forms. This is similar to the way evolutionary biologists use structural changes in genomes to discover the origins of a particular population group – or how the Big Bang theory was arrived at by reversing the observed expansion of the universe. This has traditionally been done using historical texts which reveal the changes, but the lack of physical evidence of speech before writing came along makes it impossible for linguists to reach back far enough to pinpoint the origins of language (to the extent that discussion of the subject was eventually banned by learned societies toward the end of the 19th century). However, there may be a cleverer way to proceed.

We have already seen that language can manage quite well with a relatively small number of phonemes. This means that most existing languages have many more than they actually need – and intriguingly, there is an overall tendency for the number of phonemes used in a language to reduce over time as they evolve away from earlier forms, in what is technically known as a 'cline'. Languages with the largest numbers of phonemes are found in communities in Africa with the most diverse genetic heritages – revealing their ancient lineage – whereas those with the least are found in South America and Oceania, among communities who have travelled the furthest from Africa. If speech originally developed from the digitisation of a large number of analog calls, we would expect the number of phonemes to reduce as humans spread across the globe, even as grammar became more complex – it's simply more efficient to do so. And that is actually what we see.

A paper published in *Science* magazine in 2011 used this drop-off in the number of phonemes to claim that it could be used to calculate the date and location of the origin of speech – which its author estimated to have occurred in sub-Saharan Africa around 100,000 years ago. This is in line with what the archaeological evidence so far implies – and though there is disagreement about the accuracy of the methods he used, the phenomenon of phonetic depletion itself has been confirmed by subsequent studies. Regardless of the accuracy of the timeline, this is significant supporting evidence for the idea that language first emerged from a large pool of existing calls, and then gradually reduced the number of phonemes – as theory would predict. Just with genomes, it may turn out to be possible to read the phonetic structure of languages as a living fossil that reveals how and when our analog whoops and yells morphed into digital words.

Seen as a natural and gradual progression from animal calls, the development of language is really just a question of time, like the evolution of the eye. Being able to see is also a radical game-changer in the evolution of life, but vision did not happen suddenly, either. Even Darwin struggled to explain how an organ with a structure as complex as the eye could have evolved through a long series of intermediate stages, but sight gives such an advantage that the eye has independently evolved in at least 50 unrelated species over the deep history of life on earth. Nor is the human eye the finest of these structures – among other issues, its reverse-wired optic nerve causes a blind spot in the middle of the retina. The eye of a squid offers a far more elegant solution – but our brains have proved remarkably adept at making the best of a bad job.

And that's the key to understanding why language is so effective, despite being far from logical or rational – and why the quest for a universal language is ultimately pointless. Our brains are good at making the best of a bad job because that's what they do. As pattern-recognising devices they have evolved to make sense of sensory data, no matter how noisy or poorly presented. For all their apparent inconsistencies and irregularities, both English spelling and Chinese characters work just fine, as do their very different grammars. They exist as they are because they do the job they're required to do, and are not worth the effort of reform, any more than our eyes would be better at seeing if replaced by squid eyes. Just as it is the brain that sees, not the eye, it is the brain that uses language as a tool for communication.

A fascinating insight into the ability of brains to extract patterns from data is provided by a remarkable invention called a BrainPort. This is a device which allows a blind person to see with a camera connected to a simple lollipop-shaped array of electrodes placed on the tongue. Earlier versions of the device even worked with the array placed on the skin at the small of the back, but it was found that the tongue worked better, being a more sensitive area of the skin, and having a greater density of nerve endings. What happens is that signals from the camera are routed to the electrode array in much the same way that information is sent to the pixels of a television screen. The person using the device then experiences tingling sensations on their tongue which – after a few days of training – the brain interprets as a visual image without further help. Cochlear implant technology, which helps deaf people hear, works in much the same way – as does the technology for artificial retinas, which are becoming increasingly viable.

Astonishingly, it seems that incoming visual information can be still be processed even if fed to another part of the brain than the visual cortex – as demonstrated by a bizarre experiment conducted at MIT in April 2000 where the optic nerves of ferrets were re-routed at birth to the auditory cortex, and yet the animals were still able to see. This shows that the brain is in principle able to interpret information from any interface with the real world, provided that it can match the new data with other sensory information. Whether the means of access is auditory (spoken language), visual (writing and sign language) or tactile (braille), language is our naturally evolved BrainPort – a systematic arrangement of data which allows our brain to 'see' into the mind of another person. There's nothing intrinsically meaningful about the language we grew up speaking – even though we experience it almost as an extension of ourselves and use it without thinking, it is just as artificial as an array of electrodes sitting on the tongue. Language is only ever the means of delivering information, not the message itself.

Which means it's not so surprising that speech has evolved into so many apparently unrelated languages. You don't need to believe it developed independently in separate locations to arrive at the Babel of different tongues that we have today: as an artificial medium, language can transform itself much quicker than our genes. French, Spanish and Italian have all diverged from Latin in less than 1000 years, and even in more recent times the difference between American and British English shows how quickly phonemes and grammar can change. Brits may understand American English well enough because we hear it so much in films and on TV, but despite any wishful thinking about the 'special relationship', Americans often need subtitles to understand what British speakers are saying. Even if we've only been talking to each other for 100,000 years, that's quite long enough for thousands of different languages to emerge.

All it takes for language to change is for groups to become isolated from one another; the history of human colonisation of the planet after we broke out of Africa is a history of successive isolation, with pioneer groups continually breaking off (or being driven away) to develop new territories. And once a language group breaks away, conventions can change. With genes, it's well known that the smaller a breakaway group, the greater the genetic change due to the increased likelihood of mutations being inherited: the same is true for language. We have already seen that overall, the number of phonemes in use drops away with distance from Africa because languages don't actually need them; grammar also changes and evolves over time to reflect new needs, especially without a normative media presence to provide a standard to conform to. From the perspective of a single lifetime in our wired-up world it may be hard to imagine how this could have happened, but these are changes that took place over many thousands of generations. That's quite enough to account for it. God did not need to confuse the languages of humanity – we were perfectly capable of doing that for ourselves.

The money of fools

It doesn't matter which one you speak: language is always an artificial device, and the sounds of the words we use have no meaning in themselves. Anyone working with translation soon becomes aware that there is much more than words at stake – it's not just a question of finding a dictionary and translating word by word. Each language has a characteristic way of expressing itself, and the trick is to get away from the words to what things actually mean. When a French speaker says *les carrottes sont cuites*, they don't mean the carrots are cooked. They mean it's all over. So that's the way you translate it – although there are many other colloquial idioms in English you could choose: *the chips are down, the die is cast,* or *the game is up,* for example. Each of these expressions has a different nuance, and the one you choose will depend on the context in which the French expression is being used; but the principle is the same.

The deeper your knowledge of another language, the easier it becomes to escape from the literal sense of the words and translate their meaning into your own language using words that may have little connection with the ones used in the original phrase. A Permanent Secretary is not the same thing as an Eternal Typist (an old saying about the perils of literal translation) and the expression 'pulling someone's leg' may mean 'playing a joke' in English, but in Japanese it means 'holding someone back' (whereas the Russian equivalent of 'pulling your leg' in the British sense is 'to hang noodles from your ears'). Language is being constantly renewed by its native speakers both to cope with changing needs and to keep it fresh – but we don't have any difficulty in keeping up, because words are only ever pointers to meaning, not the meaning itself.

What we don't often consider is that language is already a translation – a translation of our thoughts, feelings and perceptions into words. Some people find this process easier than others, but whatever their native language, authors are only ever expressing one version of what they want to say. There are many ways I could write the sentence I am writing just now (*there are various ways the sentence could be written,* or *the sentence could be written in a variety of ways*) and which one I choose will depend on many factors, not least the possibility that I have not yet thought of a better way to express myself. In a fascinating seminar held by the British Centre for Literary Translation in 2011, five authors writing in languages other than English spoke about working with translators to produce English versions of their work, and all agreed that experience had suggested to them new ways of expressing themselves in their 'own' language.

There is a long history of debate about the extent to which language influences, or even determines, thought. In the mid-20th century the advocates of linguistic relativity were in fashion, the famous 'Sapir-Whorf' hypothesis claiming that the structures of a language can shape the way its speakers think. But cultures have little difficulty in distinguishing between things that their language may not explicitly express. English speakers can tell the difference between male and female even though, unlike German and French, we do not generally mark the gender of nouns with grammatical forms (like *der*, *die* and *das* or *le* and *la*). Similarly, Chinese speakers are quite able to tell the difference between singular and plural objects, even though their language treats everything as an 'uncountable' noun. With language, form is not the same thing as content.

The traps that language sets for us can be illustrated by two areas that are traditionally held in high regard by cultures everywhere: jokes and poetry. Both jokes and poetry fall into two major groups, which can be distinguished by the ease with which they can be translated. Situational jokes rely on subverting our expectation of how a particular situation will work out, and often don't need any words at all – as we see from the world-wide popularity of Mr Bean – and in early generations, of silent movie stars like Charlie Chaplin. Verbal jokes, on the other hand, rely on the fact that there are many words in any language which mean different things in different situations, and exploit our expectation of one meaning by deliberately switching contexts.

The first type can be easily translated into another language because words are particularly good at describing situations: "*A mother mouse and a baby mouse were walking along, when all of a sudden, a cat attacked them. The mother mouse goes, "Woof!" and the cat runs away. "See?" says the mother mouse to her baby. "Now do you see why it's important to learn a foreign language?"* The second type is often untranslatable because the word-play it depends on does not work in another language. When Zsa Zsa Gabor says that she is a good house-keeper – "*whenever I leave a husband, I* get to keep the house" – the joke plays on the knowledge that 'keep' has two very different meanings in English, which it may not in other languages.

There is a similar divide with poetry. Shakespeare's famous phrase '*a rose by any other name would smell as sweet*' – a wonderfully poetic characterisation of the artificiality of language – survives translation intact because its poetry lies in the idea, not in the words. Hamlet's "*To be or not to be, that is the question*" seems relatively transparent, though some languages can struggle to say it with such economy. But the next line contains the kind of poetry that resists even the most talented of translators: "*Whether 'tis nobler in the mind to suffer the slings and arrows of outrageous fortune...*" The core sentiment can be conveyed, of course. Shakespeare's enduring popularity across the world is testament to that. But there is a rhythm and a set of cultural cadences to the particular combination of words that are unique to the English language (just as there are in any language) which can be very hard to fully deliver in translation.

But the difficulty of translating puns and poetry is no reason to celebrate the unique virtues of a particular language. If anything, it show its inflexibility. It may be that poetry is what gets lost in translation – as the poet Robert Frost famously put it – but that kind of poetry relies on the particular structure of the language concerned. In that sense, it's really just a decorative feature quite distinct from the meaning – almost a form of music that simply plays with the rhythms, tones and resonances of the physical sounds of the words. How these factors are reflected in translation to give a sense of the skill of the original author can be quite crucial in determining their reception, but in terms of what language is and how it works, it's just a sideshow – if a very pleasing one.

Fundamentally, language is about the communication of ideas – thoughts that arise as a result of our perceptions. We use words to think about our ideas, but this is not the only way our brains handle them. We'll all have noticed how when you can't remember something, it often only comes to mind once you stop thinking about it. Something is clearly going on outside of what we are aware of at a conscious level. Intuition and the sensation of telepathy (suddenly thinking of someone just before they call you, for example) are forms of awareness that seem to come from a different, non-verbal place. There's also the well-known phenomenon of 'sleeping on' a problem: you can go to bed worried about something, and wake up with a solution in mind, as if the screen of words had cut you off from the superior problem-solving capacity of your 'subconscious'.

It is these levels of our mind that practices such as meditation seek to tap into. Whether rhythm-based (in the form of chanting), activity-based (yoga, tai-chi) or just simple sitting (Zen), the point is not to empty your mind — something Zen is mistakenly criticized for — but to open it up, to liberate it from the restrictive categories of language. Zen is famous for using verbal conundrums known as *koans* to help break a novice's attachment to words. Seemingly nonsensical questions such as *"What is the sound of one hand clapping?"* are used to encourage the student to abandon pre-conceived notions — such as the idea that there is any-thing real about language itself, rather than it simply being an artificial medium that allows us to communicate with each other.

Which doesn't mean to say that language is not important. Without the ability to keep records of time, money and 'lessons learned', civilization would never get started. Without the ability to explain to others what we are thinking, and justify our actions, we would rapidly revert to the raw violence of the jungle. But it's a double-edged sword. To the extent that we are enabled by language, so are we enslaved by it. By taking 'our' language seriously, by using it as a badge of identity that divides us from others, we are missing the fact that it's only ever a frame of reference, abstract patterns of data our brains have to learn to decode before they can extract the meaning. As the English philosopher Thomas Hobbes sagely put it back in the 17th century, *"Words are wise men's counters. They do but reckon with them, for they are the money of fools."*

The next three chapters explore the trouble such credulousness can quickly lead to.

HOW: The Trap of Culture

"Culture is roughly anything that we do and the monkeys don't."
– Lord Raglan

The puzzle box

The first thing that language encourages is a social culture. Once you can use words to talk, however simply, suddenly there are things to discuss: instead of second-guessing what everyone else around you wants, conversations can be started, and agreements reached on how to do things. These mutual understandings gradually grow into a way of life, eventually becoming distinctive cultures that are unique to the groups that share them. For as with language itself, the heart of culture is agreement: whether it's the noises we make when we speak, the way we measure time and space – or even the side of the road we drive on – the only way we can avoid chaos is to agree on and accept a common system. As children, we don't necessarily realise that we're agreeing to anything, of course. We just automatically do what everyone else around us is doing. But it's an agreement nonetheless. And the desire to buy into that agreement seems to be deeply part of us from an early age.

In 2004, researchers at the University of St Andrews were surprised by an unexpected result in an experiment they were doing to compare the relative intelligence of chimps and young children. They found there was a particularly significant difference in the way the two groups learnt how to do things. Presented with a 'puzzle box' from which they could extract a reward (a peanut for the chimps, a sweet for the children), both groups were shown a sequence of actions involving rods that had to be manipulated in certain ways before the drawer containing the reward would open. It turned out that the chimpanzees were just as quick as the children to grasp what had to be done.

But then the box was replaced with a similar one made of clear plastic which allowed them to see that the routine with the rods was just a decoy, and did not affect the opening of the drawer. When they spotted this, the chimps immediately abandoned the dummy sequence, and went straight for the drawer. But the children didn't. Even though they could see that the rods had nothing to do with the way the drawer opened, just as the chimps could, every time they wanted to get the sweet they kept on repeating the sequence of actions they'd been shown. They continued to do this even when there was no one else in the room.

This experiment has now been repeated enough times in a sufficiently wide range of cultures to leave little doubt about the result: young children seem to be predisposed to continue to imitate what they've been taught, regardless of whether their eyes and instincts might tell them otherwise. Psychologists have coined the term 'overimitation' to describe this puzzling behaviour. But though we've given it a name and can discuss it as a scientific phenomenon, we still aren't able to explain it. Do the children do it because they like to play games? Because they don't want to upset the person who showed them? Or is it because they assume that they wouldn't have been shown if there wasn't a point, even if they can't see what that point is? We don't know.

But what we do know is that, unlike the chimps, the children have language. Even if they are only shown, not told what to do, their sensitivity to language is likely to be a factor in their behaviour. The chimps have no reason to believe anything other than the evidence of their eyes. Once they realise there's an easier way to get what they want, they simply take it, without hesitation. But language gives children a reason for doing something other than what seems obvious. Children quickly learn that what adults tell them is usually useful, and worth taking seriously – so they get used to the idea of doing things the way they're shown, even if they can't immediately see why. They may still have doubts, but language installs a voice in their head which can easily become stronger than their own feeling – especially if they are not yet confident – and so they learn to do as they are told. Language creates a split between instinct and action.

What emerges from that split is culture. If you don't trust your instincts, it can often feel safer to take someone's word for it. Conformity becomes the name of the game, and that's the struggle we all face – first as children and then as adults. Without culture we are as helpless as we are without language, as culture delivers precious knowledge that we might otherwise never discover; but it also functions as a mental strait-jacket, encouraging us to follow established ways without questioning them. Culture reinforces and supports traditional practices, which is why humans tend to be conservative: faced with a huge resource of tribal knowledge, it's always going to feel less risky to go with what you've been told than to strike out on your own.

Yet culture is mostly just a collection of lucky accidents that have been found to work, survival strategies that have been passed down the generations. Many such traditions evolve from the circumstances and choices of the people who created them, like the decision to make cheese from milk rather than grow beans to make tofu. Others emerge from necessity, like the most practical way to make fire. Ultimately, culture is about passing on tricks that can improve our chances of survival, however inefficiently. Something is always better than nothing. Just as there are many thousands of different languages in the world, all relying on the same trick of speech, different cultures have evolved customs that can sometimes seem almost incomprehensible to others, despite serving the same basic needs. But no way of life seems strange to someone brought up with it – just as all languages seem natural to their native speakers. The trap of culture is to believe that our way of life is normal, and that everyone else is odd.

Nor are cultures necessarily tied to a particular language – a point made by the old joke about Britain and America being divided by a common language. Though Hollywood's dominance of the global entertainment industry means British speakers of English are more familiar with US culture and speech than Americans are of the Brits, it wasn't always so; when the first 'talkie' movies appeared in the 1920s, British audiences complained that American accents were incomprehensible.

Attitudes can be quite different too. I can't be the only British person to have been surprised in the States at being greeted with a friendly 'Hi, how are you?' when entering a shop I'd never been to before – most British people only say that to someone they already know.

For if your accent doesn't mark you out, your reactions certainly will. The culture you grow up in imprints itself on your behavior as surely as your personal history. As well as speaking different languages, citizens of European countries dress and behave quite distinctly, as do British and Americans. And you can instantly spot US tourists of Japanese descent on the subway in Tokyo not just from the way they dress and talk, but from the way they hold themselves: Americans have mobile faces due to living in a more relaxed culture not afraid to show its feelings, and can tend to slouch instead of holding themselves erect. In contrast, the relative expressionlessness of Japanese faces works as a kind of cultural Botox, smoothing out facial lines and making them look much younger.

Humans are not the only species to have cultures, of course. Whether it's pods of dolphins or killer whales cooperating to catch fish in ways that are unique to their feeding grounds, or chimps teaching their young how to coax termites out of holes in ways that are unique to their particular troupe, you don't need language to pass on knowledge that marks you out as belonging to a different tribe. Even songbirds display regional variations – dialects, in effect – in their characteristic songs. But just as communication between all other animals is limited by its analog nature, so their ability to develop cultures is limited because they cannot discuss and agree things.

For without the ability to share detailed information, no complex culture can emerge. The decisions we make through discussion and group activity are what allow us to develop and build on earlier ideas, creating an unspoken cultural grammar that every community depends on. In the end, culture is just a long series of nested meetings, with each new layer built on the assumption of previous agreements. Though by no means always consistent when viewed from the outside, culture is the result of what's been discussed and accepted within the group it emerges from, whether that's as small as a group of friends or as large as a country: if you find it odd, it'll be because you've missed a meeting. We're all doing the same things – it's just that other cultures have learnt to do those same things in very different ways. Let's take a look at some of them.

Slices of time

A key series of meetings that all cultures have to have had since we first began to discuss things is how to talk about time. We all have a sense of time, an awareness of things that have happened and the ability to imagine things yet to come. This sense of time does not need to involve words – the behaviour of most animals shows that they remember things that have happened, and can anticipate what might be coming next. But unlike us, other animals can't talk about it – and until we agreed a way of speaking about time and had defined units for measuring it, neither could we. Even something as straightforward as *"I'll meet you on Wednesday next week at six o'clock"* contains several assumptions that are not immediately obvious until you start to think about it.

We are perhaps fortunate that the colossal cosmic collision that happened in the early days of our solar system left our planet with a distinctively wonky axis of rotation and an oddly over-sized moon. This has gifted us with several obvious units of time that are widely identified and spoken about in most cultures as days, months and seasons. It's not too difficult to recognize what a day and a month are, and we soon understand that the seasons occur regularly in a predictable cycle which we think of as a year. Most cultures have ancient words that relate to these phenomena, and as the moon waxes and wanes in a cycle of around 28 days, it's reasonably convenient to subdivide that period into halves and quarters to create more manageable units called weeks.

Or so you might think. But although agreeing on a day as a unit of time would seem easy and natural enough – the sun rises, sets and rises again in a straightforward cycle – things are not quite so simple, even so: different cultures have had quite different ideas about when the day should start, for example. We may have come to accept that midnight is the logical point to end one day and begin the next, but it could just as well start at sunrise, midday or sunset – and that's what many other cultures have decided. Then you need to agree on how long a week is going to be. We now take it for granted that it should be seven days, but history tells us that other cultures have divided their weeks into units of three, four, five, or six – and even eight, nine or ten days.

Yet even when we've agreed on how many days we are going to have in our week, we still have to decide how to name them, so that we can tell them apart. For cultures that could already count you'd think that numbering them would have been a tidy solution – as Arabic, Greek, Chinese and Portuguese do to this day, for example. But that's not been the answer that most of us came up with, and the names of heavenly bodies and long-gone deities are still widely used. We don't usually think about it, but most days of the week in English still nod to the gods of ancient Europe – Tiu, Woden, Thor and Freya – with Saturday honouring the Roman god Saturn, and Sunday and Monday named after the sun and moon. And we're not there yet: once you've named them, you have to decide which day to start the week with – another decision that varies with cultures, even when they've agreed to use the same names.

That's plenty of meetings to get through even before we start to think about how to calibrate time within a day – and without deciding that, we're still not going to be able to keep that Wednesday appointment of ours. We're all used to the idea that a day has 24 hours, an hour has 60 minutes and a minute has 60 seconds, but when you stand back for a moment, that's a pretty unusual number to choose. After all, we measure almost everything else in units of ten – a natural enough choice given the number of fingers we have – so why not time? That's what they did in Ancient Egypt, as did the Chinese for most of their history, and the Jacobins in Revolutionary France.

But with no obvious division in a day beyond the clear difference between day and night (apart from the sun's highest point in the sky, widely recognised as 'mid-day'), in principle any system of division is just as good as another, as long as you stick to it. It speaks to the innate conservatism of culture that the system now used internationally can be traced back over 5000 years through Arab culture, Ancient Rome and Greece to the Sumerians, the first people to start thinking about it – and that it originally derives from using a thumb to count to twelve with the three joints on each finger of one hand, and then using the five digits of the other hand to multiply the units of twelve up to sixty.

But even with an agreed system of dividing up the days into hours and minutes, and an accurate way of measuring them, there's yet another problem: because the sun rises and sets at different times in different places, time based on the movement of the sun is relative to the place where it's being measured. Once mechanical clocks allowed us to mea-sure time accurately enough, for much of the 18th and 19th centuries towns across England had their 'own' time that varied by several minutes from other parts of the country. The decision to introduce a standard time across the nation did not come until the invention of the railway led to a need to fix times nationally, although old habits die hard: the 5-minute difference between Oxford and London is preserved in the tradition of 'Oxford Time' – still marked by the tolling of the Great Tom bell of Christ Church college every evening at 9.05 pm (9 pm in 'Oxford time'), an ancient reminder to students to be back to their rooms before the gates were locked.

And as if keeping tabs on the time of day wasn't bad enough, tracking the length of a year proved to be much harder. Though the months come and go regularly enough, it wasn't at all easy to work out how long a year was – especially as it seemed that God had neglected to make a year divisible by an exact number of months (he'd not done a very good job with weeks, either, as a month averages 29.5 days – which means the weeks of a lunar calendar have to be constantly jug-gled between seven and nine days). There's some very complex maths involved in matching up a hunter-gatherer's simple lunar calendar to the more precise solar calendar that was required for agriculture, and although ancient cultures from the Egyptians to the Mayans did come up with a system of sorts, it was a puzzle that was not really solved until well into the 16th century.

The establishment of an accurate system wasn't the end of it – it still took centuries before most of the world caught up. The last major adjustment in the UK calendar was as recently as 1752, when 11 days were 'removed' from September – it being decreed by Act of Parliament that the 2nd of September should be followed immediately by the 14th – thus finally bringing Britain in line with the rest of Europe, where Catholic countries had been using the Gregorian calendar since a papal bull on the subject in 1582. But Orthodox Russia continued to hold out as far as 1918 – so for much of the 17th, 18th and even the 19th centuries, it wasn't jet lag that travellers from England would have experienced on their Grand Tours, it was date lag – on top of any time difference between countries, there was a difference in the date of around 10 days.

But even when we've agreed on how long a year is and how it should be subdivided, there's still the question of how and when to start counting them. When I first went to Japan in September 1978, I was taken aback to find myself among 120 million people who thought we were in the 9th month of the 53rd year of 昭和 (*Showa*, or Shining Peace). To my further astonishment, they also wrote the date 'backwards': rather than 26/09/53, they wrote 53.09.26. This mysterious number appeared on every kind of official document – on train tickets, on newspapers, everywhere. My astonishment was misplaced, of course. Japan is not the only country to count the passing years in a different way. Had I been curious enough, I would have discovered that the Arab world thought it was the year 1399 (dated from the birth of Muhammed), the traditional Chinese calendar would have told me it was the year 4676, the Hindu calendar would have said 5080, and the Jewish one 5736.

But although the 'Western' calendar is counted from the birth of Jesus Christ – a date of great significance to the people who first came up with the idea – the original meaning of the number is no longer important. The reason why the world has accepted a system based on Christian belief is not about religious doctrine, but about political influence in the world: Europe was calling the shots when it first became important to have a global standard that allowed everyone to discuss dates using an agreed point of reference. Most scholars now agree that the historical figure of Christ is unlikely to have been born in the year 1 AD, yet there's no pressure to revise the dating system because, just as with grammar, content slowly bleaches away to function. And if we all agree it serves a useful purpose, however absurd its original meaning, there's no need to change it – any more than we need to change the irregularities of our writing systems.

And what goes for time also applies to space. Given that the surface of a globe has no obvious centre, no east, no west nor even any 'up' or 'down', it's not surprising that different cultures have had different and often conflicting rules about how to make and read maps. In the west we are quite used to seeing a map of the world with Britain at the centre, the line for zero longitude running through Greenwich – but in classrooms in China and Japan you will see a very different perspective, with New York on the right (the Far East) and Britain on the left (the Far West).

Maps these days are conventionally presented with the north at the top and the south at the bottom, but this has not always been the case, and not just in non-western cultures. The idea of proportionality and scale is also relatively new, and many cultures still make maps that show important things and places larger than they actually are, which can make it hard to estimate distances. From a rational standpoint we may wonder how such maps can be of much use in the real world – but as with the erotic Japanese *shunga* prints, they too have a truth, a truth about the emotional significance of place.

The man in the moon

But culture is much more than the fractional division of time. All those meetings about time and space may have helped us put a man on the moon, but there was a man in the moon long before anyone had ever thought of going there. Or at least, some of us thought so. There's a long-standing tradition in European culture about a man in the moon, although the explanation for what he was doing there varies greatly. The Romans thought he was a sheep-thief, the Germans had a man caught stealing wood from his neighbour's hedgerow, Christian lore held that he was the man sentenced to death by God in the Book of Numbers, and in Talmudic tradition it's the face of Jacob.

The moon is a good example of how different cultures see the same thing in quite different ways. That's because – now we've actually been there – we can be certain that it is none of the things attributed to it in legend and folklore. As far as we can tell, the moon is simply a large lump of rock, about 3,500 km in diameter, which orbits the earth at a distance of about 400,000 km. Although the Ancient Greeks and possibly even the Egyptians had managed to work out a good approximation of how far the moon was away from the earth, they had no means of discovering any more about it – and most of the older and less sophisticated cultures had no idea at all. For them, the moon was simply a strange light in the night sky that mysteriously grew larger and then smaller again, and somehow seemed to have influence over tides, minds and menses.

But you can't have such a large and luminous object in the night sky without wondering about it. It's not surprising that, once we could talk about it, all manner of just-so stories grew up from all those meetings on cold clear nights when there were no other social media to distract us. In the English-speaking world we're familiar with the idea that the moon is made of cheese – a notion that comes from the way cheese was made in days when such processes were more visible and obvious, and people could see that the moon looked like a large roundel of cheese. But in other parts of the world people have had very different ideas. The moon was frequently associated with gods or goddesses (as it once was in the European tradition as well) or with life, or alternatively with death, and can be either male or female. It can be a threatening or a comforting presence, a wife or a sister to the sun, and be associated with a wide variety of animals – frogs, toads and snakes – or even a hunter in front of his igloo.

The Chinese fancy they see a rabbit in the moon – and, following them, the Japanese even believe the rabbit is pounding rice in a wooden tub to make rice-cakes, a traditional Japanese activity. You can make out the rabbit from its ears, but I've always struggled to see the tub (if not as much as the Japanese struggle to imagine the moon made of cheese, as cheese-making is not part of their culture). But moon/rabbit legends are common in East Asia, and although that might suggest a Chinese origin to the idea, similar stories are also found both in the pre-Columbian legends of South America and the lore of native American tribes. This raises the intriguing possibility that the first people to have seen a rabbit in the moon might have done so long before China existed – perhaps in some nameless Stone Age tribe whose descendants eventually crossed the Bering Strait into the Americas, taking their legend with them into a cultural cul-de-sac whose isolation was undisturbed for over 10,000 years.

In that sense the moon is a like a cosmic Rorschach test, the legends that have grown around it reflecting the cultural hinterland of the societies that created them. It makes no difference to the moon whether you see a man or a rabbit in its pock-marked disc, but decisions such as these still play an important part in our cultures. Such stories belong to the class of meetings led by poets and story-tellers, the entertainers and proto-media folk who invented ingenious ways to decorate the down time around the camp-fire, or simply to keep the children amused before bedtime. The bright strip of light in the night sky might be the Milky Way, the Silver River or the wood ash thrown into the sky by the First Girl, but once established these legends are hard to forget, because they spark the imagination. We may now know that the Milky Way is a throbbing galaxy of 200 billion stars, but it's still the girl who pleases us more.

That's why these stories and legends become part of the fabric that language weaves: and your familiarity with this colourful cloth is what determines your acceptance in the society in which it was woven. Joining a group is not just about being able to speak their language: you have to know what people like to talk about, the stories they tell, the things they take for granted. Often, this pool of shared ideas is passed on most vividly in childhood, which makes it hard for an adult to learn about them even if they have mastered the language: our knowledge of such things is a kind of cultural shibboleth, and like language itself, the set of values you are first exposed to can become hard to shake off without a considerable effort. What you learn first goes deepest.

The Piraha tribe of the Amazon have managed to keep themselves to themselves for as long as anyone knows. And no one does know, not even them. They don't have writing, and their oral traditions stretch back a couple of generations at best. They don't have a creation myth, and simply believe that things are the way they are because they have always been so. Their way of life is simple, but they are admirably secure in it, refusing to accept other ideas or doctrines. Their scepticism is so profound that they actually managed to make an atheist of the missionary Daniel Everett who had gone there to learn their language and convert them. Everett lived with the Piraha on and off for decades, slowly learning their language and getting to grips with their way of life.

One of the first things he learnt as he started to be able to understand their language was that they had a very robust view of their own language and culture. The expression the Piraha use for their own language means '*straight head*', and their word for a foreign language means '*crooked head*'. We can laugh at the naivety of this perception, but it actually gets right to the heart of the matter: deep down inside we all tend to feel not only that we ourselves are right and everyone else is wrong, but that the group that we belong to – whether it's our family, football club, country or religion – is right, and all the others are wrong. Logically, that can't possibly be the case, but until we are challenged to give it some thought, humans – like most animals – are driven more by habit and emotion than logic. The Greek historian Herodotus makes this point as far back as the 5th century BC with a story about Darius I, the great Persian king:

Darius, he tells us, "*summoned into his presence certain Greeks who were at hand, and asked them what he should pay them to eat the bodies of their fathers when they died. To which they answered, that there was no sum that would tempt them to do such a thing. He then sent for certain Indians, of the race of Callatians, men who eat their fathers, and asked them, while* the Greeks stood by, what he should give them to burn the bodies of their fathers at their decease. The Indians exclaimed aloud, and bade him forbear such language." Herodotus is philosophical: "How right Pindar is, it seems to me, when he declares in his poetry that 'Custom is the king of all'."

Whether it's a story about the moon or the order in which your write your name (many cultures find it more natural to write their personal name after their family name) humans can have diametrically different ideas about how to do things. That's all part of the rich tapestry of confusion from which we eventually learn to make sense of the world. But no matter how much we may be attached to the ways of our own culture, they are still liable to succumb to the pressure of convenience, as happened with the measurement of time. In a world far more interconnected than Herodotus could ever have imagined, we increasingly have to agree on matters that cross cultural boundaries, and learn to gracefully give up our old-fashioned, out-moded customs. In my lifetime the UK abandoned the old imperial measures of money, weight and length, and no matter how they resisted it, no one felt any the worse for it: a glass of beer is still a glass of beer, whether you measure it in pints or litres, or pay for it in pounds or euros.

Discomfort food

Whether we believe the moon is inhabited by a man or a rabbit, made of cheese or pounded rice, one area where cultural differences are felt most keenly is in what we eat. Eating is essential – after breathing and drinking, it's the most crucial thing we need to do in order to survive. There are certain key nutrients the human body needs to be able to maintain itself, but the sources we can turn to are exceedingly various – and the ways that different cultures have found to supply them are marvellously different.

Much depends on availability, climate and custom, but ingenuity, imagination and desperation all play their part. *Tepas*, a delicacy eaten by the Yupik people of Alaska, is a paste made of fish heads that have been left to rot for several weeks. *Casu marzu* is a ripe Sardinian cheese fermented by maggots, often consumed with the maggots still alive.

The chitlins (or chitterlings) eaten in many forms in poorer communities across the world are the small intestines of pigs, fried or boiled. Disgusting though all these might seem to some of us, they are usually looked on as special treats in their culture.

But before you throw your hands up at the Icelandic practice of eating ram's testicles smoked in their own dung, or at *balut*, the Filipino bar snack that's a fertilized duck egg boiled alive and eaten in the shell, remember that the humble rice pudding can turn stomachs in parts of the world where rice is something that should always be savoury, and definitely not cooked in milk. Strange though it may seem, the sense of revulsion which certain foods can arouse is often matched by the enthusiasm with which others long for them as precious memories of childhood, the comfort food we so often return to when distressed. It's almost as if we get used to food in the same way as we learn to speak – there's a certain period of time in which our basic tastes are formed, creating a resistance to anything different. Yet the difficulty is mostly mental – the thought of eating something strange is nearly always much worse than actually doing so.

A few weeks after I first started living in Japan, I began to long for some fresh bread. It wasn't that I'd not had any bread at all – at lunchtimes in the classroom where I was teaching, I was provided with bread instead of rice when we all sat down to the *bento* lunchboxes that the school supplied for the pupils' communal lunch. Each *bento* was divided into two sections, one with a selection of fish, meat or vegetables that varied with the day or season, and the other full of steamed rice with a little pickled plum. All except mine. The school had decided that as a foreigner I would be unable to eat rice, and substituted a thick slice of bread instead. As I was the only person eating bread and they bought it a loaf at a time, it took about a fortnight to get through the loaf – by which time it was getting noticeably stale. So when I passed a bakery on my way back from school one day, I couldn't help looking longingly in the window. And what caught my eye most were some beautiful soft-looking buns. I rushed in, bought half-a-dozen, and dropped into the local store for some butter. At last, I thought, a taste of home.

But when I finally bit into one, I got a terrible shock. Instead of the pure white bread I was looking forward to, there was something dark, reddish-brown and – even worse – sweet inside. Not only that, it seemed to have a very strange consistency. It wasn't jam, it wasn't chocolate – it seemed vaguely fibrous. I couldn't tell what it was. So I took one of my buns with me when I went to school the next day, and asked a fellow teacher what it was. He told me that it was *an-pan* – bread with adzuki beans mixed with sugar. This was, as they say in Japanese, a 'double punch'. Not only was there something sweet in the bread, which went against all my expectations, but this sweet thing was actually made from beans, which also should not be sweet. Of course, the only thing odd about it was my failure to imagine things being different than the way they 'ought' to be. There was nothing wrong with putting sweet beans in bread – in fact, once I got over the shock of the idea, I actually got to like *an-pan* very much.

Not all new foods are quite so easy to adjust to, though. When travelling in Africa in my student days, I met a young Sudanese man on his way back home after three years spent in Paris. He told me his parents would be holding a party at his house, and urged me to come and stay. The Sudanese like to sleep out of doors. They take their beds outside the house and sleep beneath the open sky (though inside the walls of a compound). This was already strange enough, though it was pleasant to drift off to sleep looking at the stars.

But early the next morning I was woken up by a loud shout of 'Come, come!' and a plaintive background bleating. I rubbed my eyes and rolled over to see a short man with thick spectacles approaching me, dragging a reluctant sheep by the ear. He gestured with his head for me to follow him, and not wishing to offend, I got up and followed. Around the corner was a trestle table laid out with some tools. I was just taking in this scene when he abruptly picked up the sheep by its ear with one hand, and without further warning, neatly sliced off its head with a machete he'd been holding out of sight in the other.

It happened so quickly I hardly had time to react. The next thing I knew he had the body up on the table and began cutting up the carcass, removing the skin first. With practiced movements he inserted a tube into a cut made in one leg, and started blowing into it to separate the skin from the body. Within five minutes he had the table laid out neatly like a butchers' shop, and from the pile of entrails he carefully selected the heart and laid it on the palm of his hand. With a few sharp cuts he had sliced it into small pieces, and, glowing with pride, held it out for me to take a piece. 'Eat!' he said, beaming. As I later learnt, I had been selected for this joyous experience as I was the honoured guest – this was the choicest of cuts, the essence of the beast, the warm heart of hospitality.

It certainly didn't feel like that at the time. I hadn't had any breakfast, I was hardly awake, and to be invited to gnaw on a warm piece of raw heart that was still twitching did not seem like the best way to start my day. But to refuse would have been rude: I took a piece, and placed it in my mouth. It is hard to say which was worse, the taste or the thought of it. But as soon as I began to chew, my host took his own piece and started chomping away as if it was the best thing a person could ever hope to eat. And for him, of course, it was. I was the odd one out for finding it strange.

But every country has its special foods that no one other than a native is supposed to be able to eat. One of Japan's culinary touchstones is a sticky, rather smelly dish of fermented beans called *natto*, of which they are particularly proud. These foods are often at the heart of what it means to be that particular nationality. Apart from roast beef and fish and chips, the British may not be widely famed for their cuisine, but we too have our own peculiar delicacies: think black pudding, pickled onions, spotted dick, jellied eels, pork scratchings, steak-and-kidney pie, scotch egg, haggis, marmite... It's almost a badge of honour: only 'we' can eat these uniquely odd things that we nonetheless claim to like so very much. We must be different, after all – or rather, you must be different because you don't like to eat them. Never mind that millions of Japanese people don't like to eat *natto* either, or that black pudding isn't exactly high on most British people's list of favourite foods. It's ours, and we're proud of it.

However, much of what passes for a national cuisine is dictated by what happened to be available in less bountiful days, when you had to eat whatever you could find. Even within living memory in the UK, the supply of imported food was very limited, and the British people had to make do with the meagre range of fruit and vegetables that can be persuaded to grow in their dark and damp islands. And one of the reasons Chinese cuisine is so fabulously imaginative is that in many periods of their history, you had to find a way to eat anything that came to hand. Even today, in some parts of rural China you could be forgiven for mistaking a local restaurant for a zoo – Beijing Zoo even has a restaurant where visitors can sample meat from some of the animals on display.

The distinctive treats of most countries often owe more to necessity than choice: black pudding was simply a clever way of making use of a rich source of protein – blood – that would otherwise be wasted when a pig was slaughtered. The same is true for haggis and pork scratchings, and until well into the 19th century, people in England ate almost all parts of an animal, brains, intestines and all types of offal as well as the meat itself. It's only quite recently that we could afford to be squeamish about what we eat.

A word about beards

And speaking of squeamish: the awareness of our relative nakedness compared to our animal cousins with their thick coats of fur has long provoked debate about how to manage what remains of our body hair. Quite different practices in this arena can be found throughout history and around the globe even today. Much of this may be driven by fashion, but there's usually a cultural factor in play, nonetheless. Facial hair may change more visibly, but culture can still exert an influence in the most private of areas – even those not normally on public display – and though we don't necessarily speak about such things at dinner parties, the power of persuasion is at work here as well.

The very existence of the word *merkin* reveals our difficulty with the subject. But our more ancient traditions have become disrupted by the easy availability of online porn in recent years, which appears to have radically changed the etiquette around pubic hair in the west. Even if the fashion for shaven parts stems as much from fear of infection as the desire to reveal more flesh to gawking viewers, it has now reached the point where women in particular seem to feel pressure to conform to what they believe is expected of them in that department – even when presenting themselves to a midwife.

It is perhaps surprising that the fashion for shaving 'down there' is such a recent fad in the west, given that until the end of the 19th century, depictions of the nude in Western art almost universally omitted pubic hair (to the extent that, according to his biographer, the famous 19th century art critic John Ruskin was driven to annul his marriage upon discovering his wife's bush on their wedding night, on the grounds that she was "freakish and deformed"). This is certainly not the case in other parts of the world, as the depilation of pubic hair has been the norm in many Middle Eastern and Asian cultures from ancient times, and not only for women. When visiting a *hamam* bath in Istanbul in the 1970s, the fact that I was the only person present who was not shaven below the belt provoked visible disgust from the other customers. I was only saved from an impromptu encounter with a blunt razor by the fact that I also sported a full beard, traditionally a sign of a *hajji*, or someone who has made a pilgrimage to Mecca, which luckily excused me – even though I have never been there.

But as you contemplate the cultural merits of a regular 'sack & crack' routine, spare a thought for the oddity of the traditional Japanese fashion for shaving the front of your head. Think of all those period-drama samurai movies, the Japanese equivalent of spaghetti Westerns, where the men all proudly display a chunky *chonmage* topknot, oiled and waxed onto a smoothly shaven pate. It's hard to imagine how anyone could have thought it looked good to shave off that part of your hair, or how they ever persuaded anyone else to do it. In European eyes at least, it seems just plain crazy – so much so that when Japanese men started to appear in Europe with this tonsorial arrangement, a riot nearly broke out in a Dutch theatre in 1863 when they were asked to remove their hats, exposing their freakish hairstyle.

These days, far from shaving hair off, people are willing to subject themselves to the painful process of supplementing any natural thinning with hair transplanted from other parts of their body. But in the days when that wasn't an option, it's tempting to imagine that this Japanese practice may have started as a way of compensating for the male-pattern baldness of a superior lord. But whatever the reason, it rapidly became a style affected more for fashion and status that anything else, and certainly no more absurd than the extravagant wigs that royalty and aristocrats used throughout the 18th century in Europe (a fashion that actually did start with the desire of the French kings to hide their hereditary bald patch, a tradition which comically survives in the wigs of judges and barristers in British courts to this day.)

But when it comes to shaving, the oddest custom of all is surely the shaving of faces. Until quite recently, that thought was not one that troubled many people in the west, but beards are undeniably making a serious comeback. Wherever you look, any man with pretensions to be at the forefront of fashion is growing one. Ads, TV, films and magazines are full of hairy faces, and not just those with carefully groomed 'tache and sideburns. The current taste is for the full monty, with maybe a little careful trimming to keep it in line. As a life-long beardie myself, I can only approve (although I have lately shrunk down to a goatee to avoid that ungroomed salt-and-pepper look).

But it was not always thus. Though there was a brief vogue for them in the 60s, when they were really just a natural accompaniment for long hair, beards have largely been the exception in western culture for hundreds of years, and to judge by the busts and statues they leave behind, the Romans and even the Greeks were none too fond of them either – though contrary to popular myth, the word barbarian does not in fact derive from *barba*, the Latin word for beard: more interestingly, it seems to be a reference to foreigners, whose unintelligible speech was thought to sound like '*bar-bar*'.

The Ancient Egyptians also disliked body and facial hair, resorting to all kinds of methods to remove it. But they do seem to have had a weakness for chin hair, a habit that later evolved into the custom of wearing a *postiche*, a kind of false beard made of metal, held in place with a ribbon tied over the head, which became such a symbol of authority that it was even affected by queens. The cultures of Mesopotamia were big on beards too, oiling, dressing and curling them into elaborate tiers with tongs and curling irons, and in Turkey the cutting of a man's beard was regarded as a shameful thing suitable only for slaves, who were shaven to mark their servility. Further east, the ancient cultures of India and China have traditionally viewed beards with reverence, but apart from a Tudor fashion for them when Henry VIII decided to sport a beard, the Christian world has generally viewed them with disapproval.

The most significant resurgence in recent times was in the latter part of the 19th century, when the leading figures of the day began to sprout beards as bushy as Old Testament prophets. That may have been part of the attraction – the Reverend William Henry Henslowe published a pamphlet in 1847 railing against the "unnatural, irrational, unmanly and ungodly practice of shaving", which he claimed was contrary to the "good-will and pleasure" of the Lord – but it was also a time when Victorian men were beginning to feel hemmed in by civilisation, and the beard was one way to assert their natural manliness. The Army had also relaxed its traditional stance on beards and encouraged soldiers to grow them during the Crimean War, partly to deal with the harsh conditions, so there were many fully-bearded men returning as heroes to set the tone.

But whatever the fashion or the reasons for it, there's no denying that man was not born to be clean-shaven, and – no matter what the persuasive purveyors of the three-, five- or even seven-blade fantasy shave may tell you – he can never achieve it. Those of you who have struggled with it will know that, no matter how hard you try, there's always going to be that annoying little scrap of sandpaper at some odd corner of your chin. And that's before it all starts growing back again, which it does soon enough. So why do we try to hold back the inevitable? And why did we start in the first place?

Imagine the uproar the first time a man discovered that he could liberate himself from the limitations of his secondary sexual characteristics by deftly scraping his face with a shard of chipped flint. There were practical reasons, of course. Alexander the Great worried that beards might make his soldiers more vulnerable to being grabbed. Then there's the question of hygiene – poor grooming around an orifice into which all manner of materials are stuffed is an open invitation to the spread of a rather different form of culture. But there's no need to let nature take its course – as with the hair on our heads, the solution is a neat trim, leaving the beard both manageable and pleasantly malleable.

And if you still think that growing one is weird, consider this: beards come naturally – it's shaving that doesn't. Just like circumcision, the onus is on its practitioners to do the explaining. In finding beards strange, you're no different to the samurai who thought that growing a full head of hair was an abomination. So next time you look at your clean-shaven face in the mirror or see one walking down the street, just think of a clean-shaven scrotum. And remind yourself why shaving your face is so normal.

The dog's bollocks

A friend once told me a story of a visit to Shanghai where he was attending a gig by a young band he had been mentoring. At the end, along with the applause, he could hear people shouting something that sounded to him like 'newbie, newbie...' Perplexed and concerned that they were insulting his protégés, he demanded to know what was going on, only to be told that the phrase he was hearing meant 'cow's vagina'. On further inquiry, he was told it was slang for 'awesome' and that he should be pleased that the audience liked the music. He told me this to how show weird things were in China, as he couldn't understand how it could be a compliment. On the face of it, it is quite astonishing. How could such an odd image (牛屄; or *niú bī*) be an expression of praise?

But let's not forget that British English has a phrase that is equally weird, and means much the same thing: *the dog's bollocks*. When I pointed this out to my friend, he was non-plussed: that's different, he said. But it's not different. It's actually just the same. The origin of either of these intriguing phrases is essentially irrelevant. It's an expression that the culture has adopted, and that's just what people say – and why such an odd phrase came to be used is really no more important in the case of the cow's vagina than it is for the canine testes. Just as we saw the 'semantic bleaching' of grammar, or the loss of the original sense from the meaning of 'Goodbye', we no longer know what the original meeting was about. But whether the 'dog's bollocks' is actually cunning piece of back-slang for *the box deluxe* (think about it...), or the thought that anything a dog spends so much time licking must be tasty, the force of the expression survives – perhaps precisely because of its oddity. Whatever their origin, both phrases effectively express a feeling we can all identify with, and that's the real point.

For it's not the words themselves that count, it's what they represent – as the father of semiotics, Ferdinand de Saussure, observed over a century ago. In my early days of learning Japanese I was amazed to discover that the word for nerve, 神経 (or *shinkei*) literally means 'path of the spirits' and that 病気 (or *byouki*), the word for illness, means 'sickness of the mind' – an amazement that was only compounded when I also discovered that most Japanese people are usually unaware of that, and are even surprised when you point it out. But then many English speakers are surprised when you point out to them that the word 'disease' derives from *dis-ease* – hinting at a theory of mind remarkably similar to the idea behind the Japanese word for illness – just as 'business' originally comes from *busy-ness* and 'holiday' from *holy-day*.

So we see that words can take on meanings that are far removed from their original sense, with both form and pronunciation evolving along the way, sometimes almost unrecognisably so. The word *'elixir'*, for example, with all its exotic connotations in English, actually derives from the Arabic word *al-iksir* which simply means 'the catalyst' – *'al'* is just the definite article. All a catalyst does is to promote chemical reactions, but in earlier times such substances were thought to have magical properties. *'Alchemy'* has even deeper roots. It is derived via old French and mediaeval Latin from the Arabic *al-kīmiyā* which in turn comes from a late Greek word *kēmeía* meaning 'transmutation'. But what's really interesting is that the Greek word stems from *kēmia*, an early Greek name for Egypt, which is taken from the Ancient Egyptian *kēme* (hieroglyphic *khmi*), literally meaning 'black earth', the rich loamy soil around the river Nile that was what allowed the desert sand to be transformed into the civilization of Egypt. From black earth to alchemy: talk about a transmutation of meaning!

All languages borrow words and phrases from each other as one of the natural consequences of conquest, travel and trade. English is particularly promiscuous in this respect, with as many as half of all English words coming from roots that are not immediately German or French, the basis of most modern English. This is not surprising, given the broad sweep of the British Empire and the need to pick up a certain amount of the local language, even if shouting louder in English was often the preferred option. And if another language has a better-sounding, more convenient or otherwise useful word than English, well, *hey presto*, we adopt it. Words do not always survive the transition with their meaning intact, however: *bimbo*, for example, is used to refer to a young male child in Italian, the language we take it from.

My favourite example of this semantic confusion is the Japanese word for tinplate, *buriki*, which allegedly derives from a misunderstanding dating back to the late 19th century when bricks were first imported into Japan. According to the story, stacks of bricks were transported with an outer covering of corrugated iron to protect them – a material new to the Japanese at the time. But when someone enquired what it was called, the British navvy who answered said 'brick' because he thought he was being asked about the contents, not the covering. It's a good story, even if a more plausible version is that it comes from the Dutch word for tinplate, *Blik*. So you never know, really, and it doesn't matter. Whatever the origin, Japanese use the word *buriki* without any confusion, as they already have the word *renga* for brick.

But then it doesn't matter what words you use to describe something, as long as you communicate. That's why the claims of 'untranslatable words' are so misleading. Almost any word or phrase is translatable, if you come at it the right way. The much-quoted 'untranslatable' Japanese expression *komorebi* (木漏れ日) just means 'sunlight through trees'.

That's exactly the same number of syllables in English or Japanese, no more or less difficult to say in either language. Even *Schadenfreude*, a 'word' that supposedly doesn't exist in English, is really only a fancy way of saying 'gloating' – taking pleasure in someone else's misfortune, or, as Google Translate offers, 'malicious joy' – a phrase with the same number of syllables. If the concept really doesn't exist in the other language, you can sometimes struggle to express it economically – the Inuit translation of the Bible allegedly renders 'The Lamb of God' as *'God's special thing that looks like a caribou calf'* – but these things get much exaggerated in the telling. The reason a speaker of one language can find it difficult to say what a word in their language means can simply be that they don't know the other language well enough.

Confusion can often be caused because the same idea is just being expressed differently, and you don't spot it. For many years I was mystified by the Chinese and Japanese idea of *chi* or *ki* (気) which seemed so integral to many of the traditional arts and practices of their culture, yet impossible to translate into English. Words like spirit, energy and life-force were often used, but they didn't seem right in the context. I was first introduced to *ki* through the practice of aikido, a martial art which at the time (in the mid-1970s) was translated rather grandly as 'The Way of Spiritual Harmony'. I used to attend classes in London with a very severe teacher who would berate us consistently about using too much strength when we should only be using our *ki*. None of us had any idea what he was talking about, of course; it was a mysterious force that seemed as elusive as the Holy Grail, and which you apparently had to be in a state of grace to receive – not that there was anything particularly gracious about Chiba Sensei as he hurled his students around the dojo, frequently knocking them out in the process.

It was only when I went to Japan and started learning the language that I began to realise that far from being mysterious and exotic, the word *ki* is widely used in the ordinary speech of Japanese people. 'Feeling', for example, is *kimochi*, or, 'having *ki*'). I'd struggled for years to identify and have some *ki* of my own, but in Japan this supposedly elevated and abstruse concept was being used on a daily basis, without anyone giving it a second thought. Was the entire Japanese population enlightened? They were not, of course. They were simply using a word so common in Japanese that, according to a Wikipedia article on *ki*, "*the Japanese language contains over 11,442 known usages of 'ki' as a compound*".

And no word so commonly used can be exotic or mysterious. It's only the absence of a 'proper' English word corresponding to *ki* that gives the impression that it's something strange or supernatural – whereas in fact it simply refers to what we mean by 'mind' in the sense of focused attention, or mindfulness. People in the west are no more devoid of *ki* or unaware of its workings that people anywhere: it's just that we don't use the same language to talk about it. Though English may have some older expressions and phrases that use words like 'mind' and 'spirit' in the same way that Japanese and Chinese do (such as 'I don't mind' or 'That's the spirit!'), these days we usually express most of the things that involve a sense of *ki* in another way altogether. In fact, we don't use a noun at all. We use a verb.

Perhaps the best way of understanding this is to think of the Japanese expression *ki ga au*, which literally means '(our) spirits meet'. What it really means, though, is that you 'get on' with someone. That's the sense in which it's used on an everyday basis in Japan. We all know how it feels when you get on with someone. It's not necessarily something that you can explain, but you feel it. It feels like you're in tune with the other person, that you see things the same way – or share a sense of humour, for example. Your spirits meet. Except we don't say that in English. We say 'we get on'. The word 'get' is the key here (if you'll forgive the unfortunate pun). We use 'get' in countless idioms in English that correspond to the way the word *ki* is used in Japanese. To *get into, get off on, get down (or up)* to something, to *get over* someone or something, *get on* (one's nerves) *get under* (one's skin) – you 'get' the picture.

It's not that *ki* is the same as 'get', though. It's more that the *ki* is the part of you that that 'gets' it: we're expressing the same thing in different ways. The apparent absence of a word in one language doesn't mean that the concept is missing as well – it's just talked about differently. A common mistake made by people not familiar with another language is to assume that there's a one-to-one correspondence between the words in a dictionary. That's almost never the case, even for the simplest of things. Take water, for example. In English, the word refers to the clear liquid that we call 'ice' when solid and 'steam' when a gas. But in Japanese there is a further division: the word usually used for water (*mizu*) means 'cold water' only, as there is a separate word *oyuu* for 'hot water', which is considered to be quite different. There are cultural reasons for that, of course, just as with any of the words and phrases a language uses.

But again, that's the point. It's not what a word once meant, or what its historical roots and antecedents are, or even how reliable the stories we tell about them are – it's what it means now that counts. And that is entirely up to how people use it. You can be upset about the way people say *prevaricate* when they mean *procrastinate*, for example, but if a word is used 'wrongly' by enough people, then it's you that's wrong – you've missed the meeting. Language is a plastic medium that evolves to suit what's required, and moves with the times. If we lose a particular meaning or nuance because not enough people really know what an old word means any more, we'll find another way of saying it if we still need it. That's just how language works. It's how culture works too.

Coming and going

Confusion over cultural concepts can extend even into the bedroom, however. To your surprise you will discover that in much of the orient you don't come, you go. That's particularly interesting, since physiologically it can feel as if you are 'going' anyway when you 'come' – so the mystery is more why English speakers don't say that anyway. The French supply the best answer, of course, with their charmingly jaunty '*j'arrive.*' But this confused sense of direction is not limited to sexual matters, however – speakers of languages that 'go' rather than 'come' often tend to use the words differently in other contexts as well, using the phrase 'I'm going' rather than 'I'm coming' when they're on their way to join someone, which sounds odd in English, but no more odd than the English way of saying things seems to them.

It's not just words, either. Gestures can be highly cultural, too. On one of my first days in Japan, travelling by train with a Japanese teacher to visit another school, I was surprised by a gesture that looked (to me) like it meant 'Go away.' The teacher had gone to the other end of the platform to make an enquiry at the ticket office, but then suddenly turned to me with his outstretched arm raised at shoulder level, apparently batting me away with the back of his hand, which he held palm downward. Confused, and thinking that perhaps my presence was proving an embarrassment in some way, I walked away – only to be summoned back by a shout telling me in English that he wanted me to join him.

What I hadn't realised (because I didn't know at the time) was that he was making the standard gesture used in Japan to invite someone to come towards you, as the waving hand is not seen as a dismissive gesture, but as beckoning someone to you, with the palm moving toward the body. Objectively speaking, the actual movement is virtually identical – but because the intent is different, it's quite clear to anyone who understands Japanese culture. At that time I didn't, of course – any more than he knew that in Britain we beckon people with your palm facing upward. We tend to assume the gestures we use in our own culture are universal – but even the most "obvious" ones can be understood very differently: don't try using the 'thumbs-up' sign in Iran, for example.

Basil Hall Chamberlain, one of the earliest and shrewdest observers of Meiji Japan, was fascinated by what he saw as the 'topsy-turvydom' of the Japanese, who seemed to do so many things the other way round to Europeans, particularly the British. He attributed that largely to their cultural backwardness, but really, who had it backwards? Europeans push on a saw or a carpenter's plane rather than pull on them as the Japanese do, but is it any easier or better to do it one way rather than the other? They both have their advantages, and both work as well. Japanese books start at the 'back' and finish at the 'front' – although that's exactly what they think our books do, of course.

There are many examples of 'either/or' situations where other cultures have taken the opposite, albeit equally logical, approach. Take clearing a blocked nose, for example: there are really only two options available – snorting or snorking. Should you blow, and find some means of disposing of the resultant slimy mess (many cultures find the British habit of putting a used handkerchief back in your pocket to be disgusting beyond belief) or should you suck and swallow? The point is, whichever way you're used to doing it, the other way is going to seem 'wrong'. Driving on the right side of the road feels wrong if you're used to driving on the left. Pushing on a saw seems wrong if you're used to pulling on one. And sucking in mucus... well, let's leave it at that. *"I still feel a shiver of disgust running down my spine and kindly offer them a paper towel,"* to quote the author of an online blog that addresses the subject.

Not all such dilemmas are quite so personal, but there are plenty of choices that create lifestyle issues. Consider shoes: do you remove them before entering a house like the majority of cultures around the world (perhaps replacing them with slippers), or do you follow the Anglo-Saxon practice of traipsing into a house wearing the shoes you have just walked the streets with, smearing the floors and carpets with whatever you've picked up on them in the course of your wanderings? The British and Americans seem to find this quite natural – when I first came back from Japan and removed my shoes in my parents' house, my father warned me against trying to import such an unacceptable foreign custom – but for most cultures it's considered the height of barbarism.

Personal hygiene is another area of conflict, especially in international relationships. Though things are improving, the British have traditionally had a rather parsimonious approach to baths, which they take much less frequently than in many other countries – even without making the comparison with the Japanese, who are famously fastidious in that respect. Nor is it simply a question of the frequency of ablution; even as a child I was disgusted at the idea of washing myself in six inches of tepid bathwater while still having to sit in the resulting scum, using a towel to wipe off the residue without rinsing first – but that was the way it was usually done in England when I was growing up.

And the management of one's personal space can throw up conceptual as well as practical differences. Every time a Japanese or Chinese person checks into a hotel in most western countries, for example, they have to think back to front. The simple process of registering their address requires them to upend their normal habits. Not only do they have to be able to write in an unfamiliar script, they have to write their address in a way that – to them – seems the wrong way round. In Japan and China, addresses are typically written with the name of the most important and biggest geographical division first. That means you start with the country, then the district, only then writing the town, the street, the house number and finally the name.

So if your name was Joe Blow and you lived at 10 Downing Street, London, England, a Japanese or Chinese person would think of and write this address as England, London, Downing Street 10, Blow, Joe. That's the right way around in their culture, and if you think about it from the postman's perspective, it's also much more efficient for sorting purposes. After all, that's the order in which you would naturally narrow things down from the largest category to the smallest – from country to city to road to family to individual. But things are not always so logical. The Japanese still use a concentric numbering system in which houses are numbered in the order in which they are built, and roads frequently have no names – a system reminiscent of mediaeval London. In the end, culture is simply what you do, not necessarily what's most efficient.

Just like the fish that doesn't notice it's in water until it's taken out of it, we generally don't question the ways we've grown up with until we've experienced an alternative. But when we do, it helps to bear in mind that the ways we've grown up with seem just as weird to 'them' as 'theirs' do to 'us'. In fact, it's the extent to which you think of a particular custom as weird that marks you out as being a foreigner. That doesn't make one way better than the other. Most of the time, it's not an either/or choice: we've just happened to learn one particular way of doing things, and missed a meeting on the rest.

In that sense, we're all 'us' – equally odd, equally irrational, and equally human: most of what we call 'culture' no more than a curious mixture of ingrained habit, low cunning, unexpected insight and rank idiocy – the defining hallmark of our species. Even our most venerated traditions are often just ways of doing things that have been found to work – no better or worse, in most instances, than most other ways of doing things. And once you realise that, the spell of language is broken.

The cultural differences that the trick of speech has encouraged over the millennia may be deep-seated, but – just like the sounds and grammar of language – they are largely accidental. We may feel there is an internal logic and consistency to why we do things one way rather than another (like whether or not we wear shoes indoors), but culture is more the result of historical happenstance than necessity, despite the emotional attachment we have for our own traditions. That doesn't matter, most of the time: but if you're in the business of empire-building, or simply feeling culturally insecure, it can start to seem like a weakness. You may be convinced inside yourself that your way is right, but a little more back-up can be required to persuade others.

And without logic on your side, the temptation is to make it a religious argument – a rabbit hole that language rapidly takes us down.

WHY: The Trap of Faith

"The invisible and the non-existent look very much alike."
— Delos B. McKown

The birth of belief

In these sophisticated times, it's easy to mock the absurdity of religious belief. How could anyone be foolish enough to imagine that everything just came into being at the say-so of some all-powerful yet invisible Creator – without any thought as to how it might have been done? How could we ever have led ourselves to think that the confused and contradictory words of some ancient book, indifferently translated from languages spoken by simple herdsmen, represented the sacred and settled will of an omnipotent God? To anyone who gives the matter any serious thought, the ideas at the heart of these beliefs seem such obvious fairy tales – a preposterous jumble of just-so stories with no plausible basis in reality – that it's almost incredible that we could ever have taken them seriously. But we did. And still do. All over the world.

For there's certainly no shortage of belief to go around: many of our most persistent cultural ideas have religious roots. Though faith may be in decline in urban societies, global surveys still show that as many as 85% of people around the world believe in some form of religion. The big ones are the 'Abrahamic' religions of Christianity and Islam, which together with Judaism make up more than half that number, with Hinduism and Buddhism accounting for around half of the rest. But at the other end of the scale there's a whole spectrum of smaller religions – according to some estimates there are almost as many religions in the world as there are languages, numbering in the thousands. Whatever we may think of it, religious belief is clearly still an important part of human society: hardly a culture on earth is not deeply coloured by it.

To the faithful, however, religion is much more than just another part of culture. We all feel an emotional attachment to the culture we grow up in – the foods, smells, habits and customs of our particular society – and share a secret sense that it's somehow better than all the others. But religions stake a much higher claim to our loyalty than nostalgia: though they come in as many flavours as there are cultures and peoples, their traditions, teachings, rituals and ceremonies demand a devotion to something that goes way beyond mere human authority or convenience. Religion is about reverence for, and even fear of the divine – and presents itself as being a far deeper truth about the world than we can hope to uncover on our own.

Its importance can be seen from the fact that our largest gatherings still take place in the name of religion – easily attracting tens, even hundreds of times more people than our biggest political, musical or sporting events. Through most of human history, the largest and most splendid buildings built by any culture have had a religious purpose: cathedrals, mosques, temples, shrines and pagodas – even pyramids. To those who value it, religion is about the sacred, the holy and the spiritual – it appears to speak to the most precious, significant and meaningful parts of our lives, often connected with the best of what it means to be human: kind, loving, forgiving, generous. All the more puzzling, then, that more hatred, cruelty, brutality and oppression have been dispensed in the name of religion than almost any other cause. What on earth is going on?

Religion is a uniquely human phenomenon. Though we know other species develop and transmit culture in a limited sense, they certainly don't seem to engage in any form of worship – even if some suspect that the devotion dogs lavish on their owners borders on the religious. And while we may not be able to tell what any individual cat – for example – thinks about its place in the world, or whether it believes some creator-god is responsible for its existence, we know that neither cats nor any other animal species get together for religious services at a church of their choice. That is an exclusively human habit, and – once again – language is clearly the prime suspect. For however much our biology may dispose us to have religious feelings, without words it's going to be impossible to persuade others to believe that the universe is controlled by a supernatural being or beings – let alone to follow all the rituals involved in their worship. Language may not actually cause belief, but it's an indispensable enabling mechanism.

In a very real sense, religion is the mother of all conspiracy theories; not only does it ask you to believe that things are not the way they seem, it offers solutions that are literally out of this world – relying on the convenient fact that absence of evidence is never the same as evidence of absence. For whatever form it takes, religion essentially involves accepting something that cannot be confirmed with our normal senses: the belief that an invisible someone or something with greater powers than we possess – or can ever hope to understand – is responsible for creating and shaping the world we live in. That's a big claim, and that's only the half of it – most religions also teach there is a purpose to life which can only be fulfilled by performing specific acts that are believed to please or placate the object of their devotions. If culture is a club that relies on shared understandings, religion seeks to impose them in the name of some celestial being.

How might the emergence of speech have contributed to these extraordinary claims? One clue lies in the very nature of language. We have seen how grammar emerges from the need to order the words we use so that we can express the relationships we see between things: but whichever order we settle on, the grammatical relationship between subject, verb and object remains intact. This reflects our experience of the world, that an action (as expressed by a verb) is caused by an actor (the subject), and produces an effect (on the object). If we see ripples appear on a pond, we know someone has thrown in a stone, or that something is moving in it. Experiments show that even young babies and animals expect actions to have causes – and it is ultimately the acceptance and application of this relationship between cause and effect that has allowed us to uncover the secrets of many things that once seemed mysterious.

But this quest for an explanation can have unintended consequences. Despite his bold announcement of the death of God, the philosopher

Nietzsche was well aware that language tended to bias us toward belief in a creator god, declaring *"Ich fürchte, wir werden Gott nicht los, weil wir noch an die Grammatik glauben"* (I'm afraid we will not get rid of God because we still believe in grammar). He saw language as encouraging faith by supporting the idea that all things have causes: since we are born into a world we did not create, and are often affected by events beyond our control, as a first guess it's not unreasonable to suppose the world we live in could be the action of some unseen actor or actors – super-power subjects of actions for which we are the object.

And there are other, more psychological factors that may be at work to persuade us that some powerful being is watching over our lives. As we make our way through a world that rarely seems to have our best interests at heart, it can be comforting to think that someone might be looking out for us. Freud even suggested that we are predisposed to believe in an omnipotent God because of our experience of being cared for as children. And though this nurturing experience is common to many animals – born helpless but raised by parents who go to great lengths to defend and protect their vulnerable offspring – language makes it easy for us to project our infant experience onto the backdrop of the wider universe, and agree amongst ourselves that there must be some cosmic parent who cares for us in much the same way.

But there's a simpler, much more straightforward reason why language would have taken us in the direction of religion. However clever we may have become about solving puzzles that troubled our ancestors, we still have no certain answers to the meaning and purpose of life, or whether life continues after death – and what we might be doing here in the first place. Science may have plausible explanations for almost everything that has happened since the first few nanoseconds of the Big Bang, but without turning to religion of some kind, none of us can answer the nagging question that anyone who has learnt to speak eventually runs up against: *Why am I here?* And once you have stumbled onto that question, it doesn't easily go away.

This is not a problem for other species – it's a question that only emerges once you have the ability to talk about it. Religion may arise from emotions we broadly share with other animals, but it is language that makes the difference. The awareness of animals is directed to the business of survival, and dealing with that. The purpose of survival does not occur to them, because – without words to discuss it – it cannot. Animals eat when they're hungry, sleep when they're tired, and have sex when they can. They feel fear, sadness and boredom just as we do, and may even mourn their dead or have other emotions that correspond with what we like to call 'spiritual' – chimpanzees have been observed sitting and staring at waterfalls or across distant views in ways that can only really be interpreted as demonstrating a sense of wonder. But because they have no words to describe it, they can neither talk nor even really think about it.

But humans are in a position to do both. Once we'd learnt to speak, it was only a question of time before the practical use of language in helping solve the 'how' of day-to-day issues turned to the 'why' of more philosophical questions during the down-time around those early camp-fires. Even very young children ask them, as parents are well aware. Those pretty stories about the moon and the Milky Way were all designed to answer the persistent question 'why?' – and we're still faced with the same problem today. We all arrive in this world without an instruction manual, and as we gradually come to terms with the inevitable pain and disappointments of life, words enable us to question whether it's worth the effort, what it's all for, and how we should make the best of things. Even for the luckiest of us, there are times when life can look daunting – it's a scary world out there, largely out of our control, and painful, terrible things will inevitably happen to us, including our own death.

So it's not surprising if we have felt the need for an answer, an idea which helps make sense of our pain – a mental analgesic to make the question go away. Religion provides a useful story – in very real sense, it's an early form of science, an attempt to come up with a theory, a best guess that might explain the otherwise chaotic and confusing world we find ourselves in. Having an idea, even though it may be wrong, is better than having no idea at all. It's a place to begin, at least; and language gives us a way both to start and then continue that conversation. The trouble comes when we persuade ourselves that the story we've come up with must be true: for the trap of faith is to think that believing something makes it so. And once a tradition is established, it can be hard to break: as the puzzle-box experiment would seem to confirm, if you're told a plausible story at a young-enough age by people you love and trust, it can easily turn into an unquestioned assumption – an assumption that soon becomes a narrative we end up taking for granted, the subject of ceremonies and sermons.

Dying for our sins

It's easy enough to spot the oddities of someone else's religion; but like the curious grammar and quirky tastes of our own cultures, the one we've grown up with often seems the most natural thing in the world. For Christians – the largest religious group on the planet, lest we forget – nothing could be more normal than the familiar iconography of the cross, recognisable all round the world. But take another look. What actually greets you in any church you visit, right at the centre of the lines of vision, is the image of a bloody, emaciated human corpse nailed to a piece of wood. When farmers want to keep crows away from their fields, they sometimes shoot a few birds and hang them up as a warning to keep others away. It doesn't appear to be that effective. But with humans, it seems to actively encourage them to stay. And it's harder than you'd think to identify the meeting you seem to have missed.

Though there's no more historical evidence for the existence of Jesus Christ than for the founders of most of the major religions, the standard account of his life says that he was executed by the Romans at the behest of the local authorities for claiming to be king of the Jews, and thus posing a threat to the existing order. As such he became a martyr for his cause, and like many martyrs, a cruel, unjust and premature death turned out to be good publicity as far as his teachings were concerned. The interesting thing is that martyrdom in the name of his core doctrine of forgiveness and redemption is not the story that the Church has chosen to tell over the centuries. Instead, they've preferred to focus on the fact that he died for our sins.

That has become a staple of Christian doctrine, but it it's a curious argument to make. What difference could it make to our sins to have someone die for them, even a son of a god? That was the question I eventually choked on when I first started to notice the words of the hymns I used to love singing in my local church as a boy. Try as I might, I could not get my head around that. I wasn't really conscious of being such a terrible sinner – at least, I couldn't think of anything I'd done that was bad enough to justify someone else dying for them in order to save me. Did stealing a piece of bubble-gum from the local corner-shop count? Or lying to my brother? It seemed a bit presumptuous to be signing up to such a drastic solution on such flimsy grounds.

Secondly – and I did feel rather guilty about this, given that crucifixion can't have been much fun – did he really die, anyway? I thought the whole point about Jesus was that he didn't actually die – so it seemed a bit cheeky to be claiming that our sins had been done away with as a result of a short stopover in purgatory (the exact nature of which is still argued about by theologians to this day.) And thirdly, and most damningly: even if he did 'die', I couldn't understand how the additional sin of his murder was really going to help eliminate the enormous pile of sins that humanity was collectively continuing to amass. It didn't make any sense, and no-one could explain it to my satisfaction.

Many years passed before I finally understood the context of this religious riddle. Jesus had offered himself up as a scapegoat. Originally, a scapegoat really was a goat. In the ancient Jewish tradition, whenever anything really bad happened in your town or village, the presiding priest would select two goats, one to be sacrificed to God as an 'atonement', and the other sent out into the wilderness loaded with all the sins of the community. The idea was that 'the devil's goat' would never return (it was usually pushed over a cliff to make sure) and so the community could be ritually cleansed and get back to business as usual. It's pure transference magic – a linguistic sleight of hand of the type documented in great detail in *The Golden Bough*, Sir James Frazer's classic study of 'primitive' magic and religion, where he notes that *"The notion that we can transfer our guilt and sufferings to some other being who will bear them for us is familiar to the savage mind."* And to Christians as well, it seems.

For that is the sense – the only sense – in which Jesus could be said to have 'died for our sins'. According to Christian teaching, he voluntarily took on the burden of all the sins of humanity and 'died' on our behalf, thereby somehow excusing us of them. He was a sacrificial animal, taking all our sins away with him. But then, he didn't go away. On the third day he came back again – thus demonstrating his victory over death (with a little help from his Father in Heaven) – to show that we too can be saved if we would only follow his example. This is another magical idea common to many ancient beliefs, expressed through the familiar theme of death and rebirth at the heart of the traditional fertility rituals later widely co-opted by the Christians – as was idea of the virgin birth, another key element in orthodox doctrine.

But there's worse to come. The service of communion that lies at the heart of the Christian ritual, the sacred renewal of the covenant with Jesus that forms the basis of the entire religion, is even more bizarre. Consider what happens when you receive communion. You are first offered a tasteless wafer that stands in for 'bread'. This is the first suspension of disbelief required, as it neither looks nor tastes like bread – no matter how beautifully decorated with a religious symbol. Then there is the wine. At least the Church has generally insisted on the use of real wine with an alcoholic content close to what would have been being drunk at the Last Supper. But here's the thing: according to core Christian teaching it's not wine, it's blood, real blood. And specifically, it's the blood of Jesus Christ. That is the whole point of the ritual.

And it's the same with the bread, which is held to be the actual body of Christ. So we have bread-that-is-not-even-bread becoming his flesh, and wine becoming his blood. This mysterious process is technically known as 'transubstantiation' (taken from an obscure Latin word, no clearer in Latin than it is in English) – which means that the 'accidents' of bread and wine somehow transform their substance "*in a way surpassing understanding*" into the Body and Blood of Christ, without actually doing so in a way detectable to the senses – as the Church freely admits. Just like the Emperor's clothes, which were supposed to be the most beautiful and stylish designs of their day despite not actually being visible to the naked eye, it's something we are asked to take on trust.

But even if we manage to accept that this undetectable transformation has occurred (the purpose of the ceremony, after all), what are we to make of what is supposedly taking place? If we take the orthodox teaching of the Church at face value, those taking part in a communion service are quite literally – not symbolically, in any sense – participating in an act that involves eating the flesh and drinking the blood of a fellow human, even if he is the son of a god. And all this to a magical end: the Gospel of John quotes Jesus as saying "*Whoever eats my flesh and drinks my blood has eternal life, and I will raise him up at the last day.*" In other words, the Eucharist – the most sacred of the seven sacraments that lie at the heart of Christian practice – is undertaken as an act of cannibalism that participants believe will allow them to live forever.

The inherent horror – both physical and conceptual – of these beliefs have sparked endless theological disputes down the ages. Even ignoring the inglorious squabbles and sectarian bickering about scripture that took place prior to the first Council of Nicea in 325 AD – which finally signed off on the first 'official' Christian doctrine – the onward progress of the creed has been riven with disagreement. It didn't take long for East and West to go their own ways as the old Roman Empire broke into two, each taking their own version of the religion with them. Europe is more familiar with the Catholic Church, which has played such a dominant role in its culture and history for the best part of two millennia – but as far as the Orthodox Church is concerned, it's the Catholics who are out of line. There had always been rivalry between the two main centres of Christianity in Rome and Constantinople (now Istanbul) but they have barely spoken to each other now for nearly 1000 years.

What's astonishing is how small the gap between them is. It's like regional accents: the two groups have no trouble understanding each other and use the same basic grammar, but regard themselves as enemies because of some slight differences in accent and vocabulary – much like the rivalry between Manchester and Liverpool, or Chicago and Detroit. And we are talking very slight points. One of the main stumbling blocks, the proximate cause of the Great Schism of 1054 which finally ended relations between the Orthodox and Catholic churches, was whether the bread used in the ritual of communion should be leavened or unleavened. Most of us no longer know what that means, but in essence it's the difference between thin and thick crust pizza, *chapatti* and *naan*. There was no disagreement about the nature of the ritual itself, or whether the magical concept of transubstantiation at its heart should be viewed symbolically rather than taken literally. No. The concern was over the type of bread used.

To be fair, there were other issues. There was the question of whether the Pope in Rome should be the supreme authority, or simply remain the first among equals in the convocation of bishops. Then there was a long-standing debate about whether the Holy Spirit – however this concept was to be understood – should be held to emanate from God alone, or equally from God and Jesus. But in terms of core belief in the Christian message, no difference at all. *Nada.* None. It was just that because the bread that Jesus had used at the Last Supper would have been unleavened according to the religious custom of his day, the Catholics had adopted it as representing the authentic tradition. In the Orthodox world, however, some clever wag had decided that leavened bread should be used, because it represented the 'risen' Christ. The Eastern Patriarch accused the Roman Pope of clinging to heretical Jewish practice, and that was that.

At least the Protestants had a better excuse when it was their turn to kick off. Luther was upset about the selling of 'indulgences' (essentially free passes to heaven for rich sinners who contributed to church funds) and had concluded from a study of the Bible that – contrary to both Catholic and Orthodox teaching – there was no need for a priest to intercede between God and man: brothers (and sisters) could be doing it for themselves. And once the Protestants set the precedent of going back to the Bible, and as translations of the Bible into the everyday languages of the world gradually became available – in the teeth of opposition from the Catholic Church – it was open season on interpretation. The slightest hiccup in the supposedly smooth continuum of doctrine was liable to turn into a veritable wormhole of dissent – especially in America, a country founded on the right to religious freedom.

And that's the problem with belief: with nothing solid to base your argument on, and no means of testing it, you're always vulnerable to a new kid on the block claiming that his or her version of your tradition is more authentic. Language allows – and even requires – us to dispute the finest points of detail, and holy scripture is no refuge. Because a religion based on revelation is always in a weak position, as we shall shortly see.

The house of monotheism

Long before it started splintering into endless variations on a theme (according to the Church's own estimate, there are more than 34,000 Christian sects in existence – each with their own version of the truth), Christianity itself began life as a variation of an earlier creed – Judaism. The Jews believe that one day a Messiah will come to rule in God's name, ushering in an era of justice, truth and peace across the earth. Though this paradise may seem as far away as ever, among his supporters Jesus staked a successful claim to be the promised one ('Christ' comes from the Greek word *christos* meaning 'the anointed' – which is also the meaning of the Hebrew *mashiach* from which the word Messiah derives). His teachings are essentially an update on God's earlier covenants with mankind, toning down the more vengeful parts of the Old Testament – and the entire edifice of Christianity rests on the validity of his claim.

Fast forward six hundred years, and there's a new kid on the block: Muḥammad ibn ʿAbdullāh. The Islamic faith he founded – currently the second most popular choice on the planet – comes from the same monotheistic stable as the Jewish and Christian faiths. Muslims recognise the Old and New Testaments as holy scripture, and even accept Jesus as a prophet – it's just that they don't believe he was the last or the best one, and certainly not the son of God. In its favour, Islam has no blood-curdlingly strange pagan practices, doctrinal difficulties about the nature of God or confusion about the status of our relationship with him. Allah is one and undivided, and Muhammad is his true prophet – in that, all Muslim sects agree. Furthermore, although it took centuries for Christians to agree on an official text for the Bible, Muslims have always believed the Koran is a faithful representation of the word of God as received by Muhammad and dictated to his followers.

But that's where the good news ends. The Great Schism in Islam is between Sunni and Shia, and though the argument is perhaps more substantial than the Christian spat about unleavened bread, it's still pretty thin. Essentially, the dispute is about who should be considered to be the true successor to Muhammad, who died in AD 632. The Shia sect claim that Muhammad appointed his son-in-law (and cousin) Ali ibn Abi Talib to be his successor, whereas the Sunni claim that his rightful heir was Abu Bakr, his father-in-law, the man chosen to do the job by his closest companions – who had evidently missed the meeting about Ali (although he did eventually get his turn at the wheel). The Sunni continue to believe that a religious leader should be chosen from the best candidate among the community, whereas the Shia belief is that only the descendants of Muhammad are truly qualified. It's a row that rumbles on to this day, some 14 centuries later, made all the worse by contemporary events.

And though it may not boast anything as definitively weird as the Christian service of communion, the underpinnings of Islamic practice can still raise an eyebrow among those not signed up to it. As distinct from the sacraments of the Church (important rites of passage like baptism, confirmation, communion and marriage), the Muslim faith is based on the so-called Five Pillars – the profession of faith, charitable giving, fasting during Ramadan, pilgrimage to Mecca and the performing of prayers. This last duty is a core component of what it means to be a Muslim – but as the

Koran does not specify how many prayers should be performed each day, practice relies on the accounts of Muhammad's personal instructions to his companions (the *hadith*). So far, so good – but now the story gets a little strange. The number of daily prayers to be offered is supposed to have been negotiated directly with God by Muhammad during a miraculous night journey. The faithful believe this journey took place on the back of Buraq, a winged horse which took him from Mecca to Jerusalem, where he travelled up through the heavens and was granted an audience with Allah himself.

The story goes that in the course of conversation, Muhammad managed to haggle the required number of daily prayers down from fifty to five. He was put up to this by Moses (who just happened to be there as well, along with other Bible A-listers like Adam, Abraham, Gabriel and Jesus) because he felt that having to perform 50 daily prayers would not prove a popular idea with the faithful – and sent Muhammad back to ask again. And again. And yet again. At the first go he got it down to 25 times, at the next to half that (it's not quite clear how performing 12.5 prayers was ever going to work), and then finally down to five – at which point his manners got the better of him and he felt he couldn't bring himself to hustle the Almighty for a further reduction, even if Moses was still unhappy about it. That's according to one story, anyway. In another *hadith*, it's reported that at the first try he only got Allah to bring the number down to 40, then to 20, then to 10, and only then to 5. Either way, he clearly drove a good bargain. It must have been his early training as a merchant.

When he first related this story to his circle of supporters, it was greeted with some incredulity, as well it might have been. But it wasn't the winged horse and the visit to Allah that caused concern – that was all perfectly fine. No, the fuss was over the 'impossible' distance he claimed to have travelled overnight – a problem that was only solved when Abu Bakr stated that he recognised Muhammad's description of Jerusalem, a place he could not otherwise have been to – though some cast doubt on the idea that 'the farthest place' mentioned in the Koran really was Jerusalem, and even whether the al-Aqsa mosque it refers to actually existed at the time.

But beyond the potential potholes in the story – and the tricky suspension of disbelief required – there's a much larger issue at stake for Islam: its biggest problem is in fact Mormonism. That might seem surprising, but consider this: Islam's great claim to truth is that Muhammad was the last and greatest of God's prophets, to whom God revealed his teaching in the form of the Koran. Indeed, the only real justification for rejecting the divinity of Jesus and the authority of the New Testament is the claim that through Muhammad, God provided a definitive upgrade on his previous revelations. The teachings of the Koran thus supersede all earlier editions of God's word, as the Christians and Jews are believed to have gone astray and allowed their holy texts to become corrupt. And that is exactly the ground on which the Mormons assert the supremacy of their Bible, as they believe it was Joseph Smith, the founder of their religion, who was the lucky recipient of God's last word on the subject.

We shouldn't allow ourselves to be put off by the distracting familiarity of a name like Joseph Smith. The more exotic-sounding monikers of Muhammad and Jesus were both quite common in their own cultures before the appearance of their most famous owners – and if a rose can smell as sweet by any other name, there's no reason to think that someone called Joe Smith would be less likely to be favoured with God's confidences than anyone else. And by the same token, there's no reason that the claims he made to have been be inspired by God – and visited by an angel with a set of golden plates into the bargain – should be taken any less seriously than the claims of Muhammad to have been spirited to heaven on a winged horse. As to the objection that the Koran says Muhammad was the last prophet – well, Jesus made the same claim about himself, and that didn't stop Muhammad.

Which is why the revelation argument creates such a difficulty for its supporters: it's hard to accept its validity in one case, and then dispute it in another. Though Mormons may take a more indulgent view of Muhammad than Muslims do of Joseph Smith – if they've heard of him at all – that's because they can afford to, just as Muslims can afford to take a more charitable view of Jesus than do followers of the Jewish faith. But the parallels are striking, and were noted in Smith's own time. Both claimed to have been visited by angels. Both were 'unlettered' men unaccountably chosen by God to record words they could not themselves write – they both dictated their understanding of what God had communicated to others who wrote it down at a later date. On the face of it, Joseph Smith's claim is quite as good as Muhammad's, and Muslims have no more reason to reject his word than Christians have to reject the word of Muhammad, or the Jews to reject that of Jesus. Mormonism even meets the challenge of the 23rd verse of Chapter 2 of the Koran – that those who doubt its veracity should produce a surah (chapter) like it, and provide witnesses. That is exactly what Joseph Smith did, even without being aware of the challenge.

So it comes down to whose story you believe – a difficulty that applies to all the 'people of the Book', and to the idea of monotheist faith more generally. For despite any agreement on broader principles, acceptance of their creed is dependent on the detail. The Jews believe that God will send his messenger in the person of the Messiah to save the world, and are still waiting for his arrival. The Christians believe the promised Messiah arrived in the person of Jesus Christ, as the Son of God, and revere the New Testament accordingly – and regard Muhammad as an imposter. Muslims accept the divinity of both books, but see Jesus as a prophet, not the Messiah – and hold that Muhammad is God's true and final prophet. Mormons also accept the Bible, but argue that Christianity in its modern form has become degraded, which is why God chose Joseph Smith to put things back on the right path.

It's tempting to dismiss this argument as childish. The dispute, however, is about faith – and genuinely held beliefs. But it is a real problem for anyone interested in promoting closer ties between monotheist religions, and encouraging 'interfaith dialogue'. Even if common ground can be found in terms of a shared morality, or an emphasis on peace and justice, the bottom line is that the differences between them are grounded in fundamental doctrine that cannot be resolved by rational means – because the claims rest on assertions that are essentially unprovable.

Jesus either is, or is not, an imposter, a prophet, or the true Son of God. Quantum physics notwithstanding, he cannot be all of those things. At best he can only be one of them, and none of the others. At worst – and much more plausibly – he is none of them at all.

From animism to atheism

But we are getting ahead of ourselves. The clash between rival monotheisms is a relatively modern concern – it has only been an issue for the last two thousand years. To understand how we got into this mess in the first place, we'll have to revisit what we know about the evolution of religion – because as replicants that live on in our minds, ideas evolve by mutation and adaption just as surely as our genes. Starting from the idea that an imperceptible someone or something might be influencing the world we see around us – and, more importantly, that it might be possible to have more control over our lives by negotiating with them through prayer and supplication, as we do with our fellow humans – we can begin to see how our ideas have developed in step with the growth of our communities, providing support at both the personal and political level.

From a broad historical perspective, it seems clear that the older the religion, the more spirits, deities or gods have had to be invoked, placated or otherwise engaged with to ensure our world continues as we would wish. In that sense, the history of theism is like the loss of phonemic diversity – as we realised we could make do with less of these beings, we have gradually done so. Which is not to say that religions that claim to be monotheistic are more advanced or more sophisticated: Hinduism, for example, allows believers to engage at levels of belief that range from polytheism to an almost deistic, even atheistic perspective – and the large retinue of saints recognised by the Catholic Church can make it seem more a polytheistic cult than a monotheistic creed. But though animists still exist, and sceptics have probably been around since the dawn of belief, there's a distinct trajectory to the convergence, nonetheless.

In some ways the evolution of belief through animism to polytheism and then on to monotheism and atheism can be read like an embryology of thought – a process that beings endowed with language are bound to go through as their thinking progresses. It's a simple enough logic: once you have the words to talk about any creepy, scary feelings you have, it's not going to be long before you are likely to suspect the presence of spirits everywhere. The instinctive horror that children have of monsters under the bed – and their fear of ghosts and other supernatural beings – is simply a remnant of that process: a mental virus that starts to take hold unless neutralised with knowledge of the meetings we've already had about such things. You have only to see how much animals and babies can be scared by fireworks to understand the power of language to provide reassurance in the face of otherwise frightening and inexplicable events.

So it's not surprising that the oldest belief systems of which we have any knowledge (whether or not we call them religions) appear to be some form of animism – the belief that all things have a kind of soul or spirit that can survive death and/or affect us in ways that may not always be beneficial. Given the harsh conditions of a hunter-gatherer's life – the very same precarious life, lurching from feast to famine, that animals in the wild still live out to this day – it's entirely plausible that an ability to discuss the feelings that natural phenomena and sheer bad luck induce would soon lead to beliefs about supernatural agents: beings that may be approached in ways that mirror the social practices of the tribe. And what we know of the beliefs and superstitious rituals of existing hunter-gatherer communities bears this out.

But like other forms of culture, belief does not stand still. With the beginnings of agriculture and the development of early settlements, a more systematised approach to religious practice and ritual starts to emerge – we begin to see a pattern of belief in named local deities. Gods are now worshipped in dedicated shrines or temples of the growing towns rather than in natural locations: a more complex grammar starts to develop from the analog jungle of spirits and demons that populate the worlds of our earliest societies – and a hierarchy of gods appears. Again, it's not hard to understand why: as society itself became more hierarchical, organised around more permanent social and physical structures, it was both logical and convenient to rationalise the ad hoc superstitions and create a system of worship that both reflected the new reality and could be outsourced to a specialised class – like the other emerging professions.

Polytheistic belief – the idea that there are a number of gods, each with powers in their own realm but none that have an exclusive claim on our attention – is the most common form of religious practice in ancient communities for which records survive. Every known society had a pantheon of deities, from the Egyptians to the Aztecs, the Chinese to the Greeks, the Arabs to the Goths – whose gods, as we have seen, live on in our names for the days of the week. These gods were ranked according to their powers, and worshipped according to need. If you were sick, you could call on the god of healing. If pining for a lover, you went to the goddess of love – and so on. Polytheism also made it easier for beliefs of neighbouring societies to be integrated through trade and conquest, as gods with similar functions could be absorbed into existing traditions – as happened between Egypt and Greece, Greece and Rome, and Rome and the Goths.

But over time an internal logic has driven our belief in the supernatural to converge on a single source. From within any pantheon of gods (themselves often only the highest ranking of a group of less powerful spirits), a supreme 'king of gods' emerges as the focus of worship – the other gods being seen as independent, or simply other aspects of this supreme being. This is as much a reflection of the nature of developing political structures as it is useful to those in charge of them – kings and emperors become associated with the power of the supreme god. There was a further step to be taken, though. As societies became more civilised and villages grew into busy towns and cities, the downward pressure on the number of gods grew – both for reasons of efficiency and because there was less need for them as life became more secure: it gradually made more sense to deal with a single god who could really take care of business.

Once the concept of monotheism took hold, it spread rapidly. A single creed that united believers on a universal basis was not just a useful tool for expanding empires: it was a radical and simplifying idea that was easy to grasp. Unlike the more transactional nature of polytheistic religions, the new religions promised redemption and the prospect of a better life for the faithful after death. But despite the appeal of such concepts to people with little education and fewer prospects, the task of teasing out the finer points of doctrine created knotty problems for the theologians whose job it was to explain the revelations of scripture. The devil really *was* in the detail, and much of the intellectual effort of the Middle Ages was spent devising arcane refinements to help resolve the inevitable inconsistencies of belief – even if the story about the time wasted calculating the number of angels able to dance on the head of a pin is probably apocryphal.

What's striking is how the key themes of theology recur in different religious traditions. The similarities between mediaeval Christian and Muslim thinking in scholars like St Augustine and al-Ghazali may not be so remarkable – they were both channelling the ideas of the ancient Greek philosophers in trying to reconcile faith with reason – but the overlap with Hindu theology in its quest for proof of the existence of God, debates about the nature of causality, right knowledge and the possibility of knowing objects beyond the senses (as well as traditional Chinese thinking about the nature of God being both transcendent and immanent) shows the human mind working through the puzzles that belief in a supernatural being and faith in religious teaching inevitably throws up.

One of these is that an obvious solution to the question of conflicting faiths is to conclude that they are all wrong – given the lack of evidence, any form of belief in a supernatural being is illogical. But insofar as atheism is a belief in the absence of God, it too takes on a religious aspect – the end of the line perhaps, but a position that is just as untenable as any other form of belief. We cannot know for certain that there is no god or divine 'supernatural' presence animating what we perceive as reality: it is not a falsifiable proposition, any more than belief in a god is falsifiable. All we can say is that so far, there is no objective evidence to support the claims of religion – only subjective effects, which may nonetheless be real. The only clear advantage that atheism holds over any other belief system is in terms of the principle known as Occam's Razor: it makes fewer assumptions than all the others.

Ultimately, this is the logic of language at work: once freed sufficiently from the brutal business of survival to contemplate the mystery of existence and the riddle of life, the arguments that arise from the presumption of a Primer Mover in the form of God (or whatever name we choose) reduce to the same conundrums. Take the key issue of creation – an argument that echoes through every tradition: if everything has a cause, there must be something that caused the world we live in. For many people that's sufficient proof of the existence of some kind of God – until you start to wonder what, in that case, causes God. You either have to say that nothing causes God, that s/he or it exists beyond time and space – and thus beyond any cause – or you are left wrestling with the unsatisfactory notion of 'infinite regress': the buck has to stop somewhere.

But roll that logic forward a notch, and there's a simpler, more elegant solution. If God can always have existed, why not start with the universe instead? After all, it is the only thing we can be sure of. Adding God into the mix doesn't help – as the French mathematician Laplace allegedly said to Napoleon, in response to the Emperor's question about the absence of God in his explanation: "*Je n'avais pas besoin de cette hypothèse-là.*" (I have no need of that hypothesis). It still doesn't answer the question, but it doesn't answer it any less than the notion of God does – without certain evidence to the contrary, or the ability to test it, it's simpler to accept that the universe is its own first cause. That may make no more sense than the idea that God created the universe – but as Occam tells us, it's a better place to be from a logical perspective. But not everyone is persuaded by logic. Let's remind ourselves why.

The wages of woo

Even without the complication of religious belief, we can have some pretty strange ideas about how the world works. There may be nothing as odd as other people's superstitions (why would cutting your nails at night shorten your life?), but we barely notice what we ourselves do to avoid bad luck. We might be less fussy about keeping horseshoes the right way up these days, but we still avoid walking under ladders, throw salt over our shoulders when we spill it and have a fear of bad luck 'coming in threes' – and many of us still feel uncomfortable about doing important things on Friday 13th, even if we no longer know why that date is significant. Why do we feel that way? Because we don't want to 'tempt fate.' If you've been told something is unlucky, there's always going to be a small voice in your head warning you to avoid it – because why would you take the risk? That's the psychology of those chain messages warning you of bad luck if you fail to pass them on. We still fear bad things might happen to us, don't know why, and will take precautions to avoid them – even if it makes no 'sense'.

But though language may be responsible for spreading irrational memes, it can't take the rap for what drives them. Despite the sophistication that words spawn, we seem to be programmed to sense there may be more out there than what greets the eye or ear – even those of us who would agree with H. L. Mencken that religion is *an illogical belief in the occurrence of the improbable*' are still liable to get spooked from time to time. It's not just children who imagine monsters under the bed: an unexpected noise or apparent movement in a house you believe to be empty can creep you out at a gut level without requiring any conscious belief in the supernatural. From an evolutionary perspective, that's quite understandable: we're much more likely to be the descendants of people who were alarmed when they heard a strange noise than those who weren't.

The crop circle phenomenon that swept the UK from the late 1980s is telling evidence of our tendency to jump to paranormal conclusions. In actual fact, the unusual geometric patterns that started appearing in fields of grain and other crops were being created by an artist called Douglas Bower and his mate Dave Chorley, two pranksters who had simply wanted to give the UFO enthusiasts in their local pub something to talk about. They certainly succeeded in that: the phenomenon was taken seriously enough that crop circles were even discussed in the British Cabinet, and the range of theories advanced to explain them ran the gamut from aliens to plasma vortexes to poltergeists – even "faxes from the Gods" supposedly warning humanity about global warming.

But even after the perpetrators were unmasked, the faithful were still not dissuaded: exotic theories persist to this day – despite the fact that most crop circles are admitted to be man-made – on the grounds that some still just might be 'genuine' circles with an unearthly explanation. But we're not the only animals who fall prey to this kind of speculation – other species can be spooked as well.

In a famous experiment in the 1950s the behaviourist B.K. Skinner was able to show that hungry pigeons kept in a cage and fed at random intervals via a hopper began to demonstrate 'superstitious' behaviour – in which they continued to repeat whatever they had just happened to have been doing (such as flapping their wings, lifting a leg, or stretching their head in a certain direction) when the last meal was delivered. The pigeons seemed to be making an association between whatever they had done and the probability of a desired event happening – in this case the delivery of food. Of course, since the delivery had been random there was absolutely no connection between the two, but Skinner found that if the next delivery came while the pigeons were repeating their activity, it reinforced their tendency to continue with the 'superstitious' behaviour.

In a sense, this is just bad science – the same line of thinking that starts us down the road to religion. With nothing else to explain what's happening, even a pigeon will start making a best guess. This is much the same as the well-documented 'cargo cult' behaviour of isolated tribes in the Pacific who began to imitate the actions of troops on military bases built there during World War II. In a dramatic illustration of Arthur C Clarke's famous dictum that any sufficiently advanced technology will seem like magic, the islanders apparently assumed that the appearance of planes carrying military supplies – something quite beyond their under-standing – was caused by the behaviour they saw on the base where the planes landed, and decided that this must be responsible for the arrival of the miraculous metal gods. So once the soldiers had left, they set about clearing runway strips on their own islands, marching about with sticks held like rifles, and building fake control towers in the hope that they too might be visited by the big silver birds in the sky bearing wondrous gifts. Some of them still await the arrival of a messiah, with one cult even being dedicated to the late Duke of Edinburgh.

With the pigeons there was a clear and quite short 'lag-time' over which feedback had to take place before the behaviour was forgotten – but language lets us prolong the life of such plausible theories through discussion and group reinforcement. Memes about ways to bring good fortune quickly spread, and soon whole cultures are touching wood or crossing their fingers for luck – even if the original reasons for doing so have been long forgotten (it's likely that both these practices have their roots in pagan beliefs about tree spirits and the magical power of intersections). Just as with the pigeons, the behaviour may not make any sense to anyone outside the loop, and may contradict a similar but opposite superstition in another community – like the black cat superstition, thought to be lucky in some cultures, and unlucky in others – but to the people who believe it, the idea that it may affect one's luck is a strong motivation to retain it.

And it's not just superstition we seem to have faith in. Concern for and fear about the future shows up in an intense interest in fortune-telling – whether using tea leaves, animal entrails or astrology. Despite apparently believing we can in fact change our luck, belief in a fixed fate or destiny is another idea with deep roots in our history. Records show this to have been a human obsession since the earliest civilizations (divination using flour or birds is recorded in cuneiform texts, and the first Chinese writing is found on oracle bones used in pyromancy, a form of divination by fire) – and we're still mad for it. In the course of the infamous News of the World phone-hacking trial, the court was told that though the newspaper paid their leading hacker as much as £100,000 a year for his services, this was not excessive as they paid their regular astrologer twice that amount – an indication of just how important her contribution was held to be on sales. No matter where we're from, what language we speak, or what method we use, we seem very keen to know about our future.

Somewhat counter-intuitively, this even applies to people in positions of power and influence. Though it might seem they would have more freedom than the rest of us to determine their own fate, the pressure of having too much freedom – of having to constantly make decisions rather than simply do what others tell them – can be intense: witness the speed at which the hair of our political leaders tends to go grey. History records the strong influence that diviners have had on kings and other rulers through the ages, and even in our own time, high-profile individuals from presidents to pop stars have sought out the advice of astrologers to help them make decisions. And so it is for the rest of us: given all the other voices that language installs in our heads – the cultural, political and religious considerations that so often give us pause – a visit to the soothsayer can help reassure us with the illusion of certainty. Because we have so much in our minds to distract us, it's much harder for us to just 'go with the gut' in the way that other animals can rely on instinct to guide them.

Ironically, animals often bear the brunt of our superstitions. Though there's no more reason to believe that fate could be determined by the shape of a fresh sheep's liver than by cracks in eggshells or gastromancy (divination from the sound of stomach rumbles), the use of animal parts for divination or healing due to some perceived magical quality has been widespread through history – and is increasingly driving rare species to the brink of extinction. In oriental medicine nearly every part of a tiger's body is believed to offer some sort of health benefit: its blood is thought to build willpower, its bones are said to have an anti-inflammatory effect that can cure arthritis, headaches, and swellings – while its eyeballs allegedly relieve epilepsy, malaria, and cataracts, and a tiger's penis is prized as an aphrodisiac. Nothing is spared: even its excrement is regarded as a remedy – for piles and alcoholism.

Rhino horn is now so rare it has a street value higher even than cocaine – though snorting it will do little for you: rhino horn is mostly keratin, which is what your finger and toe nails are made of. And yet, it's believed to help strengthen the liver (good for all those hangovers), enhance virility and even cure cancer. Rhino horn has been a traditional remedy for thousands of years, and given the widespread belief in Chinese folk remedies in other parts of Asia (and a lack of access to and availability of more effective forms of treatment), belief in its magical powers means that as many as a quarter of the world's population are potential customers for a rhino horn remedy. And with as few as a thousand rhino left alive in the world, it's difficult to see how the maths of that works out in favour of the rhinos. Or the tigers.

Nor are humans left untouched by such bizarre beliefs. Circumcision is a practice that goes back at least as far as Ancient Egypt, where depictions of the act have been found that date to the third millennium BC. In the absence of textual evidence, it is not known for sure why circumcision was important to the Egyptians, but the idea was faithfully and painfully passed down through the Abrahamic tradition – though its independent practice in other parts of the world with no cultural connection to Egypt (even among Australian aborigines and the Aztecs) suggests there may well be a powerful symbolic and ritual component linking blood sacrifice to significant rites of passage.

That is certainly explicit in the Bible, where the deal Abraham cuts with God is sealed with a more intimate cut: Abraham circumcised himself to symbolise his own and his heirs' relationship with God in perpetuity. There being no recorded instances of animals biting off their own or others' foreskins, we can again safely conclude that language is responsible for this perverse custom. And the brutality of circumcision is by no means restricted to the male of the species. Female genital mutilation is far more invasive and dangerous, and even within the terms of those religions that endorse it, clearly violates the teaching about doing no harm – although FGM seems to predate our more modern religions, and is a practice that probably emerges from a dark, paternalist pre-history.

Can any of this be changed? The agonisingly painful custom of binding women's feet – which involved breaking the growing bones of a young girl's feet over a period of several years, using tight bandages to force them into shape – was practiced in China for over 1000 years. But with the introduction of new ways of thinking about society and the role of women that came in with communism after the war, it was possible to finally break the spell of tradition and outlaw the practice, which has now disappeared. Belief in the magical may be the default position of our minds – one that only becomes reinforced by language and a supporting culture – but the power of language to spread education, understanding and practical alternatives can eventually make a difference.

Amphetamine of the people

Perhaps the worst danger of such beliefs is our persistent tendency to use religion as an excuse for war. It is a notable fact that the key tenets of every major religion – peace, love, justice and tolerance – are the first victims of any conflict between believers and non-believers. Not that you need to belong to a different religion to suffer the scorn of those who espouse another creed (although it helps): some of the worst violence to take place in the name of religion has occurred between sects of the same faith. Despite the horror of more recent events, the religions of the Middle East hardly provide the worst examples in history: Protestants and Catholics have fought each other mercilessly for centuries, followers of Shiva and Vishnu have a long history of violent clashes within the same Hindu tradition – and even the more saintly Buddhist sects are no strangers to sectarian violence, especially in Japan.

For once you start down the path of doctrinal dispute, there's only one conclusion. You must fight for your belief, or abandon it entirely – the logic of language means I must either argue with you if you do not agree with my position, abandon my own beliefs and accept yours, or conclude that neither is true. This point was made very clearly in an encyclical issued in November 1885 by Pope Leo XIII: "*To hold, there-fore, that there is no difference in matters of religion between forms that are unlike each other, and even contrary to each other, most clearly leads in the end to the rejection of all religion in both theory and practice."* He knew that if belief is to mean anything at all – and for a revelatory religion it must, since that is the only point on which it stands – the crucial issue is this: *"Men who really believe in the existence of God must, in order to be consistent with themselves and to avoid absurd conclusions, understand that differing modes of divine worship involving dissimilarity and conflict even on most important points cannot all be equally probable, equally good, and equally acceptable to God."*

With religious conviction as for any other belief, the fact that there are so few truths to converge on means the field is wide open to speculation, and sects and sub-sects proliferate. As soon as you have a new theory, you have a potential dissenter – as recognised many centuries ago in the Latin phrase *quod gratis asseritur, gratis negatur* ('anything freely asserted [without proof], can be freely dismissed'). Even witches are at it – when Britain finally repealed its witchcraft laws in 1951 under the delightfully-named *Fraudulent Mediums Act*, the underground world of wicca soon emerged blinking into the New Age daylight and fractious sects immediately flourished – with the founding Gardnerian tradition soon rivalled by the Alexandrian, the Georgian, the Algard, the Dianic and many other varieties of the craft.

Nor does the belief have to be in the supernatural: the devoutly materialist Karl Marx has spawned huge numbers of divergent creeds in his wake, each one disagreeing about some aspect of how heaven is best to be achieved on earth, or what exactly Marx meant in some of his more gnomic pronouncements. These include (but are by no means limited to) Left Communism, Maoism, Stalinism, Marxist Leninism, Trotskyism, Luxemburgism, Council Communism, Hoxhaism, Titoism, Insurrectionary Marxism, Eurocommunism, Third Worldism, Deleonism, Structural Marxism, Neo-Marxism, Cultural Marxism, Juche, Castroism, Autonomist Marxism, Analytical Marxism, Marxist Humanism and Liberation Theology – all disagreeing vehemently.

That's a serious problem, which has the power to transmute the soporific effect of religion – Marx's 'opium of the people' – into something closer to an amphetamine rush. Not all wars are religious, of course, and even those conducted in the name of religion are rarely religious in origin – there's always something else at stake, usually power and property. But when it comes to the grab, there's nothing better than saying you're doing it in the name of God. We may be wary of admitting it openly these days, but we don't have to look far back into our history to find a Christian past that closely mirrors the *jihadi* present. Pogroms and auto-da-fe burnings were familiar items on the menu of mediaeval European bigotry – and once unleashed, the fight for right so often turns into a campaign of evil. We don't know where to stop.

At the root of any 'religious' war is a sense of injustice. War is never 'about' religion – war uses religion as a banner, a symbol of what it is trying to achieve, an appeal to the sense of righteousness that we all recognise inside ourselves. We all understand fairness; as children, that's a key demand. No parent ever needs to teach a child how to say "That's not fair" – though they may often need to explain that it works both ways, that the demands of fairness apply whether or not you have what you want. Children also have little difficulty in grasping the idea that something is 'mine' – and the demand for fairness usually grows louder when staking your claim to something you wish was your own. We have an innate sense of what is right and reasonable within our own terms, even if we may need some help and guidance in extending that sense of justice to others around us. It's a question of where you draw the line between 'us' and 'them'.

And when that cause is about restoring honour, dignity and pride, religion steps into the breach. Whatever it becomes once power, wealth and property make it vulnerable to corruption, religion is essentially about recognising the virtues of life – the good, the just, the generous, loving and peaceful. But if people feel oppressed by the reality of their daily lives, if they are ground down by a system which keeps them barely alive and scorns and persecutes them, they will eventually rise up against their oppressors – and they will do so in the name of justice. And in societies where justice is rarely seen to be done due to tyranny and corruption – the default situation for most human societies through history – the only model to turn to is the truth and justice promised by religion. The meaning in Arabic of the Lebanese political party *Hezbollah*, for example, is 'The Party of God".

For those of us living comfortably distant from the action, it's easy to believe that there is something about radical Islam that makes it incompatible with what the rest of the world is aiming for. This was the idea articulated by George W Bush immediately after 9/11, when he said of al-Qaeda that 'they hate our freedoms'. But though al-Qaeda was not clamouring for the social freedoms that only ever evolve out of political freedom, political freedom was what they were after – as was clear from the very beginning of the movement. America was targeted for its overwhelming support for the ruling clique in Saudi Arabia, bin Laden's country of origin – a point made explicitly both in his formal declaration of war on the US in 1996, and in his subsequent writings and speeches. His primary target was the Saudi regime, which he saw as rotten and corrupt – the source of the many wrongs and injustices done to the ordinary people of Saudi Arabia. And like many before him he took up the banner of religion to press his political cause.

It is not surprising that he should have done so: his cause is much the same as that of the Puritans who sought to confront and correct the corruption, vulgarity and greed of their times by appealing to what they considered the true values of religion. This is the great appeal of religious propaganda: forces opposed to an existing regime – which is always stained by the corruption of power – can hold up a pure vision of their faith as the model they aspire to, and urge followers to support them in building their version of heaven on earth. Their followers won't necessarily be satisfied by the outcomes, but this appeal to the good and holy – the Will of God – is what attracts those who turn to them. For people with little to lose and everything to gain, the promise of a better world will always seem more worthwhile than submitting to humiliation.

The savagery of IS, though unfamiliar and shocking to us in the modern world, is little different to the savagery perpetrated for centuries by Christians in the name of the Crusades or the Inquisition, or the wanton destruction of the Puritans under Cromwell. It was they who destroyed the religious imagery in churches throughout England, smashing windows and statues, and painting over the murals that used to decorate all churches – even if this process had already begun a century before as part of the Protestant backlash against Catholicism. The threat of destruction was not limited to rival Christian sects: as a Parliamentary army commanded by Thomas Fairfax passed close to Stonehenge on its way to the West Country after the Battle of Naseby in 1645, its chaplain, Hugh Peter, urged his general to demolish *"the monuments of heathenism"*. Fortunately for us, Fairfax had other priorities and declined the opportunity – but the parallels with the destruction of monuments in Palmyra and elsewhere are instructive.

Nor are we so far from the beheadings and other 'barbaric' behaviour we condemn in the followers of fundamentalist Islam: the bitter religious disputes over the Reformation led to a spate of equally barbaric Christian burnings in which hundreds of so-called heretics were burnt alive for holding opinions contrary to the religious beliefs of the establishment. Though the Puritans were less brutal than their Catholic counterparts, a terrible retribution was practiced upon many of those held responsible for the death of Charles I, among them the unfortunate Hugh Peter, who like others accused of 'regicide' ended up being hung, drawn and quartered at Charing Cross in October 1660. This wanton brutality continued on to the latter part of the 17th century, when the penalty of burning as a punishment for religious heresy was finally abolished – although along with hanging, drawing and quartering it continued to be carried out for selected crimes for almost another century, only being taken off the statute books in 1814.

The attempt to establish an Islamic State in the Middle East was driven by an almost perfect storm of such factors: extreme dissatisfaction with the existing autocratic and unaccountable regimes, anger at the Western 'Crusader' forces who employed a vastly superior military force to support them, the sheer desperation of persecuted religious minorities – and a bitter political struggle between two opposing religious sects with conflicting geopolitical interests in the region. To say that is not to excuse what is done in the name of religion; but insofar as religion is driven by language, we have to acknowledge that – and, more importantly, understand why it causes us to do such things. There is nothing about Islam, or any other religion, that makes it violent in itself: it is simply the nature of belief – just a measure of the pain of our struggle for meaning, in the end – to drive us to violence when our desire for better things is frustrated.

Looked at through the longer lens of culture, religion can start to seem like a language: it may function as a means of communication, but its specific features – the grammar, and vocabulary of belief – are always meaningless in themselves. So the question then becomes: what is religion communicating? Language may set us up for religious belief, but like the lexicon and syntax of language itself, the particular forms it evolves into are just flags of convenience. Language allows us to pose questions that have no answer: *What is life for? Why do we exist? How did the universe come into being?* These are questions that may not necessarily bother most people, fully occupied with the business of survival and enjoyment of their lives, but if not addressed can leave you exposed to the nearest huckster when they do. And as we have seen, there are plenty of answers on offer. How can so many contradictory beliefs all satisfy so many people?

The efficacy of prayer

Given the bewildering range of choices available, the odds in favour of one particular doctrine having an exclusive handle on the truth are extremely low. From a logical perspective, rather than just one of them being right, it's overwhelmingly more likely that all religions are untrue in their particular assertions. As an accidental kludge of ideas and practices that somehow delivers the goods for those that believe in them, a religion – like any other language – is incompatible with other systems and often inconsistent even on its own terms. But at the same time, they could all contain a kernel of truth as well – at some level they must, in fact. After all, the audience has spoken. Even if many people just go through the motions of belief because everyone else does – or because it's too much trouble to speak out – religions must be delivering something: if we weren't getting a bang for our buck we wouldn't be doing it. Perhaps there's something about religion that allows it to be both true and untrue at the same time?

In his famous study of the Roman Empire – a more innocent era when monotheism had yet to make such demands on the human psyche – the historian Edward Gibbon wrote *"The various modes of worship... were all considered by the people as equally true; by the philosopher, as equally false; and by the magistrate, as equally useful."* In other words, different strokes for different folks: it could well be that what matters is whether – not what – you believe. Or as George Carlin once put it: *Religion is like a pair of shoes – find one that fits for you, but don't make me wear yours.* If we would only relax a little, that could still be the case today – religion works just fine as long as you don't ask too many questions about doctrine, makes no sense at all if you do, yet provides a code of conduct which offers psychological support and promotes social stability for those who prefer to just follow the rules and get on with life.

So what is the effect of religion? Many priests are entirely sincere in their professions of faith, and genuinely believe that they are helping their parishioners. And they are. People not only feel comfortable with their beliefs, but are comforted by them as well. Nor is it just the reassurance of having answers to questions that would otherwise nag. Belief in a religion offers membership to a club, a group of other people with shared beliefs and practices. And it's not just any old club. It's a group of people who are concerned to do right for themselves and other people, as they see it – or as they understand their gods/god/God to want it. In providing a model of goodness as a default mode to follow, organised religion encourages people to help each another more than they otherwise might. Without the charitable work done in the name of religion around the globe, there would be a great deal more suffering in the world.

But beyond the psychological reasons why religion can help people, there's another reason it can seem to work: the power of 'prayer', which is such a core part of most religious practice. Though formal studies are often inconclusive, the medical profession is sufficiently convinced of the effect of belief on our response to treatment that it goes to great lengths to prevent it through double-blind tests when testing the effectiveness of a drug. The placebo effect has been known as a technique of self-suggestion for at least a century, but we are still no closer to knowing why it works, only that it does. Though officially frowned on as a technique by doctors today, it is widely accepted that treatment is likely to work better if there is a relationship of trust with the doctor, and the patient believes in the effectiveness of the cure. So it's possible that much of the effect of religion and its appeal to those that believe in it can be explained in the same way: through the power of positive suggestion, we become the change we wish to be.

And there's another explanation, too. Why do we pray, anyway? I once saw a poster outside a church which said *"Life's knocks bring you to your knees – the perfect time to pray."* Prayer is an activity mostly undertaken when we need help, or are feeling pessimistic about some situation. That's understandable – why would you ask for help if everything was fine, after all? But if you're starting from the bottom, the only way is up. Things are rarely as bad as we tend to think, and from an evolutionary perspective, there's a clear benefit to imagining and preparing for the worst rather than just assuming, for example, that there isn't a lion the other side of that rock.

But by the same token, that means that our worst fears are often not borne out. Even if there wasn't a lion on the other side of that rock, carrying a spear and preparing myself for a possible attack would be a better strategy than not having done so. I'd have little to lose and potentially much to gain – and if I'd also prayed to my god not to let there be a lion the other side of that rock, I'd have evidence of the efficacy of prayer when it turned out that there wasn't. So by the law of averages, prayer is going to seem an effective strategy to anyone who tends to feel pessimistic about things; if you are fearful by nature, prayer is usually going to work out well for you.

What happens when your prayers aren't answered, though? You don't get that job, your friend dies, your love is spurned. It turns out that this doesn't necessarily prove that prayer doesn't work, either. The religions that encourage prayer (most of them) have clever workarounds for that. *"God had a better plan." "You didn't pray hard enough." "You didn't pray right."* Just because nothing turned out the way you wanted it doesn't mean that God didn't hear your prayer – it just shows you weren't asking for the right thing, or in the right way. This also plays to the psychology of the person doing the praying. If you're desperate enough to have turned to prayer, you're probably not holding yourself in very high esteem – so the idea that God agrees with you is not going to be such a surprise. Why should God listen to a miserable sinner? There are all kinds of reasons (that only we know – and know all too well) why he might choose not to. So even if prayer doesn't seem to have worked out, there's always a way to excuse it.

But what if just imagining how you want things to be in some strange way increases the likelihood of that thing coming to pass? Because prayer does appear to work in this sense also: if you earnestly and sincerely want something to happen, your positive intention can often in itself make the outcome more likely to happen than otherwise – if only because you are focussing your energies on achieving that goal. I cannot prove that my life is objectively better because I try to follow this principle, but I can report that my life feels better as a result. If you are looking for a parking place and you 'create' one in your head by imagining that there will be one waiting for you, you are at least going to feel better about the universe when you find one than if you just put it down to 'luck' or – even worse – expect that you probably won't find one and spend all your time grumbling about it. Not convinced? All I can say is, give it a go some time. I won't mention trying to influence the weather, but it's surprising how often that works too.

Without words to confuse us, life would be much easier. Like an animal or a baby, we would simply do what we want, and act how we feel. Language muddies the water and makes it harder to connect with what we truly feel ourselves to be. It is also the great gift that allows us to be much more than we could ever be on our own, because it gives us new ideas to work with. Religion is one of those ideas, one that has clearly helped us through the ages. But that doesn't mean that religious belief is the best solution, or will provide you with advantages not to be found elsewhere. It is quite possible to think positively about yourself and the world, become actively engaged with your community, and have a great love for and sense of wonder at the astonishing beauty and complexity of the universe without needing to rely on belief in a supernatural being.

Just as languages and cultures gradually evolve into mutually incomprehensible forms, so do religious beliefs: like biological species, they evolve, grow, fade and die – many more religions have gone extinct than are still being practiced today. No matter how pervasive their influence or persuasive their priests once were, few people now believe in the gods of the Vikings, Mithraism, or the Olmec religion – to say nothing of the beliefs of our prehistoric Stone Age ancestors. And yet the world has not come to an end, despite the fact that their gods must have commanded just as much fear, respect – even love – as those of the religions that remain. The sun still continues to rise, even though there are no Aztec priests performing human sacrifices to make sure it does.

Will the religions that dominate world culture today still be with us in 100 years? 500 years? 1000? Most of those that survive have already lasted for longer than that, but the pace of change is faster than it once was; with more mobile phones than people on the planet, the world is a very different place than it was a century ago. But despite the growing evidence for a correlation between education and the decline in religious belief, it's not that simple: the God meme is always lurking to console you when there's no-one else to love you, or support you in your fight for justice. Both may be illusions, but as the poet T.S. Eliot famously observed, *"human kind cannot bear very much reality"* – and we've clearly been keen to accept all the help at hand to avoid dealing with it.

There's no doubt a sprinkling of celestial stardust has long been effective in supporting both individuals and entire communities, even when the original point of a tradition has been lost. As the long-suffering Tevye says in The Fiddler on the Roof, *"You may ask, 'How did this tradition get started?' I'll tell you. (Pause) I don't know. But it's a tradition. And because of our traditions, every one of us knows who he is and what God expects him to do."* It's a comic moment, but makes a serious point: the religious habit is ultimately about reassurance – something that language is perfectly placed to provide.

But like other aspects of culture, it's a reassurance that is intimately bound up with our sense of identity – another comforting mirage that language so easily creates for us.

WHO: The Trap of Identity

"Identity is theft of the self."

— Estee Martin

A pronoun in the works

One of the bigger surprises for a non-native learner of Japanese is to discover that you are no longer simply a single 'I' when you speak. Depending on who you are and who you're talking to, there are several different words you can use to refer to yourself, each with distinct nuances that subtly signal other factors such as age, status, sex and education. 私 [watashi] is used for the most neutral situations, 僕 [boku] for more blokey moments, あたし [atashi] if you are a girl, and 俺 [ore] if you fancy yourself the cool dude – or are aspiring to be one. But that's just for starters – more personal pronouns soon hove into view as you become more familiar with the language: 自分 [jibun], 小生 [shosei], 儂 [washi], うち [uchi] are just some of the more common ones (Japanese-language dictionaries list several dozen variants).

It's not the only language to do this. Japanese may have more than most (though ironically, they tend to be used less), but the different pronouns are ways of indicating social status, or your attitude to the person you're talking to. You may be trying to impress them, put them at ease, suggest intimacy, create distance, or remind them of your age. Such negotiations are part of the universal grammar of social relations. To the Japanese, it's just common sense to assume that you behave differently in different situations, and that the word you use when referring to yourself should reflect that. What really shocks them is the idea that in English all these delicate nuances have collapsed into the single pronoun, 'I'. How can you function effectively in society if you have no means of indicating your position by the way you talk about yourself?

We do, of course. English may only have one first person pronoun, but there are other words we use to refer to ourselves, nonetheless. As well as the obvious 'me' and 'myself', there is the more formal 'one' – even the royal 'we' – and there are more ironic usages such as 'yours truly' and 'muggins' (an old-fashioned word my father was fond of using.) We can even speak of ourselves in the third person as well: "In this author's opinion". But that's not really the point. There are equally effective ways of indicating social status and attitude in English, as with every other language – it's just that English doesn't usually do it by switching pronouns. Instead, an appropriate level of respect, intimacy or disgust can be conveyed by choosing other words, or deploying a variety of earthy epithets not generally used in Japanese: "*How many effin' times do I have to tell you?*" has a very different nuance to the phrase "*Kindly desist*", even though it means much the same thing. Our repertoire may be different, but it is no less expressive.

But regardless of how we may say it, we rarely have trouble understanding what we mean when we talk about ourselves. Under most circumstances it feels as if we have a clear sense of who we are as an individual, the person who 'runs the ship' of our conscious awareness – the thing that is both the subject of the sentence "I am..." and the answer we give when asked to complete that same sentence. *I am a woman. I am Chinese. I am a father. I am dyslexic. I am good. I am a Chelsea fan.* We all have interlocking categories of association that we use to identify ourselves, a huge canvas of colours that makes us the person we sense ourselves to be, a picture we hope provides a suitably rich and reassuringly answer to another big question that our ability to use language eventually throws up – another question that has the power to take us by surprise with a sudden horror of uncertainty: "*Who am I?*"

Like the question "*Why am I here?*", the fact that we can ask it doesn't mean that there's going to be an easy answer: language may light the fuse to the search for meaning, but history is scarred with our attempts to find it. Peel off the labels we get from the society we live in, and just being 'me' can often seem a very lonely place – the endorsement of others, and the approval and recognition that comes with it, often function as a key component of our mental health. The instinct to belong, to feel part of a group that we comfortable with – usually the tribe or society we were born into – is one that likely pre-dates our ability to speak about it: a herding instinct is seen in most of the species we share our world with. That's understandable enough: lone individuals get taken first by predators, so it's a useful survival strategy – and to the extent that it's a heritable characteristic, we adopt it because we descend from those who had it. But language brings a whole new dimension to the game.

For we all arrive in the world innocent of notions of identity – as babies we just do as we please, and barely have a sense of self until we can talk. But by the time we start school we've usually learnt at least one language, have become attached to the food, customs and habits of the culture around us, and are likely to have been encouraged to accept the traditions and beliefs of a particular religion. All of these we soon come to consider as our 'own', though we have simply inherited them from others, and have no more personal claim on them than we do on our names. And despite any claims to the contrary by patriots and evangelists, we would feel just as comfortable in our own skins if we had been born into or brought up in a completely different environment, and adopted a completely different identity: for however much our nature may owe to our genes, the identity that comes with language is artificial, and largely a matter of chance.

The relative balance of nature and nurture in determining the person we become is a question that has long preoccupied psychologists. Much of this work has been done by studying the lives of identical twins who have been separated at birth – something that is rarely allowed to happen these days – and there can be no stranger and more instructive case than that of twins Jack Yufe and Oskar Stöhr. Born in 1933 to a Romanian Jewish father and German Catholic mother in Trinidad, the brothers were separated at the age of six months when their parents split up. Oskar went to Germany with his mother, taking her maiden name, and attended a Nazi-run school before joining the Hitler Youth – a movement he enthusiastically supported. Jack remained in Trinidad with his father where he was brought up as a Jew – staying there until he was 15 when he went to live with an aunt in Venezuela. The following year she persuaded him to travel to the newly-formed state of Israel where he worked on a kibbutz, married an Israeli woman and even served as an officer in the Israeli navy.

After their separation the brothers did not meet again until 1954, when Jack travelled from Israel to Germany to make contact with his family, but the meeting did not go well. Sharing no language, they had to rely on an interpreter to communicate with each other – and as his step-father still had Nazi sympathies, Oskar even insisted that his brother remove the Israeli luggage tags from his bags before going to his home. Despite some uncannily similarities in their appearance and behaviour – they had had no contact for 20 years, yet were both wearing similar jackets, shirts, and wire-rimmed spectacles when they met – they had little in common, and even regarded each other as enemies. Jack eventually went to America to work with his father as a businessman, and Oskar became a coal miner.

It was another 25 years before they met again, when their story came to the attention of Thomas Bouchard, a leading researcher in twin studies. To his astonishment he discovered that despite their lack of contact and their very different backgrounds and conscious identities, Jack and Oskar shared some rather distinctive personal habits: amongst other things, both of them read books from the last page first, wore short moustaches, washed their hands and flushed the toilet both before and after using it, used their ring finger when scratching their heads and had the odd quirk of sneezing explosively in public to get attention. At the same time, they had different views on a wide variety of topics, viewed each other as rivals, and could never agree on the politics of the Middle East. The sheer accident of upbringing turned two genetically identical individuals into quite distinct human beings: people who not only found it hard to communicate with each other, but disagreed when they did – the one a liberal English-speaking Jew, the other a conservative German-speaking Catholic.

Enough work has now been done with identical twins like Jack and

Oskar to confirm that there is a considerable genetic component to the type of personality we end up being — no matter how much we feel ourselves to have freely chosen to be who and what we are. Though the accidents of individual experience may modify these personal traits — a childhood trauma may make one twin more cautious than the other, for example — our core inclinations seem to be encoded in our genes. But for all such innate tendencies, what makes us human is the way we express them: and this in turn can be greatly influenced by the dominant cultural and religious beliefs of the language we grow up with — with powerful effects on our opinions and behaviour. These dominant beliefs affect the personality of whole nations: despite the equally distressing scale of the devastation, the Japanese reaction to the tsunami and nuclear meltdown at Fukushima was much more measured than the American response to the effects of Hurricane Katrina in New Orleans, for example. That doesn't mean we have to be trapped by the cultural habits of the society we grow up in, but unless we take active steps to outgrow them, they can become deeply imprinted on our sense of identity.

Like religious faith, a sense of identity can provide a warm fuzzy feeling, an instant connection in a confusing world it is otherwise easy to feel alienated from. To belong to a group gives you access to the emotional and physical support traditionally provided by families as the first, and often the only reliable form of social security. But there's a price to pay: membership of such a group requires you to follow their rules. The trap of identity is to think that belonging to a group is what defines us — for it puts us in a box from which we can struggle to escape. As the broadcaster Jonathan Meades once put it, identity "*defines people by their race and inherited culture rather than their individuality, their aspirations and their talents...To emphasise differences merely consigns people to their background, to where they come from, to their tribe, their caste, their religion.*" To an extent, that's a natural response — you need only visit a playground to realise that 'different' always has the potential to seem weird: but like the air we breathe, the thing that we don't see is the oddness of our own behaviour, of 'our' ways of doing things. The idea that everything 'we' do is normal, and that everything 'they' do is strange may conveniently embed us in the warm comfort-blanket of a shared culture, but it ignores the fact that every culture is doing the same things, just differently.

I am therefore I think

But we are getting ahead of ourselves again. No matter how strongly we may sense it within us, the source of our sense of self – the 'I' within me that recognises and identifies with my tribe, my team, my country or my religion – remains a mystery. Where can this thing that we think of as 'me' – whatever the word we use to refer to it – actually be found? What is my mind, and where does it come from? And come to think of it, how do I even know that 'I' exist? And what might language have to do with it?

These are old problems, of course. In the traditions of western philosophy, Descartes is generally credited as being the first person to come up with a formal proof for his (and our) existence, with his famous phrase 'I think therefore I am' – even if Saint Augustine probably beat him to the punch over a thousand years earlier in his seminal treatise *The City of God*. In response to the idea that he might be 'deceived' in assuming he exists, he writes *"I exist even if I am deceived. For one who does not exist, cannot be deceived"*. But Descartes and Augustine are far from the only ones to have pondered the question of existence, what it is, and how we can be aware of it: everyone from the earliest Hindu and Buddhist thinkers to the Chinese sage Lao Tsu and the philosophers of ancient Greece has been at it, to say nothing of more recent thought on the matter. Once you have learnt to use language, it comes with the territory.

Because just as language allows us to ask '*Who am I?*' (a question that our sense of identity enables us to conveniently deflect – or at least defer) it also allows us to ask '*What am I?*' – a subtler question whose trickiness becomes clearer if we frame it more accurately as '*What "is" I*'? Descartes' answer is that 'I' is the thing doing the thinking, which is how we know 'I' exist; but the question can only be asked – the thought can only be 'thunk' – in the first place because language enables us to do so. Does that mean that without words we would not exist? Do other animals not exist, in the sense of having an awareness of themselves?

This too is an old debate: one of the dividing lines between humans and other animals was believed to be that other animals are automata, not capable of thinking. But animals clearly do think, if by that we mean that they are able to come up with intelligent strategies to solve practical problems in their lives. In *The Descent of Man*, Darwin tells the story of a baboon who took revenge on a soldier who had been 'plaguing' it, carefully waiting for the chance to humiliate the officer by splashing mud on his parade uniform. "*For long afterwards*," he tells us, "*the baboon rejoiced and triumphed whenever he saw his victim.*" Just like us, members of other species can use the memory of past experience to modify their behaviour to ensure a better result the next time. But unlike us, they make that calculation in silence and alone. Animals may well have a sense of self, and be aware of themselves as separate individuals (everything about their competitive behaviour tends to confirm that) but they are not able to be 'conscious' of it – because without words they cannot think about it.

To better understand what language does for us in this regard, it will help at this point to make a distinction between 'awareness' and 'consciousness'. Awareness can be defined as the stuff of experience, the unmediated sensation of whatever we happen to be paying attention to – the raw sensory input from the eyes, ears, tongue, nose and skin, sources of information we share with all other animals. Other species can often see, hear, taste, smell and feel more detail than we can – but without words they can only experience and react to new situations based on immediate input and memories of previous experience.

Just as it is for us, their behaviour is ultimately a calculation: an action that seems to offer the best chance of satisfying their needs. But with no other voices to confuse them, animals are able to act with an immediacy that we call 'instinct'. On the other hand, because we have found a way to tag what we experience – a way to name and then discuss what we are aware of – we are able to become aware that we are aware. In other words, to become conscious: the ultimate gift of language.

This is a profound moment, so let's dwell on it a little: the very idea of self, the thing inside us that we feel is somehow connected to and responsible for everything we do, could be no more than a side-effect of words. *Surely it can't be that simple?* I hear you ask. But stay with me. The illusion is so profound because language is the only way we can express the way we feel beyond indiscriminate howls of pain or joy. We have no other means of knowing it. Words give form to our sensations, bringing them to consciousness by isolating them from experience, creating abstract tools to reckon with. But though this trick of speech allows us to trade thoughts like currency, it's still a trick – an illusion that actually disconnects us from reality.

Try an experiment for a moment. Look up from the page and see what's around you. Try to find a spot where there's no writing or any other signs. Stare at a wall, or out of a window. Fix your gaze and just look at what you see there. Don't think about it, just look and absorb it as a sensation, without analysing what you see. It's a hard thing to do, to look without thinking. People spend years practicing meditation to help them achieve this very state.

But if only for a moment, try to disconnect from your thinking mind, the constant whirl of words inside your head that is our conscious self – the running commentary on our awareness that language makes possible. Try to be simply aware, to let sensation take over. Without thinking about them, just notice colours, shapes and textures. Hear all the sounds going on around you. Notice any smells, any residual taste in your mouth. Feel the way your body is sitting. Put down this book, which is only adding another voice to your head, and just look, listen, smell, taste – and feel.

If you find that difficult, turn the page and see if this helps:

What you are feeling as you do this is your awareness – the same awareness than any living thing experiences, the sensation of being alive. A person born blind does not know that they are blind, and develops a much acuter sense of hearing and feeling to compensate – even to the extent of being able to 'see' with their ears. There's only so much attention you can pay to anything, and our obsession with words, the attention we pay to the virtual world of thought, reduces our ability to pay attention to the only certain information we have: pure sensation, unfiltered by thoughts about what it is. Even with language, our senses are still the only direct information we have – but words allow us to question and compare what we are sensing, learn from other people's experiences, and create a world of ideas that let us modify and classify the sensory data coming in. To remind yourself how abstract that world is, turn back to the last page again – and this time allow yourself to think about the first thing that comes into your head.

In this act of thinking you're suddenly somewhere else, and that's the magic of words – using them takes you away from where you are. Just think what happens when you are on the phone. You are with the other person in your head, removed from the particular space you're in. Reading does the same thing, but in a more focussed way. In a very real sense, language is the first form of television – words take you on a journey away from where you are. If I say 'An elephant in a red dress comes into the room holding a blue ball' you immediately have a very clear image of that in your head – you can't help imagining what it looks like, as if you were there. In some ways it's better than television, because the image is specific to you. Two people can read the same sentence and see very different scenes, whereas if you see something on television, you have no choice about how it looks. Books – and stories before them – were our first films.

And that is our secret, the extraordinary advantage that language gives us. By giving us the power to think, it allows us to become aware that we are aware, and changes our entire relationship with the world. Other animals who are simply aware can act from instinct – just a calculation, in the end – and do whatever seems to be best based on the information available to them at the time. Words not only allow but compel us to stand back and take another look, and reconsider what our 'instinctive' thinking might be telling us. They drive a wedge between sensation and response, corrupting Hamlet's 'native hue of resolution' with the pale cast of thought. It is from that pause, the pause to consider other options, that consciousness – and a sense of identity – emerges.

Sole survivor

The intimate relationship between language and consciousness is linked to another powerful belief with a strong connection to our notions of who we are: the idea of the soul. Almost every culture on earth seems to have believed in some non-material form of identity that survives our death – and if we are now perhaps less willing to use the word in its more literal sense, we still often use it to describe the effect of being emotionally moved by some dramatic event or artistic experience – we talk of feeling something in our soul, talk of a lover or close friend as a soul-mate, and even use the word to tag a strongly-felt cultural identity, as in 'soul music' and 'soul food'. And though no-one has been able to demonstrate how and where one might actually be found – despite the macabre efforts of a certain Dr Duncan MacDougall to weigh the departing souls of his dying patients in 1907 – many people are still not comfortable with the suggestion that we might in fact not have one at all.

The question of whether we have a soul is not one that would have occurred to most people for most of human history; studies show that even young children seem to have an 'instinctive' belief in the soul – along with ghosts and spirits – and so strong is the sense that we have one that most cultures have just taken it for granted. The experience of being alive, the felt reality of consciousness and the wings that language gives to thought induce a light, airy feeling that seems quite independent of the heavy, meaty mess of our biology. How could we not have a soul? But turn the question round, and the answer is far from clear. How *could* we have a soul? How would a 'spiritual' essence interact with a mate-rial body? Where might it be located? These are not easy questions to answer: the devil is again in the detail. It's easy enough to believe in a soul – comforting, even – but there are real problems with the idea: how, when and where might that soul enter our bodies? At conception? At birth? At some point in between?

These tricky issues have pre-occupied the minds of thinkers since the first beginnings of philosophy. Aristotle believed that 'ensoulment' (the point at which a foetus is thought to acquire a soul and become a human being) occurred at 40 days from conception in the case of a boy – although only at 90 days in the case of a girl – whereas his contemporaries the Stoics taught that it occurred at birth, with the Pythagoreans arguing that it occurred at conception. Christians have been curiously inconsistent over the centuries: in the early days they took a Pythagorean view of the matter, but the mediaeval Church generally tended to follow Aristotle's views – while later Popes, despite their notional infallibility, have gone to and fro on the issue. Perhaps God kept changing his mind, or reception was bad on the papal hotline.

Other traditions have debated this question as well. Islam is equally torn on the matter: some scholars say ensoulment occurs at 120 days (based on a *hadith*, or reported saying of the prophet) others at 40 days and yet others at the time when the baby is first felt to move. The oldest Hindu texts state that the soul enters the body in the 7th month, but the teaching changed around the 1st century AD when a new interpretation of scripture deemed ensoulment to occur at 7 weeks – and more recent teaching says that the soul enters the body at the moment of conception (which is also the Buddhist position). Whatever the reason, historically the question seems mainly to have turned on whether abortion should be treated as murder.

But if the soul enters the body at conception, as pro-life fundamentalists now insist, there is another problem: in the case of identical twins, the division into two foetuses does not occur at conception, but at the earliest on the second day, and sometimes as late as the sixth day. Would that then mean that God has to wait to provide the second soul, or that the soul somehow divides in two? And what about all those fertilised eggs that never make it past the first month (the majority of the products of conception either do not implant, or spontaneously abort within the first month of pregnancy). Would a kind, loving or even just a careful God waste all those souls? Inconvenient as these questions are, belief in the soul requires that they be answered: but scientists have been unable to find anything that might provide a hint of evidence, and neither the theologians nor the philosophers have a theory they can agree on.

Without written records, it's hard to know what our earliest ancestors thought, but the respect with which they treated their dead tells its own story. The practice of human burial seems to have begun around 100,000 years ago. As already argued, this is one baseline for the emergence of language – we wouldn't have been able to start cooperating with each other to bury our dead unless we could talk about the reasons for doing it. But the fact that ancient communities took great care over how they prepared bodies for burial is a strong indicator of their likely beliefs. We know from the texts they leave behind that the civilization of ancient Egypt had elaborate ideas about the afterlife at least as far back as 5,000 years ago, and would bury people with grave goods to ensure they were prepared for the life beyond. But even earlier burials have been found with precious grave goods, implying that such beliefs go back much further in time.

Excavations at a burial site from a settlement at Sungir in Russia, dating back almost 30,000 years, uncovered the graves of two children who had been decorated with thousands of ivory beads that would have originally been sewn into their clothing. The boy also wore a belt studded with 250 fox teeth, and the grave included several mammoth tusks over two metres long that had been carefully and laboriously straightened after first softening them in water. The burial of things that cost so much effort to produce (it's been estimated that the ivory beads alone would have taken about an hour each to make) strongly suggests that the people who did it believed in the need to prepare the dead children properly for some future existence.

But beliefs about the soul have more practical consequences than whether to bury our loved ones with grave goods. Just as the debate about the moment of ensoulment had the practical purpose of determining when abortion might be deemed legal, so ideas about the sanctity of the human soul (as opposed to other animals) still affect our thinking about the other end of life. Despite the fact that many of us are likely to live long enough to experience a greatly diminished quality of life in our final years due to dementia or some other degenerative illness, euthanasia is still a difficult topic for public discussion. Suicide was actually illegal in the UK until 1961, as it continues to be in many countries – and in most nations it is still a criminal offence to help someone who wishes to die. Given that we consider it a kindness to end the life of a pet who is suffering, it is remarkable that we do not offer the same courtesy to those of our own kind who request it, instead insisting that people with a radically reduced quality of life should put up with their agony until the bitter end. If our belief in the soul has anything to do with that, language has a great deal to answer for.

At the same time, thoughts inspired by ideas of immortality can literally be lethal: we don't even have to turn to the example of suicide bombers – whether motivated by the thought of 72 virgins awaiting them or simply the glory of dying nobly for their cause – to find examples: plenty of people in have killed themselves in the hope of a better life beyond, with Christian cults leading the way. Even those of us who feel that such beliefs are deluded can never quite be sure: and the uncertainty inevitably pushes us in the direction of accepting the famous wager of Descartes' compatriot and contemporary Blaise Pascal. He felt it was smarter to subscribe to belief in God and the immortality of the soul on the off-chance that it might be true: if you don't and it is, you'll be going to hell – but if you do and it isn't, you've not lost anything (except for all the time you'll have wasted in following the spurious teachings that advocate it, of course).

But on a more practical point, in the here-and-now – how would you actually know if in fact you don't have a soul, and what difference would it make to your life? Would you feel any different than if you did have one? This is a different question to whether you would *think* any differently about yourself in such a case, because switching to the idea that you don't might take some getting used to. But that's just a trick of words, a side-effect of language. Though your belief about yourself and your identity might have to alter somewhat, in reality nothing would have actually changed. The way you sense the smell of coffee, the way you see the colours of the sunset, the way you hear your favourite music or love your friends or family, would stay exactly the same whether or not you do in fact have a soul; only your belief about it would be different.

So the question then becomes: what benefit is there to believe in the soul? And here, the answer is clearer. First of all, there is the consolation of thinking that not only you but all the people you have known do not cease to exist at death, but go on living in some form after they die – in fact, we can even believe that life may be better for them in some other world where they no longer suffer. But there is a more profound, less visible side-effect. Belief in the soul as the unique repository of what we are, the touchstone of our identity, is another way in which language allows us to think of ourselves as special in some way – particularly compared to the 'dumb' animals, who are not traditionally considered to have a soul, or qualified to go to heaven. That's convenient given our long-standing habit of eating them to sustain ourselves, but it also buttresses the beliefs that sustain all religions – for if death were the end, there would be nothing to fear, no one to placate and nothing to prepare for.

What's in a name

John Keats once claimed that the prime characteristic required of a poet is a capacity for 'negative capability'– a quality well described by one commentator as *'the ability to tolerate a loss of self and a loss of rationality by trusting in the capacity to recreate oneself in another character or another environment.'* This is very much the quality required of a good interpreter – the ability to step out of the gravity field of your 'own' language and culture and adopt the discipline of another way of understanding and expressing reality that may have no obvious connection with the one you are used to. It is also the quality required of anyone who wishes to function effectively in another culture – whether or not a different language is involved – and helps explain why it's something people can often feel uncomfortable with: it requires you to let go of what you might otherwise consider to be your sense of identity, your belief in and acceptance of a certain way of seeing, doing and speaking about things.

In Arab culture, it's common for men to kiss each other when greeting, and hold hands when walking together without the slightest suggestion of sexual attraction – it's considered such normal behaviour that not to do so is to risk giving offense. That can feel awkward to someone brought up in a culture where men do not express intimacy in such ways, but to do so is not to lose your 'identity' in any way, or to be untrue to yourself: it's just a question of 'speaking' the local language. Even someone as culturally unreconstructed as George W Bush felt the need to walk hand in hand with Saudi guests, if only to seal whatever deal he was negotiating. In this he was more sensitive (or perhaps just better advised) than was David Cameron when he insisted on wearing a Remembrance Day poppy on an official trip to China, forgetting – or just not caring – that for his hosts the poppy would evoke memories of the Opium Wars, the military conflicts which enabled Britain to dominate China in the 19th century.

But one of the most personal parts of our identity is our name. We somehow feel it to be an intrinsic part of what we are, something sacred and inviolate, associated forever with us and impossible to surrender – even though it's simply a tag, a random noise that allows someone to attract our attention, or refer to us when we are a topic of conversation. The importance of this tiny piece of sonic magic is neatly illustrated by the prominence afforded it in the Egyptian Book of the Dead. Copies of this lengthy magical text were left in the deceased's tomb with their name inscribed in several places, to ensure they would not forget it in the hereafter – knowing one's name was held to be vital for continued existence – and there was a specific spell to help remember it. Yet one of the most remarkable things about our name is that (like everything else about our language, culture and religion) it is not actually 'ours' at all: it was chosen and given to us by our parents, for reasons that will usually have meant something to them, but can have nothing to do with who we actually are.

We may feel less resistance to the idea of changing our surname (in many societies women still do it as a matter of course when they get married, and some people change it because they wish to distance themselves from unpleasant associations or family connections). But we still tend to cling to our 'given' name as if it were vital to our sense of who we are – and if you do decide to change your own name, you may find that it involves more than just working up the nerve to do it. A few years ago my wife decided to formally change her name from her 'original' Japanese name to an English name, because she found it so much easier to be accepted in English-speaking social situations. Instead of having to deal with the awkwardness of other people struggling with the pronunciation of a name that doesn't sound 'English', with her 'new' name she found people generally accepted it – and her – without a second thought, even if they knew that it couldn't be her original name. Though it took her a while to adjust, she felt more welcomed – and it was better than being asked *"Can I just call you Susan?"* – an indignity she was subjected to more than once.

What surprised her was the reaction of all her friends who knew her by her 'original' name. People were quite upset – and not just her Japanese friends. They felt outraged on her behalf, as if the change of a name somehow changed her very identity. The strength of their reaction suggests that something more was at stake. A name, after all, is just a noise – and one that you had no choice over. But in accepting and using it, you are signing up to the principle that you 'are' what the accidents of life have made you – your language, your culture, your religion. Changing your name, the thing that stands for everything that makes you what you are, suggests that perhaps you could change other parts of the puzzle. And that seems to make many people feel uncomfortable.

Our discomfort with change shows up in surprising areas. Even the noises we make when stuck for words are highly culture-specific. Stalling for time while your brain finds the right word or expression is one of the most basic techniques we use in any language – but every culture uses different sounds. Where English speakers will say 'um' or 'er', Chinese speakers say *nay-ge*, Arab speakers say *ya'ni*, and Portuguese speakers will say *tipo*. The Japanese say something that sounds like *air-tor*. Even quite fluent speakers of English will say *air-tor* instead of 'um' and 'er'. When teaching English I used to encourage my students to say 'um' and 'er' when they needed to pause to find the right word to use. It's a tiny thing that most people don't think about, but no matter how fluent they may be, not using them immediately flags them up as a foreign speaker. On the other hand, the correct use of 'um' and 'er' – even with a relatively basic level of English – will make you sound much more fluent, even if you're being quite inarticulate: people will just think you're having trouble finding the words.

You might think that's not so difficult to do, but try it yourself. We're so used to saying 'um' and 'er' when stuck for a word, that most of the time we don't even notice we're doing it. But next time you're talking, try switching to the Japanese version instead. *Air-tor*. It's surprising how 'foreign' it feels just to make those two little noises – for they aren't really even words, just 'filler' sounds – even if everything else you are saying is English. That's how alert we are to the slightest breach of social and linguistic protocol. You can say the most unlikely thing that's ever been said – "*Colorless green ideas sleep furiously*" – and people will accept it more easily than if you make an unexpected noise in the stream of speech, because the whole point of such filler words is that they smooth over the flow of speech with 'invisible' noises that everyone accepts (and does not notice): using any other noises shatters the illusion.

Our sensitivity to such trivial details is well illustrated by the predicament of those who suffer from an unfortunate condition known as Foreign Accent Syndrome. This happily rather rare affliction involves internal trauma to the brain, usually a stroke or seizure of some kind, which does physical damage to the areas that control speech and prevents a person from speaking with the precision that most people take for granted. In other words, the smooth oral choreography that allows us to speak normally is interrupted. This has at least two rather startling effects. Firstly, from the point of view of anyone so afflicted, they no longer feel 'themselves'. They can no longer speak as they used to, struggle to find certain words, and mispronounce or omit others. They are very conscious of this, and find it frustrating. It feels like their whole identity has changed.

Secondly, the inability to speak 'normally' appears to mimic the difficulties that a foreign speaker of a language faces. A foreign accent is typically characterised by the inability to produce and pronounce words the same way as a native speaker, with incorrect phonemes, intonation patterns and grammar. These are all symptoms that occur with the sort of mild impairment of language function that is the cause of Foreign Accent Syndrome. It is not actually a 'foreign' accent, but to friends, family and any native speakers not familiar with another language, or how language works, it will simply sound 'foreign' – and will typically 'sound' like the foreign language that the community is most familiar with, or used to hearing, even though a more careful listening will show that the speaker still has a fluency way beyond that of a normal 'foreigner' – knowing slang words and expressions that are usually beyond a foreign speaker's competence.

But the worst of it is that the inability to speak 'normally' results in social ostracisation. A particularly unlucky case was the Norwegian woman hit by shrapnel during World War II who started speaking (or sounding as she was speaking) with a German accent – a most unfortunate consequence when everyone in Norway was on the lookout for German spies – but even in times of peace, a 'foreign' accent usually results in being treated differently, even if well-meaningly so. People may ask you where you're from, compliment you on your ability to speak their language, even try to correct your grammar. This is the experience of every learner of a foreign language, trying to make themselves understood – it's the most obvious sign that the community does not regard you as one of their own. That's something you can cope with if you have a sense of belonging to another community – even if you are cut off from them, temporarily or otherwise. But the most upsetting thing for people suffering from FAS is to be treated as a foreigner in your 'own' community just because your speech patterns have changed. There's nowhere else to go. You are 'home', but you're not treated as if you were.

Gender benders

Blue is for boys, pink is for girls, right? Except when it isn't – and for most of the world, most of the time, it hasn't been. As recently as a century ago, it wasn't even the case in America: a 1918 article in Earnshaw's, a trade magazine for children's clothing, stated *"The generally accepted rule is pink for the boys, and blue for the girls. The reason is that pink, being a more decided and stronger color, is more suitable for the boy, while blue, which is more delicate and dainty, is prettier for the girl."* The modern preference for pink for girls seems to have begun during the 1950s, a fashion driven by President Eisenhower's wife Mamie (whose favourite colour was pink) at a time when colour TV was just coming into people's homes. Despite any appearances, gender stereotypes are not nearly as clear-cut as they seem.

Although the impact of social and cultural constraints on sexual preferences has been debated for decades, it's only recently that gender has been seen as anything other than a binary distinction. Certainly it was rarely thought of as a choice – the division into one sex or the other was taken for granted, as it still is in most cultures around the world. That may have seemed reasonable enough when we mostly lived in small isolated communities where exceptions to the rule would have been rare: the mechanics of reproduction require two different sexes, and you were supposed to be either one or the other. But though that may be the overall tendency, nature is not that straightforward – like most biological attributes, it turns out that gender is a spectrum: according to the Intersex Society of America, as many as one in 100 people have bodies which "differ from standard male or female", and up to one in 1500 people are now estimated to be 'true intersex' (with neither XX or XY chromosomes).

That's over 4 million people worldwide, and in a country the size of the United States, around 200,000 people who are neither male nor female. So there are a lot of people who are going to have difficulty 'iden-tifying' with the conventional division into male and female, with all the cultural expectations and rules that apply. For even with a 'standard' body, sexual orientation can be 'non-standard', a fact now slowly being acknowledged through the acceptance of LGBT rights and the recognition of same-sex marriage – but this too is a very recent trend: within my own lifetime homosexuality was still illegal in Britain, and still has a long way to go before being fully accepted around the world.

The issue of 'transgender' identities might still be far removed from what most people experience in their lives. But however much it may seem a minority issue, it serves as a powerful metaphor for the dangers of ste-reotyping that the pressure of language and our conventional notions of identity inevitably encourage. If 'you' are not part of 'my' team, not recog-nisably wearing the same physical or mental uniform, then you become an object of suspicion and even scorn in proportion to the extent that I identify with my chosen group. If I identify strongly as a heterosexual, the idea of gay or transgender people might make me feel uncomfortable. If I identify strongly as white, I am liable to feel less comfortable around people of another ethnicity. And the same holds true for strong identifica-tion with any group, whether linguistic, cultural or religious.

Much of the difficulty and suffering that such discrimination brings is due to a lack of real contact with those perceived as 'other'. A striking example is provided by the case of John Dutcher, a 61-year-old 'Trump supporter' from Nebraska, who in 2017 surprised himself and everyone else by befriending two Muslim families who had moved in next door to him as part of a resettlement programme. Previously someone with an avowed hatred of Muslims – he'd considered himself "one of those guys who would want to put a pig's head on a mosque" – his dislike had been primarily driven by the events of 9/11, and he'd never actually met any Muslims. But once he began to have personal contact with the fami-lies and their children, and heard about the harrowing experiences they'd been through as refugees, his attitude gradually began to change. In fact their positive and grateful approach to life was so different to the people who had lived there before that, "they took the hatred out of me," as he put it.

This is the kind of transformation that language makes possible, because words exist in an abstract space, free from any physical badges of identity. With written language in particular, all that matters is what is said, not who is saying it: the essence of the exchange becomes clear and transparent, untainted by perceptions of race, sex, colour, class or any other category that we use to artificially distinguish 'them' from 'us'. This is even so in the case of other species: as we saw in Chapter 1, Kanzi the bonobo's ability to understand and act on what is said to him brings him into our world in an astonishing way. Though particular words can have specific cultural associations, language has no colour or gender – the assumptions we make are what keep people apart, but our perceptions are driven by our common biology: ultimately any case you have to make stands and falls on the validity of your argument, not the accidents of birth or the circumstances of your life.

Just as with the soul, the notion of 'identity' is not one that was much discussed by our ancestors. Either you belonged to your tribe or group, or you were a foreigner; the idea that you might have a separate identity within a community was rarely discussed until it became an issue with the civil rights movement. But then you don't need to be aware of your identity if everyone else is behaving the same way – and it is particularly hard for the members of a dominant group to notice their inherent elitism, because they do not suffer its consequences. As a white British male lucky enough to have received a good education, it was a salutary experience to realise that I was being looked down on and patronized for my ignorance of Japanese language and culture when I was living in Japan. And the closer I got to fluency, the more I felt I was being excluded – a sentiment often expressed openly: I was even told that I would never be like a Japanese person however much I tried, because I was a foreigner and there were just some things I could never expect to understand. But this reaction is not unique to the Japanese: almost every culture imposes that feeling on its members as a default setting, the sense that 'they' can never understand 'us' – because otherwise what would be the point of 'us'?

Like the British, the Japanese sense of nationality is particularly strong. Not only do they feel a very clear sense of who they are, it's a sense that in their own minds distinguishes them from every other nationality on the planet. But the Japanese believe themselves to be especially different – not just because they have a different culture, language and religion to other countries, but because they almost feel themselves to be biologically, even genetically unique. There may be no specifically religious component to this, but there is an unmistakable spiritual dimension, nonetheless. Again, this is by no means only a Japanese phenomenon – every culture is at it, whether a nation or not, and whether consciously or not – but the Japanese are perhaps unusual in the extent to which they take it. Go into any Japanese bookshop and you will find a whole shelf of books about what makes the Japanese so different to everyone else.

But reality has a bad habit of confounding such wishful thinking. The confusion that mistaken ideas of cultural uniqueness can cause is beautifully illustrated in the case of Jero, a popular *enka* singer in Japan. *Enka* is a form of nostalgic ballad music as distinctively Japanese as country music is American, and appeals to the same sort of audience – conservative, traditional, sentimental, and patriotic. In any poll of what most captures the soul of Japan, *enka* would come high up on the list. But Jero is not from Japan. He's a young African-American artist from the mean streets of Pittsburgh, Pennsylvania. Though neither of his parents is Japanese, as a young boy he was brought up largely by his Japanese grandmother, who taught him how to sing – and along with hip-hop, *enka* made its way to his heart.

And Jero can sing *enka* with the best of them. Not only can he sing, he can tremble and twitch in truly authentic *enka* fashion, so much so that he won a Best New Artist award in his first year in Japan, earning the respect of his fellow singers. But rather than dress in traditional Japanese style, he insists on wearing the clothes he feels most comfortable in

– which further compounds the cultural shock. Visually, he looks like a regular hip-hop dude, but put him behind a screen and you'd never know it – a fact that Japanese TV was not slow to exploit, fooling a respected musicologist into thinking they'd found a new *enka* star. Which they had, of course – it's just that he's not Japanese. But the shocked look on the faces of the studio audience of invited celebrities when he revealed himself to them was something to behold – rather how people in Britain might react if they had just seen a cat singing the National Anthem.

They couldn't help it, of course, and didn't necessarily mean anything bad by it. It's just that their expectations had been confounded – and in the case of Jero, their very sense of identity was being questioned. If someone from such a different cultural background could master such a definitively Japanese art, what does that say about being Japanese? Is it just a set of skills that can be mastered? Surely only a 'Japanese' person could do something so Japanese? A similar shock in a different cultural context was delivered by the rapper Eminem, whose phenomenal rhyming skills and distinctive flow propelled him to chart success in a genre that had until then been largely identified with black culture. But no cultural activity is exclusively the property of a particular group or ethnicity. Humans are humans, and the beauty of language is that once the barriers of identity are down, our knowledge and skills can be shared equally.

Identity crisis

For all the conflict it spawns, there can be no doubt that religion has had some positive effects as well. For one thing, in its modern forms it has accustomed us to the notion of uniting over an idea in ways that can cut across more tribal divisions – sometimes even splitting families with different religious loyalties. For another, it has provided a broader sense of identity that allows people to feel part of a community of shared values – and for the major modern religions, those values include compassion for the poor and destitute. Much of the slack in society's disregard for the disadvantaged has traditionally been taken up by charitable activities of a religious nature. This doesn't mean that without religion this would not take place; more that religion has found a way to encourage and formalize behaviour that comes naturally to our species – most modern charities are secular in nature. But it has often proved an important precursor for concepts that we now take for granted (like social security and even science), even if we no longer accept the faith that once went with it.

The origins of the Latin word *religio* from which we get the English word 'religion' remain obscure, and are still argued over by scholars. The classical interpretation, attributed to Cicero, was that of 'careful consideration', whereas others – most notably St Augustine – saw it as being more about binding oneself to the law: but either way, in practice religion is about observance of rules and rites. In many religions, the word used for their key doctrine means 'the way' or 'the law'. In Islam *sharia* means a way or path, the Sanskrit word *dharma* – a key concept in Hinduism and Buddhism – means the natural order or law of the cosmos (a concept mirrored in Taoism), and the Hebrew word *halakha*, often translated as the Jewish law (which all Jews should follow, whether religious or not) more literally means 'the path that one walks'. And the path that religion enjoins you to walk is circumscribed by rules. Any doubts that the Christian religion, following Judaism, is not based principally on the observation of rules can be easily allayed by reading the Old Testament – particularly the Book of Leviticus, which will put you straight on almost anything you might have ever considered doing (including several pages on who or what you should never find yourself naked with.)

There is no doubt that the most contentious part of our identity is tied up with religion. As we've already seen, conflict over religious doctrine can lead to some of the worst violence and vindictive cruelty perpetrated between people. The Catholic Church may be famous for the iniquities of the Inquisition, but Islam has also dealt severely with apostasy or abandonment of the faith, and authorises *jihad* ('the struggle') to be performed to protect it. But these external battles – what Islam calls the 'lesser *jihad*', pale into insignificance compared to the agony of the 'greater *jihad*', the inner spiritual struggle to make yourself conform to your beliefs. Given the more flamboyant and violent nature of the struggle for the minds of others, the struggle for consistency in your own mind may not seem as visible: but the letters of Mother Teresa reveal the agonies of doubt that can afflict even the mind of someone whose life was devoted to charity and good works. In the absence of certainty – something that faith can never ultimately deliver – strict adherence to religious doctrine is often a discipline that cannot be achieved without severe cognitive dissonance.

Even for those on a less elevated plane than St Teresa, the struggle to maintain an identity consistent with their spiritual beliefs – while still satisfying their more material desires and requirements – has the potential to drive the faithful to absurd extremes. In the 17th century, pioneers busy at the task of conquering America had such a strong desire for meat that the Catholic Church was at one point forced to concede that beavers – who spend most of their time in water – could be recognised as fish, so that the faithful might sustain themselves during Lent and on other days when only fish was allowed to be eaten; other animals to have ended up being classified as fish for the same reason include species as diverse as puffin and alligator. Nor is the desire to elude inconvenient religious rules limited to Christian countries: in Japan, the ancient Buddhist prohibition on eating the meat of animals that walk on four legs was got round in part by re-classifying rabbits as 'birds'. Remarkably, this classification still lives on in the language today: the word used as a counter for rabbits in Japanese is 'feather'.

This is not something that is confined to ancient history. As recently as 2007, a *fatwa* was issued by Dr. Izzat Atiya, then head of the Department of Hadith at Al-Azhar University in Cairo, advising women at work to consider breastfeeding their adult male co-workers as a means of legalising what could otherwise risk being seen as an unlawful meeting in the workplace between a man and a woman who are not related to one another (contrary to popular perception, a *fatwa* is not a pronouncement of a death sentence or a declaration of war; it's simply a legal pronouncement relating to a particular issue in Islamic law). This *fatwa* was based on an ingenious adaption of a common – if already somewhat odd – practice in the orthodox Muslim world, whereby sisters will breastfeed their siblings' children so that they can become 'breastmilk siblings'. This means that cousins of a different sex will not later have to be segregated, and their aunts will not have to cover themselves in front of them.

The implication of Dr Atiya's wheeze was that if a woman were to 'breastfeed' a co-worker of a different sex (a process nominally requiring 'five fulfilling breastmilk meals' to be valid) they would notionally become 'related' – thereby allowing them to get around the proscription on meetings between otherwise unrelated co-workers of different sexes, a severe inconvenience in a modern business environment. This ban can be quite rigidly enforced: in 2009 a 75-year-old woman was sentenced in Saudi Arabia to 40 lashes and 4 months' imprisonment (followed by deportation; she was a Syrian national) for the crime of meeting two men unrelated to her in her house when taking a delivery of bread, even though one of them was in fact her nephew-in-law.

This *fatwa* was met with consternation and even ridicule in Egypt, and was quietly dropped, but was revived three years later in Saudi Arabia (where the ban is more restrictive) when a further controversy erupted. But this time the question was not whether the suggestion was borderline insane and practically unworkable from the get-go, but whether the breast milk had to be delivered directly from the breast, or could be equally well expressed into a cup and imbibed separately – by, say, a male driver who needed frequent access to the home and could thus be converted into a 'relative' to avoid any potential breach of protocol and the dire consequences that might ensue. This ingenious workaround suggests that Dr Atiya missed a lucrative career as an advisor on financial affairs and could have been usefully employed in some offshore tax haven dreaming up creative ways of re-interpreting tax legislation – though sadly the world is not undersupplied with such people.

But the daddy of all get-arounds must surely be the *eruv*. For those who don't know, this fabulously ingenious contrivance is a way of allowing orthodox Jews to observe the sabbath without having to follow all the rules that forbid certain activities on that day – like carrying or pushing objects. These are activities that are permitted in the home, but not outside it, and include such everyday acts as carrying a house key – so locking your house and taking the key with you to go to the synagogue, or pushing a wheelchair so that an elderly relative can go with you are technically a breach of religious law. People have got round it in the past by 'wearing' a key instead of carrying it – using it as part of the design for a tie pin, for example – but the genius of the *eruv* idea is to extend the concept of the 'home' to a group of buildings that are theoretically linked (as they might have been, in more ancient times, by being built around a large courtyard).

This is done by making sure that the area designated for 'enclosure' is notionally connected by contiguous physical features, like walls and hedges, railway lines and roads. Any open spaces between these existing features can be filled in by erecting poles with thin transparent wire (such as nylon fishing line) strung in between. And we're talking serious real estate. The largest one in the UK (in Manchester) has a perimeter of 13 miles, and one built in Los Angeles in 2002 encloses a whopping 80 square miles. The poles and lines are deemed to create 'doorways' in the boundary – the poles are the sides of the door and the lines are the 'lintel' across the top.

What's most astonishing is that those who accept this seem to find it plausible that an all-knowing, all-powerful God would not see through their ruse. However, the authorities are apparently agreed that – even if he did – he would approve of their ingenuity. Just as long, or course, as the boundary remains intact: so the flimsier parts are inspected every week to check that none of the almost invisible fishing line or poles has fallen down, thereby placing the faithful in danger – at an annual cost of £30,000 in the case of the Manchester *eruv*. So it's an expensive illusion to maintain – especially since the rules it is designed to overcome were never made by God in the first place, but were devised by rabbis who 'interpreted' God's law.

You'd think that a moment's reflection about the absurdity of such an arrangement would immediately cause you to question its validity, but as we saw in the chapter on religion, when it comes to belief, the need for consistency trumps common sense. If you believe that God has decreed certain rules, and your identity is tied up in following them, then the only way to deal with the inevitable cognitive dissonance is to find a way to square the circle, however ridiculous it may seem. That's the power of identity, and explains a great deal about religion.

The scoundrel's refuge

International support for the people of France after the terrorist attacks in Paris was demonstrated at football matches and other events by the singing of the French national anthem, The Marseillaise. It was a touching gesture – even a fine example of supra-national solidarity – even if few non-French people really know the words, or what the song is about. In fact it dates back to the French Revolution, and is a stirring hymn of defiance to the reactionary forces trying to snuff out the new Republic and its desire for self-determination. But it's curious how easily the sentiments could be taken as a rallying cry for supporters of IS. Translated, it reads: *What! Foreign cohorts would make the law in our homes? What! These mercenary phalanxes would strike down our proud warriors? Everyone is a soldier to combat you! If they fall, our young heroes, the earth will produce new ones, ready to fight against you! To arms, citizens, form your battalions! Let's march, let's march! Let an impure blood soak our fields!*

The British National anthem is no better, openly harnessing religious sentiment to political ends – as the words of the less-well-known second verse make crystal clear: *O lord God arise, scatter our enemies, and make them fall! Confound their knavish tricks, confuse their politics, on you our hopes we fix, God save the Queen!* Of course, even if they know them, most people pay no more attention to the words when singing the national anthem than they do when singing hymns in church: any meaning it once had has long since bleached away to leave an empty husk of patriotic symbolism – though it's always instructive to be reminded of what lies at the heart of the ritual. Dr Johnson notwithstanding, nationalism has always functioned as a reliable bastion of support for those searching for or seeking to harness a sense of identity. But how secure is the ground you build on when pledging allegiance to a particular nationality? Lest I offend anyone else's national sensibilities, let's look at the credentials of my own country.

To begin with, the very name 'Britain' is hardly British – it comes from the Latin word *Britannia*, meaning 'land of the Britons', a people the Greeks described as *Pretani*, meaning 'tattooed folk – scarcely a compliment, despite the recent resurgence of interest in inking. The Romans used the term to mean 'The British Isles', the largest of which they called Albion (from the Latin for 'white'), and presumably named them after the white cliffs of Dover, their initial point of contact. So Albion is the first name that comes down to us from history for the land we still refer to as Great Britain (which excludes Northern Ireland, the other part of the United Kingdom), though in fact the name has got nothing to do with any greatness of the British Empire: it dates back at least as far as the Middle Ages, when it was used to distinguish it from 'Lesser Britain', the part of France now known as Brittany (also home to 'Britons' – or *Bretons* in French). These lands were originally a single territory only separated when the glaciers melted after the end of the last Ice Age some 8,000 years ago – causing the seas to rise, and creating the English Channel (or *La Manche* as the French call it after its shape – *manche* means sleeve – thus refuting the English claim of ownership). Pause for breath.

The Roman invasion of Albion caused the Britons to retreat to the less hospitable mountainous areas of the island, leading eventually to the creation of the independent kingdoms of Scotland and Wales. I was born in England, a country named for the Angles, a German-speaking tribe who invaded Albion together with the Saxons and the Jutes after the Romans left. The English (as they became) then had a hard time with the Vikings, who invaded from the north, but no sooner had the country settled down as a single kingdom than it found itself invaded yet again from the south, this time by 'north-men' (Normans) from France who were originally from Scandinavia. The new English (who had now changed their language to French with German vocabulary) eventually annexed Wales, invaded Ireland, and by the 18th century had formally absorbed Scotland into what became known as the United Kingdom. So whether I call myself British or English, I am using a name that was never given to the land by the people who originally lived there – and besides, the blood of any of my forebears who might have actually lived in the land named after them is by now so thin in me as to be virtually meaningless.

Then there's St George, the patron saint of England, who has no more claim to be English than the majority of the kings and queens who have occupied the throne of England for the last 1000 years. Quite apart from the fact that he is also the patron saint of countries as diverse as Romania, Ethiopia, Georgia and Portugal – the motto of whose army is still *Portugal e São Jorge* ("Portugal and St George") – the man who became St George, if he ever existed, was most likely a Greek-born Roman soldier executed in Turkey by order of the Emperor Diocletian while Britain was still a Roman colony. Oh, and by the way, the chief shrine in which he is venerated is in Israel, close to the international airport at Tel Aviv. So that's something to keep in mind next time you're tempted to hoist the standard of St George as an emblem of national pride – along with the fact that it was first adopted by Richard I, a man who spent most of his life on foreign crusades and was so little attached to his country that he once said he would have sold London if he could.

That's not a whole lot to be proud of – and the hinterland of most other countries is littered with similarly mixed histories. Of course, I've been selective. I could have chosen to focus on the more glorious aspects of my nation – Britain as the birthplace of democracy (except that they invented that in Greece), the rule of law (which actually dates back to the Code of Hammaburi in Babylon) the Industrial Revolution (OK, we were first out of the blocks on that one) or the triumph over Hitler (though we couldn't have done that without the Yanks). But whether these are things to be proud of or to regret, they are still nothing to do with me personally. I may have grown up bathed in the reflected glory of my ancestors' deeds, but neither my DNA nor my cultural inheritance is something that I created, even if they have shaped me. I simply grew up in a country where these things either did – or did not – happen.

The reason we tend to think our culture, our religion and our identity is the best – or worst – is that often we don't know another one well enough to be able to judge. How could we? Growing up, it takes nearly two decades to get sufficiently up to speed with the culture we're born into to be considered a fully-functioning adult, and to learn that much about another culture

— enough to discover that they too can express all the grades of thought and feeling we fancy ourselves uniquely capable of — is a commitment few people are prepared to make. We don't think another culture can be as sophisticated as our own because we rarely have enough experience of another one to find out, especially when there's another language involved.

When I first left the UK, at the age of 19, I had a strong sense of being British. In fact, if you'd asked me, I would probably have said I was English. That was the culture I'd been brought up in: white, right — and proud of my heritage. A couple of years living in the Middle East did nothing to dent my sure sense of identity, although I did make enough friends to discover it was perhaps possible to be fully human and yet not British after all. But after I went to live in Japan, a curious thing began to happen: I slowly started to realise that I was in fact European. That came about through regular contact with fellow students of Japanese from other European cultures — French, German, Spanish, Italian — with whom I clearly shared a common cultural background that I did not share with Japan. Even though we did not speak each other's languages particularly well — to the point that we sometimes found it easier to speak Japanese with each other — it was somehow easier to communicate, crack jokes and generally make myself understood with them than it was with my Japanese acquaintances.

If I'd left Japan at that point, that's probably where my understanding would have stayed. But as my grasp of Japanese improved, as I learnt more about the background history and culture — slowly catching up on the essential references that an adult speaker of any language takes for granted in conversation — I found that the gap began to close. In fact one day, after about seven years in the country, I had a sharp moment of epiphany. I can still see it now, over 30 years later. I was riding a motorbike down a hill behind a bus, reading the advert on the panel below the back window — for toothpaste, as I recall. Suddenly, as I noticed I was reading it as easily as if it were English, I realised I no longer felt I was in a foreign country. It wasn't that I felt Japanese — though I felt as comfortable living in Japan as I did at 'home' — it was that it no longer seemed to matter what country I was from. I was at home where I was.

There is a curious parallel between the limiting effect our notions of identity can have on our consciousness and the specialization that takes place in cells. Every single one of the tens of trillions of cells in our bodies contains the entire sequence of DNA required to make every other part of our body, yet each cell only 'expresses' a very small portion of that DNA in performing its particular function as part of a larger whole. We now know it is possible to reset the expression of DNA in any cell from its 'differentiated' form back to an undifferentiated, embryonic state, allowing it to be transformed into any other type of cell. This suggests the intriguing possibility that – as the Buddha taught some 2500 years ago – our individual selves, hemmed in by artificial notions of who we are and ought to be, may be no more than the limited expression of a far greater potentiality within us: that in the right circumstances we have the potential to reach out to every other human on the planet, and possibly all living things. How otherwise are we to explain our empathy for those we do not know, whether or not we act on it?

Without anything else to compare it to, our language, culture, religion and sense of identity can form a hard shell that compels us to act in certain ways whether 'we' like it or not. The more we commit to a certain way of doing things, the more difficult – and more scary – is the thought of doing things another way. This fixed and rigid attitude exacts a high psychic toll: the more disciplined and 'civilised' a country becomes, the more constrained and impoverished the individual lives of its citizens – as the Victorians found and the Japanese know. But by virtue of the very fact that it is unnatural, eventually a break is called for: sooner or later you're going to need some kind of lay-up. For despite the artificial divisions and restrictions that our love affair with language inevitably imposes on us, we have always sought – and even been driven – to discover ways to evade them: whatever form they may have taken through history, the formula of "sex, drugs and rock 'n' roll" has proved a powerful and effective antidote to the straitjackets of culture, religion and identity.

It's time to see why we are so keen to turn to them for help.

ESCAPE: Sex, Drugs & Music

"I gotta get out of it before I get into it."

— Dinah-Moe Humm

The Id-entity

The first part of this book has looked at the ways we limit ourselves by falling for the trick of speech: how our almost unconscious identification with the virtual world of words leads to the unfortunate – even fatal – side-effects that emerge from our attachment to misplaced notions of culture, religion and identity. That's because the flip side of the sense of identity that language fosters is always going to be division. The idea of 'us' can only ever exist in opposition to some other group we think of as 'them', and to the extent that we believe our group offers the best of all possible worlds, 'they' can only ever hope to be second-rate: interesting, perhaps – exotic, even – but not to be taken seriously. And there's worse: at moments of social, political or economic crisis, groups appearing to have different values to our own can easily be seen as a threat, something to be shunned, rejected – and even eliminated.

At root, it's about survival. If there's an argument over resources, someone has to be fingered as the enemy whose treasures can be looted without a qualm – and even with a sense of achievement: and when the going gets tough, the people most likely to be targeted are those who look or sound different. These resources can be human as well as material: slavery is the most obvious form, a humiliating practice that leaves a long and shameful stain throughout history – and such discrimination all too soon spills over into genocide, with people of one 'race' being slaughtered wholesale by those of another. The irony is that in the human context, race does not exist: certainly not in the sense that it was used in Darwin's day, when he wrote of the struggle for life and 'the preservation of favoured races' – by which he meant species. In that sense, there are no human races – we can and do interbreed freely because we are all members of one genetic family: the range of variation within any local population of human genes is much greater than the average variation across the genome as a whole.

Race is essentially a cultural concept with no basis in biological reality, as both scientists and anyone who has fallen in love across its artificial boundaries will tell you; like dialects of a language, our differences are nothing compared to our similarities, significant though they can initially seem – especially to other members of 'our' group. Yet the pressure to create division is only magnified by the dreams of empire that have so often driven world history; the domination of weaker nations and groups by more powerful countries is sustained and justified by an implied and unquestioned sense of superiority. And whether based on military prowess, better technology, economic power or the more subjective ideas of race, language is the tool with which we impose it – both in our own minds and those of the people we seek to control.

A sense of fundamental incompatibility with the inhabitants of colonised nations was a clear, even celebrated part of British imperial consciousness, and the phrase *"East is East and West is West, and ne'er the twain shall meet"* still echoes through the mental corridors of those brought up in its wake. The line is from a poem by Rudyard Kipling, a man who in later life became an unashamed apologist for Empire, with his writings often used to build support for Britain's fading glories after the First World War. It occurs in the chorus of *The Ballad of East and West*, a lengthy work chronicling the struggle between two young men – one British, one Indian – who are fighting for their honour in colonial India. It's quoted with much approval by people who have usually never read it.

But even without knowing where it comes from, it's a phrase that summarises the almost instinctive feelings of alienation that cultures with different languages and heritages can arouse amongst people who have had little exposure to them. What's much more rarely mentioned, though, is the unexpected punch-line that follows this famous refrain, delivered as the two face off in the climactic scene:

> But there is neither East nor West, Border, nor Breed nor Birth
> When two strong men stand face to face,
> > tho' they come from the ends of the Earth!

Despite the chauvinism of the times, Kipling is clearly acknowledging that when it comes to the crunch, the artificial categories of culture, class and race have no meaning: once you get past appearances, the deeper values of loyalty, bravery and devotion to a cause are found in every society around the globe. East may be East and West may be West in terms of our day-to-day behaviour, habits and customs, but beyond that we're all human. No matter where we may be from, how different our cultures or the colour of our skin, we're dealing with the same dilemmas in the same ways: we're all subject to the same biology, and the maths of social engagement ensures that we converge on similar values, even if we express them differently. As Kipling's poem shows, the best of us is what's the same, not what's different.

This chapter looks at some of the ways in which, almost despite ourselves, we are constantly driven to reconnect with what most unites us – the unfiltered and directly sensual aspects of our awareness, the base on which everything else that we are is built. Language is an astonishingly powerful tool, but – as we've seen – it abstracts us from reality: it's a device for artificially identifying and isolating our perceptions to enable communication – but our animal nature cannot be fooled. No matter what stories we tell ourselves about what and who we are, lurking beneath our artificial sense of identity is a raw presence that Freud named *das Es* ('the it'). This has traditionally been referred to in English using the Latin word *id*, which, through a happy accident of the English language, can also be thought of as the 'id-entity' – the largely unconscious source of urges which we sense most vividly through the joys alluded to in the phrase "sex, drugs and rock 'n' roll." Each of these three categories – taken in their broadest sense – are where we find enjoyment and satisfaction that goes far beyond words, because each of them offers the opportunity to take us 'out of ourselves'.

If "sex, drugs and rock 'n' roll" can seem rather old-school in a more straight-edge 21st century, it's following a formula familiar from history – and one that is unlikely to prove unpopular any time soon. In fact, it falls within a grand old tradition, expressed in more innocent times as "wine, women and song" – and similar phrases can be found around the world, stretching at least as far back as Sanskrit and the expression *Sur, Sura, Sundari* (or "music, wine and woman"). But despite the implied chauvinism, there's no denying that some of the most liberating moments for those of any gender can be had through the joys of sexual activity, the use of recreational drugs such as alcohol, and the 'rock 'n' roll' of exuberant behaviour – pushing back against the artificial boundaries of culture. These things can all be appreciated, enjoyed and shared without the need for language, uniting us in ways that are a powerful antidote to the forces of tradition.

And as such, of course, they continue to be frowned upon: the potential threat these appetites pose to the established order is shown by the fact that they have frequently been subject to social and legal restrictions. There may be few laws against consensual sexual activity in most modern states today (though despite its claim to be the oldest profession in the world, prostitution is rarely tolerated openly) but it was not always thus. Free sex is seen as a moral threat because it can lead to marital strife and family breakdown, and challenge social norms – and even where the act itself has not been outlawed, sex between the wrong types of person has often been subject to harsh penalties. Homosexuality has a long history of repression, and the crime of miscegenation (which despite its fearsome Latin name, simply means 'mixing of types') was not restricted to the apartheid era of South Africa or the slave days of America. Throughout history, dominant cultures have resisted anything that might sully the purity of their blood – if only because the existence of mixed-race children throws the very idea of race into doubt, and questions the notion of genetic superiority.

Drugs also have the potential to disrupt and threaten the orderly and civilised ways of society, and despite the attempts to control their use in more recent times, have generally been much used by artists and other creative spirits as an aid to their desire to break down the bonds that hold the rest of society in check. Alcohol is probably the drug with the largest back catalogue in our history, but the use of opiates and cocaine go back much further than we tend to realise: as long ago as 3400 BC the Sumerians called the poppy *hul gil* ("the joy plant") and its use spread from there both to Egypt and along the Silk Road to China in ancient times. Coca leaves, the source of cocaine, have been used as a stimulant throughout South America since at least the third millennium BC, and the use of *cannabis sativa*, the hemp plant, goes back even further: it is one of mankind's earliest cultivated crops, dating back over 12,000 years.

Music has a still older pedigree. We can't be sure how long we have been using it, whether to enhance ritual or simply to entertain our communities, but the oldest musical instruments so far discovered – flutes made from the bones of birds and mammoth ivory – go back more than 40,000 years. If not as potent as sex and drugs, the ability of music to stir emotions in ways that threaten to break down the barriers of language and culture make it a powerful tool, and it too has fallen foul of moral crusaders. Elvis may have upset the matrons of middle America in the 1950s, but religious fundamentalists had long railed against its apparent frippery: the Puritans wanted to ban music from church, and in banning music altogether the Taliban quote a *hadith* which states "*Those who listen to music and songs in this world, will on the Day of Judgement have molten lead poured into their ears.*" Even Plato had his reservations, making Socrates argue in *The Republic* that music should be controlled "*because more than anything rhythm and harmony find their way to the inmost soul and take the strongest hold upon it.*"

But whatever the attempts to restrict them, sex, drugs and music have not gone away – and are unlikely ever to do so. The secret of their appeal is that they all offer ways to escape from 'our' selves, allowing glimpses of a world in which the 'common sense' that divides and rules our normal lives can melt back – if only for a moment – into something larger and more meaningful. For the ego – the little scrap of consciousness we like to think of as 'ourself' – is just a middleman, mediating in the conflict between our sense of identity (the 'super-ego' voices of society in our head that tell us what we 'ought' to do) and the desires, feelings and impulses that are what most make us feel alive. They open windows onto a primordial world that is both before and beyond language, a world where the normal limitations of our individual lives, so reinforced by language, can be released – allowing us to return to the realm of the senses, subsuming identity into the raw id-entity as we reconnect with our true, unrestrained feelings. For if the price of language is the repression of instinct, our bodies tell us that we are healthier for staying in touch with our inner beast, however briefly. Let's take a look at why that is.

Beyond words

Like many other languages, English is remarkably awkward when it comes to finding the right words to describe an activity that we spend so much time, effort and heartache trying to engage in: 'coitus' is too medical, 'intercourse' too formal, 'love-making' too prissy and 'fucking' too graphic – and yet 'sex' is a strangely blunt and unlovely word for something that has the potential to be so profound. Sex can indeed be a blunt and unlovely act, especially if conducted without the full consent of one of the participants. But done in the right way with the right person, it delivers one of the most sublime sensations most of us are likely to encounter – a blissful, invigorating and fulfilling experience far more powerful than anything produced by a mere drug. Which is why, of course, we keep going back for more: nothing else comes close to the extraordinary intensity, the deep emotional and physical satisfaction and sense of release that sex is capable of offering – even if the reality doesn't always measure up to expectations.

It's also one of the few human activities that language can do little to enhance. In much the same way as the desire to eat, sex is a primal appetite that requires no explanation, and – unlike most forms of eating

– virtually no preparation: it's the 'plug and play' concept in its most elemental and unmediated form. And although sex with someone you share no language with is probably not part of most people's experience, it works just as well – and has quite probably played a significant part in human evolution. That's because sex is about feeling, not words: the sexual attraction we feel for a partner is mostly at a level that requires no language – and even if we do share some, it can be successfully conducted and enjoyed without needing to know any more than the fact that it feels good. In fact, as the sexual tension rises, talking becomes positively distracting; sex is a sensation you want to feel, not describe.

For at its heart, sex is an intensely wordless experience. The acme of pleasure, the agony and ecstasy of sex takes place at a level beyond the reach of language. Though not every culture feels the need to invoke God when it comes to announcing the arrival of orgasm, a great many do – and even those that don't will be having an experience that can really only be described as divine. Some people do like to talk dirty – but that's just part of the foreplay, a transgression of social and verbal codes that can provide extra stimulation through an added sense of breaking the rules. But when things get serious, the only noises that most people want to or even can make are an animal howling and wailing, a getting down to business with your pre-verbal self. If you doubt this, try talking your way through an orgasm – or if your nerve fails you, convince yourself by watching someone else trying to (you could always check the YouTube video of three girl singers from the Dutch band ADAM attempting to sing whilst coming. Spoiler alert: they can't).

What's more surprising is how bad we are at talking about sex when we're not doing it – even in the overtly sexualised times we live in. Two generations ago, you could hardly mention sex in the English-speaking world: it was all innuendo and implication – the strangulated world of the film *Brief Encounter* and the 'Say no more' Monty Python sketch. You have only to think of the fuss that 'Elvis the Pelvis' created with his overtly sexual gyrations back in the fifties and early sixties – moves that seem positively timid in comparison with what soon followed – to realise how far we have come. But being able to mention it is not the same thing as talking about it. It may be that sex still sells: ads constantly exploit the visual sensitivities of men – and women – using images which suggest that purchasing a particular product will somehow make you sexier and more likely to attract the well-hung hunk or bimbo bombshell of your dreams. But though magazines with covers promising "10 things to spice up your sex-life" may still increase sales more reliably than anything else, when it comes down to it, they're giving nothing away. It's about titillation, not information – let alone knowledge.

We just don't seem able to talk about sex in the way that we do about food, for example. Food writers and restaurant critics have no qualms about describing the finest details of taste and pleasure a good meal can deliver, even if they remain silent while enjoying it – but somehow sex is different. Even down the pub with the lads (or the girls), the intimacies of the act itself are rarely discussed – let alone how it might make you feel – unless the partner in question was little more than a casual shag. This is strange, since its overwhelming importance to us is shown by the huge vocabulary of euphemisms we have available to refer to 'it': from 'hanky-panky' to 'hiding the helmet', the endlessly creative ways in which we re-imagine sex through language tells us more about our focus on that activity than any other way we have yet been able to measure it.

This reticence to discuss sex means scientists are often still reluctant to take it seriously as a subject for research. And it can't be the easiest of tasks to persuade a person to masturbate publicly inside an MRI scanner. But the brain scans of individuals brave enough to have volunteered are revealing. They show that as sexual feelings take over, regions associated with touch are first activated. But from there on, a number of seemingly unrelated brain areas – among them the limbic system (involved in memory and emotions), the hypothalamus (involved in unconscious body control), and the prefrontal cortex (involved in judgment and problem solving) – fire in turn, each showing heightened levels of activity, and by the time the Big O arrives, over 30 major brain systems are in play. Which means that far from being restricted to a particular area, orgasm is a sensation experienced throughout the brain – as our subjective experience would tend to suggest. The scans further reveal that there seems to be little difference between male and female orgasms, also confirming research done in the 1970s when men and women were asked to anonymously write down how an orgasm made them feel without reference to body parts, and it was impossible to tell their descriptions apart.

But brain scans show other things too. The observed behaviour of the brain during orgasm corresponds closely to patterns observed in subjects experiencing a heroin rush or listening to pleasurable music – even being given a monetary reward. It seems that orgasm somehow disables the brain's control and anxiety centres and releases a cocktail of chemicals inside our heads, flooding our craniums with dopamine and oxytocin – 'feel-good' hormones well known to induce feelings of pleasure and promote bonding. So whether we're in the sack with a partner or pulling our own chain, it's essentially a drug-induced feel-good factor that we're bathing in, a temporary liberation from the cares of our day, and – if we're lucky – the joy of someone to share it with.

These results are hardly surprising. Sex demands our full attention, and generally gets it. The undistracted sense of concentration we experience just before orgasm is unlike anything we feel in any other activity. There's an almost desperate edge to the urgency with which we focus on reaching the point of release, that unambiguous moment when mind and body collapse into an unbounded sense of unity between yourself and your partner, even the entire universe – for that is what it can feel like, when nothing else seems to exist or matter, and the very boundaries of the self can appear to dissolve. In almost every other moment of our lives, some contradictory voice may be threatening to sow confusion in our mind, yet at the point of orgasm it's as if every cell in your body is shouting out an unambiguous cosmic YES – with no need to communicate beyond a moan of pleasure, the same animal sound that lies at core of every utterance we make.

It's a drive we share with most other animals on the planet. Take giant tortoises, one of the most ancient species that still survive. It's a humbling experience to watch them mate, especially if you are male. After all, these lumbering beasts have been around since the days of the dinosaurs: parallels between their sexual urges and ours are written deep into our DNA. First of all, it's interesting to see why the Chinese refer to the male sexual organ as the 'turtle head'. Normally withdrawn quite close in to its shell, or carapace, and retracted even further at the slightest sign of danger (the shrivel syndrome), when fully extended the head and neck of the tortoise resemble nothing so much as an erect male member, the pert little face adding an extra comic touch. Then there's the groaning and the drool. As he mounts the female, utilising the convenient hollow at the bottom of his shell to maintain his balance on the hard, slippery surface of her carapace, the male extends his neck fully downwards in an almost touching attempt to bring his face close to his partner, and then begins to emit deep groans of the most harrowing longing, together with copious amounts of drool which dribble down onto the head of his lucky partner – who seems almost entirely oblivious to his attentions.

But lest this description of the joys of sex seem overly phallo-centric, let us consider how things stand with the females of our species. Though they may not always have them as often, when they feel free to discuss them women typically report multiple, longer and more satisfying experiences than their male counterparts – and failure to achieve them has been known from antiquity to have deleterious effects on feminine health. The condition known to the Victorians as 'hysteria' (named from the Greek word *hystera*, or 'uterus') – whose symptoms included chronic anxiety, irritability, insomnia and loss of appetite – was found to be curable only by means of what was delicately referred to as a 'pelvic massage'. A doctor would apply manual pressure to a patient's genital area until she underwent what was coyly termed a 'hysterical paroxysm' – after which the symptoms would be miraculously relieved. With no shortage of repeat customers, it was a remarkably lucrative business for Victorian doctors.

The reluctance to discuss such matters openly was so strong that this procedure was not even considered a sexual experience. Indeed, the male doctors who usually carried it out found it such a chore that one of them eventually invented a device that would relieve the manual strain – and achieve the desired result more quickly and efficiently. Thus was born the vibrator: at first produced solely for the use of the medical profession, from the early years of the 20th century it was made available as a consumer product that rapidly became a must-have item for legions of sexually-frustrated gentlewomen, and was openly advertised in quality magazines (at least until vibrators began being featured in early pornographic films). In fact, the demand for and popularity of the vibrator was so great that it was one of the earliest domestic appliances to be electrified – along with sewing machines, fans, kettles and toasters – and some ten years ahead of such modern household essentials as the vacuum cleaner and the electric iron.

The manufacturers clearly understood their market.

Sexual healing

But why did we evolve to have sex in the first place? It wasn't always this way, after all. For the first two and a half billion years of life on earth, organisms reproduced quite happily by just dividing into two. That was a good way to increase numbers quickly, and saved the trouble of going out looking for a partner. But sometime over a billion years ago, life-forms began to reproduce sexually. There was a pressure to do so: in more challenging environments, asexual reproduction doesn't produce enough mutations to allow for a speedy adaption to changing circumstances. For despite any larger numbers, lack of variety in the genome leaves a species vulnerable to extinction when disease spreads through an ungendered population. Unlike asexual division, which simply clones the parent cell, sex allows the genetic material of both parents to recombine, creating a new individual with similar but uniquely different traits: it's a throw of the genetic dice which allows the winners to evolve and thrive.

The origin of the orgasm is perhaps more of a mystery. This all-absorbing moment of zen is so pleasurable and fulfilling that poets have frequently felt it worth dying for – indeed the French still refer to it as *la petite mort*. And as a way to go, it must surely take a lot of, ahem, beating. But how and why did evolution take us to the point where the emergence of so sublime an experience was the deal-maker? In terms of biological function, it's a reasonable bet that people would still be having sex even if it wasn't half as much fun. Even if it was only marginally more exciting than the sensation of emptying your bladder, we'd probably still be up for it. So what exactly was the path that led from not having orgasms to having them? That's not a single evolutionary step, a chance typo in the genome: like language itself, it didn't just happen. At the very least it must have ramped up from just 'feeling good' to 'feeling better than anything else you might have been thinking of doing' before it ended up being something you'd do almost anything to feel again. Why did that amount of incentive need to be built in to ensure we had sex? Was whatever else we were doing back in the day so rivetingly interesting that there was a chance we might otherwise go "Yeah, whatever. Maybe later"?

The answer, of course, is competition. From a purely statistical perspective, the more sex you have the more children you are likely to have. So the more you want to have sex, the more children you are likely to leave behind, and the genes of those with the enhanced urge will spread through the population. But sexual reproduction comes with a cost, too: you have to devote time and energy to finding a mate, and only half of your genes are passed on. So to be successful, you need motivation – and the female, the partner who bears the child (and in many species does most of the child care) has to be pickier about the genes she chooses to share with. No one knows what's really driving the choices we make when we choose our sexual partners. A huge variety of genetic, physical and psychological factors may be involved, and many more besides. But there is one constant: we don't need to be told who we're attracted to.

That's something we all just know, whether or not it is necessarily reciprocated. And it is not a choice that necessarily always meets with approval, especially when it comes to humans. For sexual attraction is something that operates at a much more fundamental level, one at which the artificial barriers of culture can suddenly seem irrelevant. This is the universal appeal of the story of Romeo and Juliet – the very archetype of lovers who transgress the social divide, a tale of forbidden love that resonates in almost every culture. Unlike our animal cousins, there's often a huge cultural component to take into account in our own couplings: a female tortoise may be making a choice based on size and status in her group, but it is her choice – we humans have a whole range of social and political rules that can create obstacles to our sexual happiness.

And obstacles there have certainly been. As we have seen, tribal divisions of language, culture and religion loom large in our perception of others, and – more importantly – our judgment of them. Whether at the level of the individual or the state, humans will often actively persecute members of a group who do not share the same cultural codes as their own. The most explicit example in recent times was Hitler's Reich, which forbade not just marriage but any form of sexual relations between those defined as belonging to different ethnic groups – but the horror of contamination is one that echoes down the ages. Records of such racially motivated discrimination go back at least as far as the Rig Veda, the holy scripture of Hinduism, where God is thanked for "*scattering the slave bands of black descent.*" But we can be pretty sure that they didn't start it – the Ancient Egyptians took an equally dim view of the Nubians, and the disappearance of Neanderthals and other early hominid groups from the archaeological record suggests that they weren't that popular with the Cro-Magnon types who went on to become us.

This fear of contaminating the blood is by no means a 'black and white' issue: Chinese culture is still very protective (Li Hongzhi, the exiled leader of Falung Gong, openly says that children of mixed blood will not be welcome in heaven) and laws have been issued through their history to prevent it – from a Tang dynasty edict in 836 banning Chinese from forming relationships with "people of colour" (meaning foreigners in general) to as recently as 1989, following anti-African riots in Nanjing, when regulations were introduced to restrict African men from consorting with Chinese women. In Japan too, there is great sensitivity about race. Though my marriage to a Japanese woman caused consternation enough in own family in the UK, my wife's family were no more welcoming, as they considered white men to be culturally and morally inferior.

Such anxiety about diluting the purity of race is puzzling given that breeders of animals have long known that cross-breeds are generally stronger, healthier and more intelligent than 'pure' breeds. Pedigree dogs are more liable than their mongrel cousins to succumb to disease and various hereditary conditions, and the same is true for humans: the history of royalty shows the damage that a limited gene pool can inflict. The fact that children of 'mixed' marriages usually grow up around different cultures and languages (and even religions) disposes them to be more flexible and quick-thinking – and they are often better-looking, too. There's another component as well: marrying within your own social group can almost be a form of cultural incest – you run the risk of trapping yourself in the assumptions of your tribe, tradition and wider community. And the narrowing of mental horizons that can result if you are not challenged to question these assumptions is every bit as damaging as the defects that physical incest is known to lead to.

But then these things are not to do with 'race' as such. Like dogs, humans are all one race – and what keeps us apart is in the mind, not the body. The use of language in human societies inevitably results in a complex web of social, cultural and religious rules that limit our ability to act freely. In a sense, every community constructs its own form of social neurosis, a neurosis that is expressed in a particular way of being: quite apart from the quirks of the language they speak, people in any community develop restrictively 'normal' ways of dressing, gesturing and behaving. This is easiest to spot with members of the same language group: think of the differences between Americans, British and Australians – and even between different regions within those countries. But the same is just as true for communities whose language and culture we are not familiar with, and therefore cannot 'see'. Every society – just like every individual – has a characteristic way of holding themselves that reflects the tensions that maintaining this cultural fiction involves: a phenomenon that the psychologist Wilhelm Reich, one of Freud's leading disciples, memorably described as 'character armour'.

It is this thick cultural carapace from which sex offers the easiest escape – and why it can feel so liberating. The *id* wants out, and sex is one of the most accessible ways to achieve it. Because sex is about release, and allowing yourself to be yourself, the transgression of social and cultural codes – if only in private – is empowering. And the intimacies of sex naturally spill over into intimacies of speech, because we like to tell the person we love about the things we are proud of, things we've experienced or thought that we may not have had the opportunity or courage to talk about before. It's a sharing of the burden, but not just that: it's a bridge to consciousness, because it allows you a chance to become aware of your taboos and insecurities, and perhaps free yourself from them – with the help of honest feedback from someone you love and trust.

Whether spouse, partner or 'significant other', those we feel closest to are important to us because we trust them to know and understand the things we would not necessarily tell anyone else. Our past. Our shame. Our fears. Our joys. Our daily niggles. Having someone you can talk to intimately means that you get a new insight both into yourself and what it means to be human, for you see your partner exposed as well as yourself. And that's what you don't get from the society around you. A confidante. A partner in crime – a 'crime' that takes you to a place more intensely real and authentic than almost anything else available to you. It fulfils an urge, an insistent hunger to connect intimately with another person that only a sexual relationship can really satisfy. The whole point of the expression "about as much fun as you can have with your clothes on" is that nothing can be more fun than sex. And that's its secret. It's the most addictive of drugs, the antidote par excellence for the stresses and strains of civilization.

Unbinding the mind

But sex isn't the only drug we can't get enough of. While the evidence may yet be circumstantial, it's quite possible our Neanderthals cousins were using psychoactive substances, including opium, as far back as 50,000 years ago – and as already noted, we've been cultivating hemp (the plant that gives us *marijuana*) since the first days of agriculture.

We'd probably been using it before that, as well: like other animals, the hard conditions of life in the wild meant our earliest ancestors would have tried eating almost anything that looked even slightly edible, and we would have been just as keen to remember and pass on knowledge about things that relieved pain, or made us feel better, as about those that were tasty – or were likely to harm us. The pharmaceutical effects delivered by natural substances would have been a key part of our prehistoric tool-kit, and quite aside from any pain relief on offer, the feel-good factor that plants like coca, betel, tobacco, khat, peyote and psilocybin provide has been recognised for millennia.

Our desire to become inebriated, whether for recreational or ritual purposes, is clearly ancient and deep-rooted. There are references to alcohol and opium going back to the beginning of writing, and archaeological evidence shows that we have been brewing beer and making wine at least since the first human settlements began. We clearly have a strong desire to 'get out of it' – even if the destination we may be in search of is less certain, and not obviously shared by other animals There is evidence that other species like to gorge on over-ripe fruit that naturally ferments to alcohol, but their use – or abuse – of it is insignificant by human standards. Could our desire to get wasted be another unintended consequence of language? Certainly, we have not been slow to pass the word about drugs whenever we have discovered them. And there are good reasons why the trick of speech might encourage us to use them.

For the 'it' out of which we wish to get is our 'normal' state of mind – a state of mind which, as we have seen, is highly influenced and affected by the artificial constraints that language is so effective at inducing and spreading. Given that our behaviour is so hemmed in by rules (whether social, cultural or religious), the need to protect our sense of identity often keeps us from acting – in public at least – in ways that would conflict with the expectations placed on us by the society in which we live. To be accepted by and share in the community around us, we have to conform to what is expected of us. But the constant fight between who we feel ourselves to be and how we 'should' behave necessarily creates a psychic tension – not to 'toe the line' can result in losing a job, breaking a relationship, being ostracised or even arrested and sent to prison. To the extent that this means we are not able to be authentically ourselves, we all live with a degree of cognitive dissonance, which we experience as stress – the 'discontents' of civilization identified by Freud. And drugs offer the prospect of relief.

They offer relief because drugs act on the parts of our brain that control our social behaviour. Alcohol, the most popular recreational drug – apart from tobacco, the only other one that is currently legal – works primarily by inhibiting regions of the brain that control our behaviour. Scans show that the greatest decrease in activity is in the prefrontal and temporal cortexes. The prefrontal cortex manages decision making and rational thought, and also plays a role in preventing aggressive behaviour, and the temporal cortex houses the hippocampus, the part of the brain responsible for forming new memories. Alcohol also decreases energy consumption in the cerebellum, the region of the brain that coordinates motor activity. It's not hard to see how that's consistent with the subjective experience of having a few drinks with friends – an alcohol-fuelled evening can easily lead to loud, liberated and clumsy behaviour.

But release from the restraints on our behaviour is only one side of the story. As we have seen, for all its benefits, culture can also limit the way we think – and anything that acts to release that restraint is bound to stimulate creativity. It is no accident that the greatest champions of psychoactive drugs have been engaged in artistic activity – though in many cases, this has not been to the benefit of the individual concerned. The road is littered with famous corpses, people whose demise has been hastened by their dalliance with both legal and illegal substances. Drugs are not always good for you, particularly if you aren't sure of their quality, or don't know when to stop indulging in them. But then that's true of most things – and not an argument for preventing the use of drugs, only of controlling it. And in many ancient societies their use was controlled by restricting it to sacred rituals with the purpose of enhancing religious experiences.

This seems to have been true even for alcohol, but even more so for drugs that have mind-altering properties, and specifically the so-called psychedelic substances which can seem to transport you into different world – a world both familiar in the sense that you are still physically where you were, but different in that neither 'you' nor the things that surround you feel the same. Part of this is an enhanced sensitivity to perception – shapes, colours, tastes, textures and above all sounds seem vividly fresh and new – but it's as if a new dimension has opened up in your world, a dimension in which time no longer exists and you are just intensely present in the here and now. Above all, there's a strong sense that the boundaries between 'you' and your surroundings are much less certain, and you are often suffused with a powerful sense of awe. There's an astonishment at the sheer profundity and interconnectedness of everyday things that is often described as a religious feeling, even by non-believers, leading some to suggest that this class of drugs should be labelled entheogens, or 'god-inducing' substances.

We have a much better understanding now of how our brains react to drugs and what is going on when we take them, but that still doesn't help explain or describe the subjective experience, or what that can make you feel or think. Whatever a drug is actually doing to your brain and to the processing pathways that allow us to perceive our world as we do, and however artificial the state they induce, the end result of such per-turbations can often be highly therapeutic. Before LSD – one of the more potently psychoactive drugs – was banned, it was widely tested in the 1960s on people suffering from otherwise untreatable mental disorders, with overwhelmingly positive results. Recent revivals of these experiments have produced equally good outcomes, and have shown beneficial effects with people suffering with psychological problems ranging from chronic depression to substance addiction and post-traumatic stress syndrome.

Why is that? The short answer is, we don't know. At least, we don't know in the way that scientists like to be able to say when they have shown something to be clinically proven. We don't have enough data (not least because of the restrictions on using such drugs in a scientific setting) and what we do have is inevitably highly subjective. If someone claims to have seen God there is no known way of testing to confirm it. How would we know what they mean by that, anyway? Except that what matters is that they feel that they have seen God – and if you have taken the drug and had the experience yourself, you will certainly know what they mean. 'God' is a culturally loaded concept, after all. You might not claim that you had seen God if you were a Zen Buddhist, or a Zoroastrian. The same thing is true for bipolar patients with grandiose delusions: those from a Christian heritage may say they feel that they are Jesus, whereas Muslims may feel possessed by a djinn or evil spirit, or Hindus believe they are a god or goddess. What they're trying to express is that they feel all-powerful, all-seeing, all connected.

But the reason people are attracted to drugs is not just the release they bring, although that can be of great help. The so-called 'mind-altering' qualities of drugs can cause you to call into question almost everything that you thought you believed, and that can be very liberating. It can of course be very frightening – if you've staked your sense of self on an identity that is essentially linked to the artificial categories of society, culture and religion, without help and guidance an experience with a psychedelic substance can be very disorienting and disturbing. Many people who experimented with drugs in their youth stop using them when the anxiety about identity that drugs induce is no longer pleasant – or the pressure to conform to social norms becomes so great that they can no longer afford to question them. This goes a long way to explain the attraction of alcohol – a drug that tends to numb you to such thoughts.

But drugs with the potential to stimulate contemplation, such as cannabis and LSD, can lead to intense experiences which allow you to experience 'reality' in very different ways. People who have 'seen God' are trying to express the powerful sense of sacredness and love for the world – in all its myriad forms – that comes over them. It's not something that you need or want to do all the time, or even many times, but in the right setting it's a profound experience that leaves you feeling at peace and in love with the world in a way that only sex – or music, as we will see later – can make you feel. But you don't have to see God to enjoy drugs. It's enough to feel 'high' – a heightened state of awareness or arousal at any level is always stimulating, and can not only help you to see things differently, but even to accept and understand things that previously seemed unthinkable. Aldous Huxley, who championed the use of mescaline as a tool for enlightenment (and asked to be given a dose of LSD on his deathbed), thought of the experience as a sacrament that everyone should experience on reaching adulthood.

Quite aside from any medicinal use, drugs have been used at all times and in all societies as anything from social lubricants and aphrodisiacs to sacraments in initiation ceremonies, and still are. The Victorians got through the darknesses of their century under a haze of laudanum, and Freud was addicted to cocaine – as was the fictional Sherlock Holmes (and presumably his creator): one can only wonder how much their flights of fancy owed to enhanced states of mind. Some of the great achievements of the modern age may have had some chemical help along the way: Steve Jobs admitted to being influenced by LSD, and even if Francis Crick's discovery of the structure of DNA predated his known enthusiasm for LSD, the more memorable of the Beatles' albums would certainly not have come into being without the help of drugs. It's quite possible that Shakespeare may have had some creative assistance, too: traces of cannabis have been detected in 400-year-old tobacco pipes found in his garden – so whether or not it was him, someone in 17th century Stratford was definitely getting high.

Breaking good

And why not? The idea that any drug should be prohibited is a relatively modern idea. Though a law by the name of "*An Act for Repressing the Odious and Loathsome Sin of Drunkenness*" was passed in the English Parliament in 1606 – and even the Sumerians appear to have had regulations for the consumption of alcohol – it was excessive indulgence rather than the activity itself that usually attracted opprobrium. Indeed, the ancient world generally had a high regard for the effects of drinking. In the *Epic of Gilgamesh*, the wild man Enkidu is turned into a civilised human being by 'seven cups of beer', and alcohol was widely used in rituals and celebrations for its ability to make people feel 'exhilarated, wonderful and blissful.' These are the sensations that people seek when they use drugs for recreational purposes, whether through drink or any other means. When nitrous oxide was first discovered to have such side-effects in 1799, the Regency dandies who indulged in it at parties called it 'the gas of Paradise'.

In part, drugs have rarely been banned in the past because there were relatively few of them – and those that did exist were so widely available or easy to prepare that control was virtually impossible: our ancestors knew they grew naturally, were not particularly potent, and were not difficult to get hold of. Opium is a dried form of the juice that leaks from poppies; coca leaves literally grow on trees. Even in the case of alcohol, wine and beer more or less make themselves through natural fermentation, and are likely to have been discovered by accident from spoiled stores of grain and grapes in the early days of agriculture. The oldest evidence of beer is from Iran some 7000 years ago; the first wine that we know of dates back a similar length of time to Armenia in around 4000 BC. Written references to beer (in the form of a recipe) date back nearly 4000 years, and evidence for the use of wine has been found in Egyptian tombs dating back to 3000 BC.

Hard liquor is more recent. Although the ability to distil liquids was known to the ancient Greeks, the first practical application to the distillation of alcohol was in the 12th century, when these strange 'elixirs' were at first mainly used for medicinal purposes, particularly during the Black Death. But by the 15th century the technique had been applied to the distillation of beer, and the drink we know as whisky was ushered into the world. The application of industrial techniques to the refinement of other drugs was only a matter of time: pure cocaine was extracted from coca leaves in 1859 by a German chemist, Albert Niemann – though not much use was made of it, medically or otherwise, until the 1880s – and heroin, originally available as an over-the-counter consumer product and named from the German word *heroisch*, meaning "heroic, strong" was derived in 1874 from morphine (another product of the opium poppy – first isolated in the early 1800s, and named for Morpheus, the god of dreams).

But the first attempts to control the availability of drugs by law did not began until towards the end of the 19th century, partly from a desire to restrict the misuse of these more potent forms of drug – especially opium and its derivatives – but also through a growing concern about the dangers to society posed by the recreational use of drugs in general. This latter concern took a firmer hold with the introduction of the Prohibition in America which banned the production of alcohol – though not its consumption. Through a classic example of the law of unintended consequences, this left the door wide open for organised crime to take up the slack, an opportunity they seized with gusto. After 13 years it was realised that the attempt to suppress a trade involving what economists call 'mutually beneficial exchanges' was doomed to failure, and for the first and only time an Amendment to the US Constitution – the 18th – was repealed.

The battle was not over, however – nor the lesson learnt. In the early 1970s, the Nixon administration introduced its Controlled Substances Act and launched the so-called 'war on drugs' – a term popularised after a press conference given by President Nixon in 1971. But just as earlier attempts to ban *marijuana* had been more to do with social and racial concerns than any medical issues, so the focus of the Nixon administration's legislation was elsewhere. As John Ehrlichman, Nixon's chief policy adviser, later confessed: "*The Nixon White House had two enemies: the anti-war left and black people... We knew we couldn't make it illegal to be either against the war or black, but by getting the public to associate the hippies with marijuana and blacks with heroin, and then criminalizing both heavily, we could disrupt those communities. We could arrest their leaders, raid their homes, break up their meetings, and vilify them night after night on the evening news. Did we know we were lying about the drugs? Of course we did.*"

But like the Prohibition, a war on drugs can never be won. Just as with the trade in alcohol, a ban on the sale of illegal drugs is ultimately doomed to failure. You cannot legislate against popular human activities, especially when they cause no harm except to the individual concerned. People vote with their behaviour. Surveys indicate that over a third of the UK population admit to having taken an illicit drug, with nearly half that number having taken a class A drug. These are the numbers of people admitting to having done so – so it's safe to assume that the real figure is greater, especially when almost 60% of those surveyed believe that 'soft' drugs such as cannabis should be treated more leniently or decriminalised – a much better indicator of people's actual behaviour, as not everyone will admit to doing something illegal, even anonymously.

Whether we like it or not, drug use has become almost endemic in the western world. Even if they don't indulge themselves, the parents of teenagers know that most of their children have been, are or will be experimenting with illegal drugs, and it's likely that the majority of the current generation of politicians have experimented with them too – although whether they will admit it is another question. The major music festivals of the day – Glastonbury chief among them – are known to be bacchanalian parties where everyone over the age of 12 is likely to be 'off their face' for days at a time: the experience is set up to cater for that, and those that go there know it. We may not choose to acknowledge that as a society, but an honest conversation with anyone who's been there will soon dispel any lingering doubts. It may suit us to turn a blind eye and allow drugs to be openly consumed even though they are nominally illegal, but long term, that's not a sustainable policy. As a society – as a civilization – we need to have a proper, grown-up meeting about this: a situation where a large number of young people, and particularly our more intelligent and sensitive ones, are effectively being criminalised for behaviour they consider to be normal, will hardly encourage them to be law-abiding.

The 'problem' of drugs can really only be effectively tackled by legalising them, not by banning them. Once we finally accept there is both a constant demand and a legitimate use for recreational drugs, we can begin to control the factors that currently cause the most concern. Just as with alcohol and tobacco, licencing the production of these drugs would allow them to be properly regulated and enable control over both quality and use – the absence of which lead to most of the dangers that drugs pose. On top of that, their production could also be taxed – again like alcohol and tobacco – bringing in a huge potential income. In the UK alone, Home Office estimates the market for illegal drugs to be around £4-6 billion. That's close to the amount Britons spend each year on lottery tickets, another form of addiction – albeit a legal one. The most recent UN estimate is that the total world trade in illicit drugs is worth about 1% of global GDP. With the market value of an acre of cannabis being over 1000 times that of an acre of wheat, the income that governments could derive from taxing or producing recreational drugs is clear – income that could be put towards education and health. Revenue from the national lottery (as pernicious as any drug in terms of its potential to ruin the lives of those who can least afford it) is used to fund good causes: why not from drugs as well? Why let criminals make all the money, and spend a fortune trying to control them?

Though the decriminalisation of drugs in Portugal since 2001 seems to have been a resounding success, the unabashed promotion of such a policy in most of the English-speaking world still looks like electoral suicide for a politician – despite the recent liberalisation in some American states. But for how much longer? Are we really going to keep pretending that we don't like to enjoy – and even benefit from – the occasional holiday from our language-constrained 'reality'? The value of recreation has long been recognised, especially in the more regimented societies we have created since the start of the industrial period, and perhaps particularly as we become more used to spending increasingly long periods of the day in front of computer screens – a virtual world that takes the artificial world of language to new levels of abstraction: the video gaming industry is now worth more than the market for music and film combined.

Physical recreation in the form of sports and other 'leisure' activities may be seen as essential to maintain health and fitness, but we pay much less attention to the importance of mental recreation. Lured by language into accepting the status quo, the stress we experience in maintaining our sense of identity and conforming to the norms of society around us is very much real. It seems only reasonable that these recreational activities should include the occasional use of 'recreational' drugs to help loosen the artificial boundaries that language imposes on us – whether simply as a licence to temporarily ignore them, or an opportunity to go beyond.

The condition of music

And an opportunity to go beyond is what music offers. As the Victorian critic Walter Pater once said, all art *"aspires to the condition of music"* – and it's hard to disagree with him. If drugs provide an artificial escape route from the constraints of culture, music seems to have an innate ability to sidestep our filters and mainline directly to the heart of whatever it is we are. Not for nothing were the itinerant musicians of mediaeval England known as 'glee-men': in a world with few other forms of entertainment, they were the costermongers of delight, dealers in dreams, minstrels who brought joy to their audiences through the power of pure sound alone. For music needs no explanation, no cultural gloss: it's accessible to us all, without the need for translation or other form of mediation. As we feel it work its magic on us, music almost wills our bodies to move, as if tapping into an animal instinct, drawing us inexorably to the beat.

But here's the strange thing about music: other animals don't seem to get it. It's possible that they do appreciate it passively (there are studies that show cows produce slightly larger amounts of milk – about 3% more – when listening to calming music) but for most species there's no overt, observable hint that they are either enjoying it, or even hearing it as anything other than noise. There's the occasional dancing parrot, head-bobbing sea-lion, and monkeys that may perhaps enjoy beating a drum. But play music to a dog, and they remain unmoved; they show little reaction beyond occasional irritation. They show no reaction. The same is true for cats. And horses. Or chimps. We've seen how most of the things that 'we' do and other animals don't seem to come down to our ability to speak. Culture, religion and a sense of identity, the three things that most distinguish us from other species, are all by-products of language. So could it be that music is, too?

It was Darwin who first suggested that music and language might somehow be linked. His idea was that language must have evolved from music, which he saw as having developed as a form of elaborate sexual display or courtship – as we see in the calls of song-birds, for example. But there's another possibility, too. Perhaps the reason we associate music with a range of emotions, thrilling to its tensions and resolutions, its highs and its lows, its soothing and inspiring qualities, is that these emotions are what language inspires in us – the psychic consequence of the legacy of words explored in the first four chapters. If other animals act according to instinct, live in the present and do not agonise over the choices that culture, religion and identity force on us, it may be that they have no need for, or are just not conscious of the emotions we find in music.

Of course, spoken language can have a musical quality to it – whether consciously or not, politicians and other public speakers make use of melody and rhythm to emphasise the more important passages in their speeches. But for all that, there's a world of difference between language and music. Instrumental music is essentially decorative: like the peacock's tail or the blackbird's song, it seems more about a desire to impress than the ability to express. However much we are moved by a piece of music, it's hard to say what it's about in specific terms, no matter how deep the feelings it may arouse in us. Language, on the other hand, is the other way round. Though a simplistic speech may sound impressive in the mouth of a populist politician, the role of words is to express clearly defined meanings. Sound may be the way most animals communicate, but language and music have refined that core ability in quite different ways.

If you've ever watched a mother sheep struggle with a wayward lamb, you'll know that a simple 'baa' sound can be used to express a number of different moods from irritation to relief, and the same is true for other animals – be it the barking of dogs, the lowing of cattle or the hooting of chimpanzees. Most species only make a rather small number of noises, but they use tone, timbre and volume to alter the way in which they express them. What's interesting is just how similar the strategies used by different animals actually are, even though each species has its own unique niche of frequencies and registers: in 2014, the artist Marcus Coates created an exhibition called *The Sound of Others*, which manipulated the natural sounds of species as diverse as blue whales and crickets to show how their very different calls and cries almost seem to blend into one when adjusted to similar frequencies – as does human speech when similarly treated.

Those visceral sounds are the starting point for both language and music. But though the trilling of a nightingale may inspire us to poetry, its song is not language (although birds are the most adept at mimicking human speech, perhaps because of the attention they pay to the detail of their song.) The crucial difference between language and music is that language is mnemonic: each word has a unique sonic signature that identifies a particular meaning – whereas despite its uncanny ability to evoke feelings of sadness or joy, excitement or tranquillity, by itself music does not transmit or encode any specific information along with its emotional affect. Yet this only seems to heighten its force. All art may be about communication, but music – without words or images – seems able to touch us the most, even to the point of 'eargasm'. As Victor Hugo sagely put it, *"Music expresses that which cannot be said, but about which is it impossible to remain silent."*

What we are responding to when we listen to music? What is the itch that music lets us scratch? To understand that, we'll have to look at what we know about how music works. Even without musical training, most of us can hear the notes in a scale and tell if an instrument is out of tune, even if we don't know why – or how to correct it. In the same way, most people can sing, hum or whistle a familiar tune in a form recognisable to others. But how are we able to do that? How can we tell notes apart so easily? As the Ancient Greeks discovered, it's all about ratios. All sounds are just vibration at a certain frequency, which our ears hear as pitch. Men's voices are lower than those of women and children because their vocal cords are longer (they lengthen during puberty) and vibrate at a lower frequency, which gives men a deeper-sounding voice. In fact, on average women and children speak about an octave higher than men. But the high note in an octave turns out to be exactly double the frequency of the lower note – and this simple relationship is what makes the octave interval seem so obvious to us.

In the same way, the familiar notes of the sol-fa scale (DO-RE-MI-FA-SO-LA-TI-DO) also come down to simple ratios. If an octave is a ratio of 2:1, a fifth (the SO in the sol-fa scale) is a ratio of 3:2. A third (MI) is 5:4 and the sixth (LA) is 5:3. Together with the second (RE), a ratio of 9:8, these five notes form the so-called pentatonic scale used in folk music around the world from the earliest times (bone flutes dating back 40,000 years are tuned to a pentatonic scale). This is one of the easiest scales to hear, sing and play with simple instruments, but as our tastes became more refined, other notes were gradually added, resulting in the now 'standard' chromatic scale of twelve notes with equal spacings between them. These are the black and white keys on the piano, on which musicians weave their magic maths: the jazz pianist Thelonious Monk – noted for his dark, angular melodies that cut playfully across the implied beat of the music – once said that all musicians are mathematicians, whether or not they know it.

Why should these sounds touch us? How can the ratios of frequency that make up a melody move us to tears? Perhaps it's because what our brains do best is to find patterns, and we are simply exploiting a sensitivity to such distinctions that developed through language, enjoying what Steven Pinker called 'auditory cheesecake'. In much the same way we can understand language spoken by a woman, man or child, or in a different accent or speed, we can recognise a tune we know even when it's played in a different key, by a different instrument, or in a different time signature. That's because a tune, like a sentence, has a signature: with music it's the relationship between sound and rhythm; with speech it's the relationship between sound and meaning. In both cases we're not just remembering a specific instance of a particular tune or sentence, we're remembering what's common between them: the pattern of frequencies that marks them out as unique. And when the patterns of tension and release between notes correspond to the emotional tension we feel within ourselves – everything from gratitude to grief – we sense the music as a feeling: a feeling that words may help to define, but can only ever be felt as melody, harmony and rhythm.

That feeling exists in language in the form of what linguists call 'prosody'. Prosody is the melody and rhythm of speech, the tricks we use to emphasise the feeling and emotion behind our words. Written words may be defined by spaces between them, but naturally spoken language is an unbroken stream of sound made up of phonetic 'bits' whose particular combinations form the 'bytes' of sound that we call words, with their unique meanings. But the carrier wave for the information that words allow us to exchange – the stream of sound conveying the data – is the very same mooing, cooing or whooping that all animals make when they communicate with each other: open vowel sounds that we turn into words with consonants. And just like other animals, we can alter that basic sound to calibrate the urgency or intensity of what our words are trying to say. Just as a mother sheep can change the tone of her 'baa' to mean 'Come here NOW', so we use stress, intonation and tone to alter the emphasis of our words.

Because we generally focus on the message, we may not always realise it – but we constantly use language in musical way. Think of how you might greet people at the start of a day in a public setting, say in front of a class or a meeting. A cheery 'Good morning' will often be pitched on three distinct notes: a fifth (SO), the octave note above (DO1), and the lower octave (DO2). SO-DO1-DO2. *Good mor-ning*. But if we meet a friend in the street, we may use a different intonation pattern for exactly the same words: a seventh (TI), followed by the fifth below (SO), followed by the octave note (DO) above: TI-SO-DO. Because we mostly hear language as meaning, our minds are immediately taken to the abstract world of the content, but there is a musical flow to what we say, a contour that adds another layer to the meaning. You can test this for yourself by reading a sentence out loud, but with your mouth firmly shut: your vocal cords will buzz with pitch noises, but because your mouth is shut, the modulation of consonants that define meaning cannot work – so nobody can understand what you're saying, though they may get some sense of your mood from the 'tone'.

What cannot be said

But the place that language and music come together most naturally is in song. People in modern societies rarely sing, but song played an important part in the world of our ancestors, as it still does in tribal cultures today. During field studies in Lesotho, the anthropologist James Ferguson once found himself honoured yet embarrassed to be asked to sing publicly as part of a traditional tribal ceremony. When he declined on the grounds that he 'couldn't sing', the astonished villagers responded with *"What do you mean you don't sing? You talk!"* I found myself in a similar situation when I first went to Japan. At a formal dinner with my new colleagues, I was horrified to learn we were all expected to stand up, introduce ourselves, and sing a song – which they all did in turn, without the slightest trace of awkwardness or embarrassment. But they were then just as astonished to discover that not only could I not sing, I didn't even know the words to an entire song (in the end I had to make them up and hope they didn't notice).

We are so surrounded by music in the developed world today that making it is a skill most people have almost entirely lost, just as few of us now make clothes or bake bread. With an industry of people with the interest, motivation and opportunity to do it for us, the easy availability of recorded music means the need to try for ourselves is greatly reduced (along with our chances of embarrassing ourselves). In historical terms, this is a real anomaly: folk music has existed in all cultures since the earliest times, and before recording technology was invented, singing was the main form of entertainment that ordinary people could enjoy, even in the latter part of the 19th century when pianos and other instruments became more widely available. Sales of sheet music were the biggest source of income for composers for some time after records began to appear – early records were seen more as a way to encourage people to buy the sheet music.

That's understandable: the good vibrations of song reach us directly, whereas language is always one step away from what it is trying to express: whether you say 'I am sad', 'Je suis triste' انا حزين or 私は悲しい, the sounds of the words are like the shadows on Plato's cave, unrelated to the emotion they encode. But no matter what language you speak, music taps back into our analog roots: the sound of a major chord is cheerful in any culture, just as a minor chord makes us feel sad. The huge international success of popular artists in the modern world shows that music is universal in the way that no word-based art-form can ever hope to be. Nor is it merely about the power of advertising: studies done with Mbenzele pygmies in the Congo, one of the most remote and isolated of cultures, show that their reactions to music, even music they were not previously familiar with, are very similar to those of us in thrall to Hollywood.

In that sense, music is a universal language – a language of feeling. It is not a passive object you engage with aesthetically or intellectually, it's an experience that launches itself at you in real time, a stream of pitch, tone and rhythm that we ride like surfers on a wave. You can't step back from music: it demands our attention in the moment, engaging us holistically in ways that other dynamic arts like dance and film can struggle to achieve – as shown by the nearly ubiquitous use of music in soundtracks to films. Nor is it just our brains that get fired up in a state of unity when we listen to music – music has the power to bring communities together, as the popularity of anthems show. And despite the almost total ban on producing musical instruments during World War II, music was judged important enough to improving the morale of front-line troops that the US government even commissioned Steinway & Sons to produce 5,000 special pianos, nick-named 'Victory Verticals', strong enough withstand being dropped by parachute.

The best performers have always been valued for their ability to move audiences, and even the names of famous mediaeval troubadours survive

— though their performances were usually only ever heard by royalty and the aristocratic families who would have employed them. Most ordinary people only came into contact with music through folk song (with the occasional thrill of the 'glee-wood' harp played by the itinerant glee-men) or hymns in church – which no doubt accounted for some of their popularity. As public performances became more common through the 17th and 18th centuries, the names of individual singers and musicians began to be better known: but concerts were expensive and the fame of musicians was still eclipsed by writers – especially poets, whose work could be more easily reproduced and read at leisure. This was particularly so at the dawn of the Romantic era in the 19th century, when the infamy of Lord Byron – arguably the first 'rock-star' poet – was such that he had to flee abroad.

It was Edison's invention of the phonograph that changed the game. Printed music allowed people to study and play popular and historical pieces for themselves, but the ability to record music as it was played – capturing a slice of time that could be reproduced and enjoyed forever – brought these early artists to the attention of an audience undreamed of by earlier performers. The voice of Jenny Lind, 'The Swedish Nightingale' and darling of the European and American opera and concert hall circuit in the mid-19th century, was probably heard in person by no more than a million people in her ten-year professional career – even though 'Lind Mania' drove as many as 30,000 people to greet her when she arrived in New York in 1850. That was 10 times more than the number who came to JFK airport to see the Beatles arrive in America just over a century later – but though the Beatles probably played live to no more than a million people either, their recordings allowed them to reach out to a much bigger audience: they still hold the record for the largest number of 'certified units' sold: 275 million discs.

The first million-selling record dates back to 1904, after a young engineer from The Gramophone Company (later EMI) hired Enrico Caruso, the legendary Italian tenor, to sing for two hours in a hotel room in Milan. Caruso was paid the enormous fee of £100 (around £10,000 in today's money) for his time, and probably received as much as 40% in royalties –

a nice little earner, as the price of a phonograph disc was about £50 in today's prices. How times have changed. To earn barely the minimum wage from recorded music these days, you need to generate around a million plays a month on a streaming service. At the other end of the scale, the most popular artists attract billions of views on YouTube – at the time of writing, the top music video was *Despacito* by Luis Fonsi, with 7.3 billion views – almost one view for every person on the planet.

But just as music is not limited to rock and roll, so 'rock and roll' is not limited to music. In the broadest sense, 'rock 'n' roll' is now really just a short-hand for anything that is exciting to do, any activity that is immediate, adrenalin-driven and does not depend on words. The thrill of doing and achieving things with our bodies means that sport is a universal language as well, even though it too has clear rules and distinct cultures, because it taps into a fundamental sense of joy. It's no accident that football thrills people all over the world, whatever their cultural background. Because it does not need to rely on words, it easily crosses borders – and successful international athletes are paid as much (and treated like) pop stars. Like music, sport connects with the human part of whatever we think we are, and has been a powerful force in helping the world learn to think of itself as a single culture. Just as with music, the forces that draw people to sport know no boundaries – a fact that international promoters, managers and entrepreneurs have not been slow to appreciate: as if hiding a cynical (and highly successful) business model in plain sight, the name of Japan's most famous boy band in recent decades was SMAP – an acronym for *Sport and Music Assemble People*.

Even if it does not always achieve the condition of music, all art speaks to us at levels that the shadows of language can only hint at. Whether figurative or not, art is the representation of an essence, the result of thought and observation, an expression of something we may have sensed, but never seen before. Art is about enriching our lives, stepping outside boxes, and pushing the limits of convention that language, culture, religion and identity all foster. But there is still a long way to go: despite the huge success of the Beatles, John Lennon was sadly incorrect to claim they had become 'more popular than Jesus'. The heady days of Beatlemania and their ongoing popularity around the world notwithstanding, the Bible still tops the list of the most popular books ever printed (estimates put the total figure at 7 billion copies) and bibles continue to be published – in one or other of the 80,000 versions that exist in the 2000 languages into which it has been translated – at the astonishing rate of 100 million copies per year.

Sex, drugs and rock & roll may help loosen our categories sufficiently to keep us in touch with our core selves, and act as a safety valve for the tribal tensions of culture: but without action to eliminate the source, the pressure is always going to build – no matter how effective the antidote. For when the excitement of these occasional thrills gives way to the mundane realities of living with others, making a living and managing a family, the heavy lifting in the struggle against ignorance and prejudice – the most pernicious effects of established culture and tradition – has to be done elsewhere.

It is to that battlefield we now turn.

INFORMATION: The Appliance of Science

"If you're not part of the solution, you're part of the precipitate."
— Henry J. Tillman

Stick and shadow

One of the great benefits of language is that it allows us to discuss, compare and think through things that puzzle us, and try to work out an explanation. That was one of the main functions of religion, as we saw in Chapter 3: it's about allowing us to understand appearances that otherwise seem mysterious. Yet while we may still get lost in the traps that words lay for us, it is science – in its original sense of 'knowledge' – that is the real fruit of language. For once you break through the barriers of tradition and 'common sense', you're on a level playing field: a desire to know the truth and resolve intellectual contradictions is a trait of consciousness that transcends religious, ethnic and linguistic boundaries. You can't have Muslim mathematics, Christian chemistry, Russian biology or Chinese astronomy: the insight that comes from applying the logic of language to the natural world applies to anyone living in it, no matter what their heritage. But this realisation has been hard-won; let's remind ourselves of some of the struggles we've faced on our journey to understand the universe and our place within it.

It's easy to forget just how recently we have learnt what we now know about the world. The detail with which we understand the processes underlying almost everything we see around us is extraordinary compared to what we knew just a few hundred years ago. Even as recently as 1850, we had no idea how old the earth was (beyond a wild guess based on adding up the ages of everyone mentioned in the Bible), had no understanding of evolution or how life came to be so diverse, only a rather recent grasp of how far away we were from the sun, were completely unaware of the size of the larger universe – and knew nothing of atoms, germs, genes, or our relationship to other species. Given that, it's not surprising that religious explanations made as much sense as any other: Newton may have worked out why the heavenly bodies move as they do, but there *was* no other answer for almost everything else.

It's even easier to forget how vanishingly unlikely it is that we have found out any of this in the first place. The fossil evidence suggests that life began at least 3.5 billion years ago. Measured against the lifetime of an individual, 3,500,000,000 years is an almost inconceivable number, so let's put it in a more human perspective: 3.5 billion is roughly the number of times your heart would beat if you lived for 100 years. With that as a scale, and counting a year for each beat, for life's first 75 years we were little more than microscopic scum – single-celled organisms slowly evolving more complex proteins in the otherwise lifeless oceans. We didn't even get onto land until we were well into our eighties – the dinosaurs appeared when we were 93, and died out five years later. It was as recently as nine months ago that our brand of tail-less apes evolved away from monkeys, and it took another seven months before the human line struck out on its own.

At that point (about 6 million years ago, in real time) we were essentially just chimps: large furry apes living in trees with a brain about a third the size of the one we have now. It took yet another month before we started using tools, expanding our brains and losing our body hair, and it was only just two or three days ago that we began to look like modern humans. We were still a long way from how we live now, however. Farming and living in permanent settlements didn't really get going until about two or three hours ago, and any certain knowledge of the world, the larger universe and our place in it had to wait until literally the last few minutes: we have only discovered the secrets of atomic structure and DNA in the last 60 seconds of the whole hundred years that life has existed on that scale. That's how long it's taken to figure it out. That we did so at all is entirely due to language; without it, no other species gets even so much as a look-in.

Yet that knowledge is not something we can take for granted. Given what we now know, it might seem astonishing that there are people who still believe that the earth is flat, but despite all the confident advances of science, they have never really gone away. In fact, their numbers even seem to be growing: there are several Flat Earth Societies who are actively recruiting members. For how, actually, can we be sure that the earth isn't flat? How many REs (or Round Earthers, as supporters of the flat-earth theory call the rest of us) have personally verified their belief? Unless we have refined our observational skills, for most of us the earth just seems to extend horizontally in all directions, with the sun and moon going round it at regular intervals – just as it would have always seemed to our ancestors. So if you think the earth is a sphere even though you can't see it and can't prove it yourself, how is that different to any other religious belief?

That is the essence of the flat-earthers' argument, and they have a point. If you don't maintain a sceptical attitude to the beliefs and traditions you grow up with, you're in danger of believing all kinds of nonsense – as human history abundantly proves. It's always wise to question even the most sacred of beliefs. But there's a key difference between a religious belief and a scientific one, nonetheless. Religious beliefs are a matter of faith, something you just have to take on trust. You either believe human sacrifice will placate the gods, or you don't. You either accept that Jesus Christ was the son of God, or you don't – you can't prove it in any meaningful sense. But scientific ideas can be tested and proved – and more importantly, can thus also be disproved. This is the heart of the method that lets us escape from the thicket of superstition and fear that language can otherwise trap us in.

So how do we know that the earth isn't flat, exactly? To begin with, we have to think back to why you would ever imagine that it wasn't. It doesn't look curved, after all. A sailor might start to see another boat disappear below the horizon at a distance of about 3 miles, but before the invention of telescopes, and in days when seafarers rarely ventured beyond sight of land, you'd be unlikely to notice. But things are different at night. Travellers who pay attention to the night sky know the stars you can see depend on where you are – a strong hint, as Aristotle pointed out, that we live on a sphere. Then there's the moon: the way the shadow on its surface changes over a month can really only be explained by seeing it as a sphere that orbits the earth between the earth and the sun. It was that thought which enabled a very smart Greek mathematician by the name of Aristarchus to calculate the distance from the earth to the moon as long ago as 300 BC (a calculation that turned out to be accurate within a few percentage points) and then – if rather less accurately – the distance from the earth to the sun.

He did this using basic trigonometry (a scary-sounding word for the maths-allergic, that really only means 'measurement with triangles'), which at least proved that the sun was much further away from the earth than the moon, and extremely large. But the moon offers an even better clue: the phenomenon of lunar eclipses, which happen two to four times a year – at least in partial form. Unlike a solar eclipse, when the moon comes between the earth and the sun, causing a brief blackout, during a lunar eclipse the full moon enters the shadow of the earth as it blocks the light from the sun, and as the shadow passes over the surface of the moon, the edge is visibly curved – another strong hint that the earth might be a sphere. But how could you prove it?

The answer came from a remarkably simple piece of maths. Less than a century after Aristarchus, another smart Greek mathematician named Eratosthenes heard about a well near Aswan where the midday sun shone down on midsummer's day without casting any shadows – meaning it must be directly overhead. He also knew that where he lived in Alexandria, due north of Aswan, the midsummer sun was not directly overhead at midday. His stroke of genius was to realise that the angle made by a vertical stick and the length of its shadow on the ground where he lived would be the same as the angle separating Alexandra from Aswan along the circumference of the earth. This in turn meant that the circumference of the earth could be calculated by measuring this angle and the distance from Alexandria to Aswan. The angle of the shadow turned out to be just over 7° (about 1/50th of the total circumference of 360°) and as the distance was around 500 miles, the circumference of the earth must be 500 x 50 = 25,000 miles – a figure accurate to within 1% of the actual value.

This was such a clever trick that other early mathematicians tried to confirm it using similar methods. Just over a century later the philosopher Posidonius made his own estimate of the earth's circumference using observations of a star called Canopus. His method was ingenious, but his measurements were less impressive – he ended up with a figure about one third less than that of Eratosthenes. Unfortunately, his method made a stronger impression on Claudius Ptolemy, the Alexandrian mathematician who later became the most respected and influential geographer and cosmologist of the Roman Empire – and it was his estimate which, some thirteen centuries later, ended up in the hands of a man keen to test it: an ambitious Italian sailor called Cristoforo Colombo.

This was not the only unreliable piece of information Columbus was working with: he'd overestimated the eastward extent of Asia – then known as The Indies. By combining these two errors he concluded that if the world was round, the distance from Spain to Japan (the easternmost part of the world then known to Europeans) should be around 3000 miles – instead of the more than 10,000 miles it would in fact have been, had America not been in the way. To his dying day, Columbus believed the place where he made landfall – the islands we now call the Caribbean – was the other end of the Indies, reached by sailing west, not east (which is why they are still called the West Indies).

Ultimately, the honour for the first successful westward journey to the East Indies was left to a Spanish navigator called Magellan over a generation later, his crew finally managing to prove that our planet is a globe by returning home on the well-established route via India and the Cape of Good Hope – though Magellan himself was not so lucky, meeting his end at the hands of angry natives in the Philippines while trying to convert them to Christianity. But the success of his voyage did finally make it impossible for anyone paying serious attention to the discussion to continue to believe in a flat earth. Nonetheless, this did little to dislodge the widespread assumption that the earth was at the centre of God's world – the so-called 'geocentric' theory of the universe. It was this that became the next cherished belief to fall foul of the logic of language, though it was a much harder and bitterer struggle than proving the earth was round.

The fog of lore

It's a curious paradox that though religion can seem at its most absurd when it asks us to believe in 'nonsensical' ideas like the Virgin Birth and the Resurrection, the ideas we have arrived at through a careful scientific study of the universe reveal a world far stranger than any religious tale. Even the most startling of creation myths would struggle to beat the idea that the entire universe emerged out of a single point of nothing at a temperature of 100 million trillion trillion degrees, was too hot to be able to release light for the first 380,000 years, is now some 13.8 billion years old, has a diameter of 1000 billion trillion kilometres, and accommodates at least 100 billion galaxies each having around 100 billion stars – meaning, amazingly, that there are more stars in the sky than all the grains of sand on every beach on earth put together. Then there's the extraordinary fact that, like so many other stars, our friendly old sun is actually a massive atomic explosion nearly a million miles wide. We orbit this vast nuclear conflagration on a tiny dot of rock which, if the sun were the size of a football, would be over twenty yards away and as small as a grain of rice. Who'd'a thunk it?

Put like that, the story science has to tell seems no different to the fabulously inventive creation myths humans have told each other over the millennia. But there is a crucial distinction, however. Whereas the key to religion is observance, science is driven by observation: like the devil, the truth is in the detail. Just as the realisation that the earth was a sphere took a long time to come, the idea that our planet was not the centre of the universe required some left-field thinking. After all, there was very little reason to suspect it wasn't. There was just one thing that didn't quite stack up: the planets.

The word planet comes from the Greek word *planētai* meaning 'wanderer', a name chosen because unlike all the other stars in the sky, the visible planets do not always move in the same direction. The so-called 'fixed' stars rotate slowly across the night sky, always in the same relationship to each other. This allowed people all around the world to measure time and direction at night using groupings of stars as markers, like the Big Dipper or the Southern Cross. But the five planets that the ancient world knew about would sometimes seem to move with the other stars, while at other times they would appear to slow down, stop, and even go into reverse or 'retrograde' motion.

These erratic motions were a source of fascination to our ancestors, who – in the absence of social media or other nocturnal distractions – spent much more time than we do looking up at the night sky. Along with other portents and alarming natural phenomena, the planets had been the subject of intense astrological speculation long before anyone sat down to work out how their odd behaviour could be explained – once we dared to stop believing they were gods, that is. It seemed clear that in some sense, they must go round the earth: but it is no easy matter to explain their movements if you assume that the earth is at the centre of the universe – as almost everyone did. The Greeks eventually came up with the idea of epicycles (small circles that move round larger ones) which – along with other geometric tricks called deferants and equants – was quite good at predicting planetary motion. But it was very complicated.

The idea that the earth might go round the sun rather than the sun going round the earth had been around since at least the days of ancient Greece, when it was proposed by the same Aristarchus of Samos who'd first attempted to estimate the sizes and distances of the sun and moon. His reasoning was quite simple: if the sun was in fact so much bigger than the earth, it made more sense to think that the earth must be orbiting the sun, not the other way round. There is some evidence that the writers of the ancient Vedic texts in India also believed – at an even earlier date – that the sun might be at the centre of the universe, and the astrologer-priests of Ancient Egypt may have been onto the idea as well. But without the instruments they would have needed to be able to prove it, the theory was never widely accepted – if only because it ran contrary to the evidence of our senses: why wouldn't the earth be the centre of God's world?

Though he was not the first to suspect it, the mathematician and astronomer Nicolaus Copernicus was the first person to prove that a helio-centric (sun-centred) model of the universe offered a much simpler solu-tion to the problem. His ideas had been circulating in manuscript form for around 30 years before he finally got round to publishing them in 1543, the year he died, but he was worried about the reaction of the authorities. Even Luther had thundered against *"this fool who wants to turn the art of astronomy upside-down"*, and although Copernicus was convinced of the truth of his theory, he was keen to avoid being censured by the Church. He presented his argument simply as a thought experiment intended to help calculate the movement of the planets more accurately, without making any claim that it was the literal truth – and as such, his system was used as part of the calendar reform undertaken by Pope Gregory in the 1570s.

Things changed in 1609 when a lute-playing former medical student and sometime art teacher named Galileo Galilei got hold of a telescope, then still a very new piece of kit. So new, in fact, he had to resourcefully make it himself after having obtained a reliable description of the device from a friend (he also managed to make a microscope). This rather basic instrument – it had a magnification of only 20 times – still allowed him to see that the planet Venus had phases, like the moon. This meant that it must be in orbit around the sun, thus proving at least that there was something wrong with the existing geocentric model of the universe, based on the long-established authority of Ptolemy.

He set out his ideas the following year in a pamphlet called *Sidereus Nuncius* – usually translated as "Starry Messenger", though 'Message of the Stars' is much closer to what he meant. His championing of the heliocentric model left no doubt as to the 'message' that the stars had to tell, and the Inquisition soon got involved – claiming that such a view threatened the Holy Faith by "rendering Holy Scripture as false." Copernicus' book was promptly banned, and Galileo warned to watch his mouth. He didn't need to be told twice – he was well aware that the philosopher priest Giordano Bruno had been burnt at the stake just ten years previously for advocating a similar heretical teaching.

His argument that the Bible need not always be taken literally fell on deaf ears, even though it was the same line taken by the venerable St Augustine over a thousand years earlier. Fretting over the contradictions between the apparent meaning of Holy Scripture and the persuasiveness of "better explanations", Augustine had claimed that the Bible was a work of 'divine poetry' containing spiritual rather than literal truths: he hoped to scotch the concern that insistence on literal interpretations would cause an unbeliever to "scarcely keep from laughing when he saw how totally in error they are." But even with the authority of this saintly precedent, Galileo was hauled up in front of a religious court, where – threatened with torture – he soon agreed to *"abjure, curse and detest the aforesaid errors and heresies"* and was sentenced to house arrest for the rest of his life.

It's not entirely fair to lay all the blame for this at the door of the Church. No matter how sure he may have been that his theory was correct, Galileo still did not have enough evidence to conclusively prove it – and even some of his fellow scientists found his ideas too much to take. Many still supported the ideas of the astronomer Tycho Brahe, who had come up with a compromise solution consistent with Galileo's evidence, which had the other planets going around the sun, but kept the earth at the centre of the universe. But the Church was clearly rattled. If it were to admit that the universe was not arranged the way the Bible claimed, then its other teachings might also be up for question.

Still smarting from the clash with Protestants over the right of individuals to interpret the Bible as they pleased, their opposition was more about maintaining authority than pursuing the truth. It took nearly 150 years for the prohibition on books advocating heliocentrism to be relaxed – and it was as late as 1992 before, under Pope John Paul II, the Vatican finally admitted the Church had been wrong to condemn Galileo. So when Charles Darwin finally mustered the courage to publish his ideas about evolution some 250 years later, the Church was in no mood to yield more ground. Though they were careful to avoid an explicit condemnation of his theory, it was clear from their opposition that the suggestion that life might have evolved without the help of a creator God was likely to leave a divine being with worryingly little to do with his time.

But just as it did with Galileo, the mounting evidence meant the Church had to find a way to back off from denial. Pope Francis has distinguished himself by a surprisingly liberal line on these ideas, though the bottom line for Catholics is still that drawn by Pope Pius XII, that the Christian faith *"obliges us to hold that souls are immediately created by God."* Darwin may not have had to wait as long as Galileo for a formal apology, which came in 2008 – but it wasn't from the Vatican: on the 200th anniversary of his birth, the Church of England announced *"an apology for misunderstanding you and, by getting our first reaction wrong, encouraging others to misunderstand you still."* The message of religion is still that revelation is more important than observation.

But the genius of science is that it is descriptive, not prescriptive, reporting on what it sees and changing theory to fit the facts as they are known, rather than sticking to theory and attempting to change (or ignore) the facts. Whether religious or otherwise, the forces of tradition often act to hold back advances in knowledge, if only because of the power and influence of those whose authority, position and influence in society are threatened by it. But however strong the forces of opposition, the tide of truth cannot be dammed forever. The insistence on dogma leads to divergence and conflict: yet the hallmark of science is its tendency to ultimately converge on ideas that emerge from the inconsistencies of incorrect assumptions. As the physicist Richard Feynman put it, it is better to have questions that can't be answered than answers than can't be questioned – that leaves room for progress, whereas dogma leaves none.

The naming game

There is little in our everyday language to suggest the underlying reality of the chemical elements of which we are all made. There is no obvious sense from the word 'hydrogen' that it is the simplest and lightest element in the universe, nor any clue – unless you have studied Greek – that it will form water when combined with oxygen, let alone why it might do that. Things are even worse when it comes to compounds. The chemical make-up of *verdigris*, the attractive green colour that forms on copper when exposed to rain and wind, is actually a very precise combination of copper, carbon, oxygen and hydrogen – $CuCO_3.Cu(OH)_2$ – a combination that was once produced in France by placing copper plates in distilled wine to create *vert-de-Grèce*, the 'green of Greece' pigment so prized by artists as the most vibrant green available to them before the 19th century. Even the word 'water', the noise we make when speaking English to refer to the key building block of life, gives no clue to the breath-taking truth of what it really is: one part oxygen and two parts hydrogen. Put the two gases oxygen and hydrogen together, add a little energy, and *hey presto!* you get water. It's that simple.

It's partly the words we use for things that makes this so hard to believe. The accidents of history mean we have known about many elements for much longer than we have known what they actually are. The first one we managed to isolate was probably copper, which has been useful to us in tool-making for at least 10,000 years. It occurs naturally as a raw metal and is easily smelted at low temperatures from ores, but its name gives no clue to its true nature as an element with an atomic number of 29: the English word 'copper' comes from the Latin phrase *aes Cyprium* or 'metal of Cyprus' – the place where the Romans got most of their copper. Oxygen, on the other hand – the most important element for life – was only identified in the late 18th century. It was named from the Greek words *oxys* ('sharp') and *genes* ('forming') because it was thought at the time to be an essential component of acid – although that turned out not to be true.

The ancient Greeks – yes, them again – were the first to have the idea that all matter was composed of small, discrete, indivisible units. These they named atoms, mainly for philosophical reasons (the Greek word *a-tom* means 'un-cuttable'). They had no means of proving it – but the idea turned out to be correct: over 2000 years later, experimental evidence slowly started to show their idea was right, when the chemist John Dalton used the idea to explain why elements react together in the same small ratios. Not that the notation chemists use helps much either: the stick diagrams that are usually used to represent molecules and their interactions bear as much relation to the reality of what they are as musical notation does to music: to experts it is an open book – to most of us, a source of mystery. Yet the complex interaction between molecules is as precise a piece of choreography as you will see in the design for a computer chip or a score by Stravinsky – or the endless interplay of meaning that language allows us to express.

For as we gradually uncover the deeper secrets of the world around us, we find that the fine grain of reality appears to be entirely digital. This is not just an inadequacy in our ability to measure things, a limitation in our equipment or an error of perception. Whether at the atomic or the genetic level, the ultimate structure of matter turns out to be incremental, not continuous. That means that everything is built up in units – like bricks – not freely formed as if poured in concrete. Just like the language we use to describe it, at its core everything around us is digital. What we experience through our senses may seem smooth and analog, but that tells us more about the way our brains process input than the true nature of what we're dealing with. Think of films: despite the seamless illusion of continuity, they are literally 'moving pictures', simply a series of still images (themselves no more than millions of digital dots or pixels in one of just three colours) projected at the rate of 24 frames per second.

In just the same way, everything we see around us is made of a relatively small number of chemical elements. Around ninety of these occur naturally, though most only exist in very small quantities. In fact, 95% of everything on earth consists of combinations of just four of them: oxygen, iron, magnesium and silicon. Not only that: 97% of all living matter, ourselves included, is also made up of just four elements: carbon, hydrogen, oxygen, and nitrogen. Every colour, smell and taste – from the shimmering iridescence of a dragonfly's wing to the pungent aroma of a porcini mushroom – is a precise combination of a small alphabet of signals sensed by a tiny range of receptors in our eyes, noses and tongues. To say that is not to diminish the endless variety of subjective experiences we enjoy, but rather to marvel at the astonishingly clever mechanism by which nature generates the maximum effect from minimal means: digitization.

And these elements, whether we think of their constituent parts as particles or waves, are simply modular arrangements of different quantities of the same stuff. Though we may still be puzzling over the precise nature of the elementary particles that form the basis of all matter, in the bigger picture all atoms are just different combinations of three basic interchangeable building-blocks: electrons, protons and neutrons. Electrons and protons have equal and opposite charges, whereas neutrons are a kind of neutral packing material, and have no charge. And that's it. The difference between hydrogen – the simplest, lightest and most plentiful element in the universe – and osmium (the densest known material) is just the number of electrons, protons and neutrons involved.

This is an incredible fact. The world we experience, with all its variety of sensations, is no more than simple combinations of the same small set of elements. Hydrogen, a gas, has one proton and one electron. Helium has two each. Each new element is larger by just one electron-proton pair (its nucleus packed out with neutrons as necessary) as the number rises through more familiar elements like carbon (6), oxygen (8) and iron (26) until we come to uranium, the biggest atom of them all, with 92. In the laboratory we can create even larger atoms, currently up to oganesson (118), though these monsters are unstable and quickly break back down into smaller elements. These are not random increases in size, as we expect in the analog world of quantities we deal with in our everyday life. Though we use standard units for ease of measurement, in real life things break down at the edges. Bricks crumble; tyres wear. Atoms do not. Like phonemes, in essence they are precise, fixed quantities – and the language they speak is our reality.

But although atoms behave digitally – they chemically combine and separate from each other according to strict rules governed by their atomic number and valency – we now realise that atoms are also divisible, if not indefinitely. In order to explain the strange behaviour of some atoms – particularly the radioactive ones – we have had to find ways to prise apart the nucleus of atoms to discover the units they are composed of. Thanks to the work being done at CERN and other institutes that work on 'smashing' atoms, we are close to confirming a complete picture of the so-called 'standard model' of atomic structure. That too may one day prove to be inadequate, just as the first atomic model we came up with once did – but what we do know is that at these vanishingly small sizes and distances, their behaviour is best explained by quantum theory.

To most of us, most of the time, the mention of quantum theory is enough to make our eyes glaze over. It's a short-hand for incomprehensible, even nonsensical theory about things that aren't real. If even its leading exponents can say that if you think you understand quantum physics, you don't! – what hope is there for the ordinary person? And yet, the thought at the heart of quantum theory is really quite simple: at the most fundamental level, everything – energy and/or matter – can only exist in certain discrete quantities or 'quanta' ('quantum' is the unit). And though few of us have the stamina to follow the maths, the implication of this theory, which is now well-established through detailed observation, is that reality appears to be digital all the way down.

The fundamentally digital arrangement of nature is also evident in a rather more familiar domain: the structure of DNA. We've all heard of the double helix – the twisted strand of genome that contains all the information that makes us what we are – and the idea that this genome is actually composed of sequences of four 'letters' that form a code that tells our cells how to reproduce themselves. These 'letters' are in fact the nucleic acids adenine, cytosine, guanine and thymine (known as A, C, G and T), and they stack up in a long row along the backbone of the double helix, forming a sequence of some three billion letters. This amazing figure is roughly the number of letters to be found in not just one but forty entire sets of the 23-volume *Encyclopaedia Britannica*, still one of the greatest stores of information ever assembled in one place. These digital 'letters' act as codes for amino acids, the building blocks of proteins, and they hold yet another digital secret. The nucleic acids code for amino acids in groups of three, known as triplets, and all the proteins in your body (some tens – perhaps even hundreds – of thousands of different types) are ultimately made from unique combinations of just 20 amino acids.

This means that despite the familiar terminology, nucleic acids are not really like the letters of an alphabet. They are much more like numbers – numbers that act as a digital code for the amino acids. The linguistic analogy is much more apt if we think of the 20 amino acids themselves as 'letters' – letters that quite literally spell out the protein 'words' that form almost every part of our bodies. And here's the fascinating thing: just as words only really make sense in the context of their grammatical relationship to other words in a sentence, most proteins can only carry out their biological function once they fold into more complex tertiary and quaternary structures – structures determined by their relationship to adjacent proteins. This is remarkably similar to the way sentences are formed of complex sub-clauses and recursive structures: as above, so below.

But the words we use to talk about the things that language has allowed us to discover around us often do little to help. That's because we have usually given random names to the objects we found before we knew what they were, which makes it all the more difficult to grasp the simplicity at the heart of complex phenomena. But just as we saw with English spelling, the effort required to retrospectively impose consistency would not really be practical or even very productive – let alone poetic. Insisting that 'water' be referred to as 'H_2O' to reflect its chemical structure might please pedants, but would probably be less than popular with most of us. In the end, it's the effort you make to understand something that counts, regardless of the name you use to describe it.

Facing the facts

Shirking that effort doesn't much matter if there are no real-world consequences: the world goes on much the same way whether or not you believe in God, the soul, fairies or Santa Claus – until someone decides to make it a political cause. For most people most of the time, the sun might as well be going around the earth as not: the truth of the matter doesn't really affect our daily lives – if we believe the earth is flat, the only consequence is that we look stupid. But there are things we now know through science where ignorance can be far from blissful: a refusal to allow blood transfusions, the denial of germ theory or the 'anti-vax' movement can have fatal consequences. And some things are far worse than that, because the consequences of failing to understand or accept the science are global rather than simply personal. We have only to think of the world-wide problem of the plastic clogging our oceans, or the air pollution in our cities: the failure to heed the warnings of experts affects us all.

It's not that experts can't be wrong. Progress in understanding will always involve overturning some established 'expert' opinion. But that can only be done if you take the time to understand what they know. Unless you have a grasp of the facts, you can't challenge an expert opinion simply on the basis of the way you feel. The advances of science that make our lives so comfortable – the easy availability of plastic bags, the convenient car we keep parked near our house – do not exist in a vacuum. We have been used to behaving as if our use of these things is free of consequences, but our planet is not an endless resource – if we pollute and degrade our environment with garbage, it doesn't just go away. Through most of history and prehistory, the planet has seemed almost immeasurably large: and compared to the size of individuals – and even to individual countries – it is. But we now know that it has limits, and our throw-away habit is coming home to roost. We need a different way of thinking about it.

The single most important issue where a refusal to listen to experts has real and lasting consequences for us all is the question of climate change. Climate change is difficult to understand in day-to-day terms because its effects are not immediate – by the time they are bad enough to be noticed, it is almost too late to do anything about it. But the scientific consensus is clear: the world is warming at an unsustainable rate, and human activity – mainly the burning of fossil fuels – is the most likely cause, by far. This too is a hard thing to understand in common sense terms: how could such seemingly small amounts of anything in the atmosphere (CO_2 is just 0.04% of it, after all) have such a big effect? It doesn't 'make sense'. But just like the counterintuitive idea that the earth goes round the sun, that doesn't mean that it isn't or can't be true – if you make the effort to look at the science behind it, the reasons for believing it are quite clear. But here's the thing: even if it wasn't true, it still makes sense to act as if it was – we have nothing to lose by doing so if we're wrong, and yet everything to lose if we aren't.

On the occasion of his 89th birthday, Sir David Attenborough issued a challenge: in conversation with President Obama, he suggested that the US commit to finding a way to produce a source of clean, sustainable and storable energy within ten years, just as in 1961 President Kennedy set a goal in for America to put a man on the moon by the end of that decade. Obama declined to take him up on it, making instead a vague assertion about how they were 'shooting for' that target, if not making as much progress as they'd like. It was a real missed opportunity: we can easily imagine what might have happened to the Apollo programme if Kennedy had not made a national commitment – other priorities would have come along, budgets would have been diverted, and the horizon would have slipped. Unrealistic though they may seem at the time, deadlines work. It's often the only way creative people actually make any progress – and scientific work, through the process of discovery and invention, is as creative as any other field.

It's not as if we don't know how it can be done. The only two truly sustainable sources of energy on our planet are solar and geothermal, and we already know how to tap both. Though our technology is still in its infancy, heat from the sun and the earth's core are effectively inexhaustible supplies of energy, and our ability to harness them can only improve with time. Think how the technology of cars and aeroplanes – to take the most obvious examples – has improved over the last hundred years. In just over a century we have gone from a world where cars and planes were flimsy, largely hand-built and semi-experimental devices to one where we all have access to extremely reliable, highly sophisticated mass-produced precision machines that we use on a daily basis – a world where not just the rich but ordinary people can use them to travel the globe easily, efficiently and cheaply. These days, their absence is unthinkable.

This did not happen by accident, however. The aerospace and automobile industries were – and still are – the beneficiaries of massive state support. Similarly dramatic progress could be made with solar and geothermal energy if these industries were given the same kind of government help. With sufficient investment, smart ideas follow. The gas and oil industries have continued to receive huge government subsidies over the years, and continue to do so – the most recent IMF estimate for the annual direct and indirect benefits that the fossil fuel industry receives worldwide exceeds $5 trillion, over 6% of global GDP. And while figures vary according to the source, it is clear that this is some 20-30 times greater than the subsidies available to the renewable energy industry.

More energy falls on the surface of the earth per hour than is needed to power human civilization for a year. That sentence is worth repeating: *more energy falls on the surface of the earth per hour than is needed to power human civilization for a year.* What does that mean? It means that even with the solar panels we have available today, which are only about 15% efficient, we'd have enough energy for our global requirements if we covered an area 200 miles by 200 miles with solar panels. 40,000 square miles sounds like a lot: in real terms it's about the size of Ireland. At the same time, that's only 0.02% of the total surface area of the planet. Our cities already account for way more than that – nearly 4%. And if we put them in a place that's not being used for anything else (like the 3.6 million square mile Sahara Desert) you'd hardly notice it.

Just 1.2% of the Sahara Desert – a perfect location for collecting the energy of the sun – could supply all of our energy needs. How much would that cost? Averaging $50 per square metre, that would cost around $5 trillion to install. A lot of money. But the Iraq war cost more than half that amount. And it's far less than the $8 trillion spent by President Obama to prop up the US economy after the last recession. It's also a mere 10% of the cost of building enough nuclear power stations to deliver the same amount of carbon-neutral energy, without any of the problems of nuclear waste and radioactivity. Of course, we have to work out effective and scalable systems of storing the spare capacity so that it can be used when needed, but these too are within our grasp: hydro-pumping, fly-wheel storage and gravitational energy are all potential solutions

And here's another astonishing fact: 99% of the entire volume of the earth is above the temperature required to boil water. Scale the earth to the size of a football, and the depth you would have to drill to reach rock at 100°C is no more than the thickness of a sheet of paper. In real terms, that's about 5km – but with the techniques developed by the oil and gas Industries, we already have the ability to reach it. The heat which radiates out from the centre of the earth – effectively a large ball of molten iron – is mainly caused by the decay of radioactive isotopes. So by harnessing the heat from this natural atomic reaction to boil water to power turbines, we would simply be using the same process already used in all nuclear power stations – but without generating any nuclear waste. Not only that: we would have a secure and inexhaustible energy source for the entire planet, and eliminate any further damage to the global climate.

In the early days of oil exploration, the natural gas released with crude oil when oil fields are tapped was considered a problem rather than a potential resource, and ended up being 'flared' or burnt off as waste product. This was partly because the techniques for exploiting it had yet to be developed, but also because its value was not fully appreciated – it was cheaper and easier to simply dispose of the gas. We are in a similar situation today with heat. Oil from more than a few thousand metres down is so hot it has to cool down before it can be safely handled – the average temperature gradient as you burrow into the surface of the earth is around 25°C per kilometre. Deep coal and gold mines, some of which go as far down as 2.5 kilometres, have to have ice slurry pumped into them to allow miners to work in conditions where rocks can be as hot as 60°C. Using that natural heat to generate power is a no-brainer.

Though this may not be practically feasible right now, it is certainly doable with political will and investment of modest resources. America already produces more geothermal power than any other country (due to investments made at the time of the oil price shock during the 1970s), and even under the administration of George W Bush, the US Department of Energy estimated that using existing technology, it would already be possible to generate 10% of the country's power with the expenditure of as little as one billion dollars. The Stone Age did not end because we ran out of stone, as a former Saudi Arabian oil minister once put it, and neither will the Age of Oil – it will require the application of new ideas and new technology. For not only do we now have the ability to create and store energy by more sustainable means, the reality of climate change – whatever its cause – means we have an ever more urgent reason to do it.

Thinking ahead

Language is what gives us the ability to consider all these possibilities rationally, and predict outcomes based on them. In a remarkable episode of the BBC show *Horizon* broadcast in 1964, Arthur C Clarke talks about cities of the future and how he imagines people will be living in the year 2000. Standing in front of a model city that looks very like modern-day Dubai, he makes spookily accurate predictions about the effects of satellite communications, saying *"These things will make possible a world in which we can be in instant contact with one another wherever we may be – where we can contact our friends anywhere on Earth even if we don't know their actual physical location."*

He's describing the mobile phone – at a time when a land-line phone was still a luxury not everyone could afford – and he goes on to predict that almost any professional skill could be practiced remotely: *"I am perfectly serious when I suggest that one day we may have brain surgeons in Edinburgh operating on patients in New Zealand."* And indeed, remote surgery has now become routine practice: worldwide, more than 1.5 million patients receive so-called 'telerobotic' treatment every year.

But then he knew what he was talking about: in 1945, as a young man of 27, he had been the first person to suggest the idea of geostationary satellites, the key to modern mobile phone technology and GPS systems – though it took nearly 20 years before they became a reality. He begins by saying that the audience will only be able to grasp the future if what he tells them appears absolutely unbelievable – and in doing so, he hits the nail on the head: what prevents us from visualising a better future is our inability to imagine anything different from our present. Galileo's contemporaries could not imagine that the solid ground beneath their feet (the "*hulking, lazy body, unfit for motion*" as Tycho Brache put it) could possibly be a rotating planet orbiting the sun – but not only did that turn out to be true, we now know our sun is a quite unexceptional star: it may be the centre of our solar system, but it's only just one of trillions of similar stars that exist in our universe.

Prediction is the greatest test of the value of knowledge, a practical application of the logic of language. Ultimately, it is a confirmation that the ideas underpinning your theory are correct: if you have understood the principles that explain a hitherto mysterious phenomenon, and can recognise the patterns that underlie it, you will know how and when it is likely to recur. In ancient times, when people were more sensitive to unusual natural occurrences, there was no more spectacular demonstration of this power than the ability to foretell an eclipse – widely considered an inauspicious omen at a time when the movements of the heavens were of much greater concern than they are today to ordinary people with little else to distract them at night.

Lunar eclipses may be easy enough to predict (the Earth's shadow is about 12,000 km wide at the distance of the moon, which has a diameter of only 3,500 km), but a solar eclipse requires a much better understanding of the Moon's orbit. For one thing, the shadow of the Moon on the Earth's surface is only 100 km wide, making it quite hard to work out where it will be seen, even if you know one is going to happen. Yet Chinese astronomers were building observation towers to help them do that as early as 2300 BC, as a solar eclipse was believed to be crucial to forecasting the future health and success of the Emperor, and failure to foretell one correctly could result in arrest and execution – a risky business given that several millennia would have to pass before eclipses could be predicted with the certainty that heads would not roll.

We also know from the historical record that the Babylonian,

Egyptian, ancient Greek and Mayan civilisations were all very interested in predicting eclipses, although we don't have enough detail to know how sophisticated their knowledge was. The Greek historian Herodotus records the successful prediction of a solar eclipse by the philosopher Thales of Miletus, a feat considered disturbing enough to end a battle in an ongoing war between the Medes and the Lydians in 585 BC, with both sides anxiously suing for peace as a result. It's not known how Thales managed such a prediction as it is thought that the Greeks would not have had enough information to do it – and there is no record of a repeat performance – but we do know that it did the trick.

Prediction is still at the heart of science. Shortly after publishing his General Theory of Relativity in 1915, Einstein wrote *"The chief attraction of the theory lies in its logical completeness. If a single one of the conclusions drawn from it proves wrong, it must be given up; to modify it without destroying the whole structure seems to be impossible."* There are echoes here of Pope Leo XIII's argument about the impossibility of yielding on points of doctrine, for fear of destroying the whole system of belief – but with a crucial difference: Einstein's ideas were not only logically compelling, they were testable by prediction and observation, and have proved to be so. The claimed truths of Christianity and other religions, which conflict both within the faith and externally with other religions, rely on unsubstantiated belief and cannot be tested. The religious argument has nowhere to turn but the revelations of prophets and the interpretation of scripture: but with the right tools, science can read the book of life itself.

The Large Hadron Collider at CERN in Switzerland is the largest machine ever built. That's quite an irony, given that its purpose is to measure the smallest things that exist – things that are so small (and short-lived) that we can only measure their existence indirectly, and not see them physically. That may sound little different to the excuses once given for the inability to see angels or ghosts, but not only does the LHC have a far better track record, it is the culmination of decades of research and theory about the fundamental structure of all matter, and is designed to test out the predictions of theory in mind-bending detail. Housed some 100 metres below the ground in a circular track with a length of some 27 kilometres, the construction of this huge high-precision device required some equally mind-bending engineering interventions along the way: an underground river between the mountains and lake where the LHC is sited had to be frozen with liquid nitrogen for two whole years while diversionary channels were built.

One of the major purposes of the LHC was to find the elusive Higgs boson, an elementary particle that theory predicted should be a key part of the so-called Standard Model of nuclear physics. This was important because although there were good reasons for believing it existed, no actual evidence for its presence had ever been discovered – and without that, no-one could ever know whether the theory was correct. The failure to find it was not entirely surprising – a Higgs boson only hangs around for a vanishingly small 1.56×10^{-22} seconds on average – around twenty billion trillionths of a second in everyday language – and is 100 times smaller than a proton (hardly a large particle itself, at about a millionth of a billionth of a metre). If you're looking for something that small, you'll need a pretty accurate ruler.

But in mid-2012 CERN announced that they had found a particle 'consistent with' the predictions of the theory, and the next year Professor Higgs was awarded the Nobel Prize for physics. Was it worth the money? Did we really need to know? It's difficult to quantify these things, but compared to how much we spend on destroying things and then building them back up again – the World Bank estimates that the bill for rebuilding Syria will be at least $200 billion, to say nothing of the human and cultural damage – the cost of constructing the LHC, at just over $4 billion, is only slightly more than what the UK spends on cut flowers each year. As the price of confirming that our understanding of the universe is correct as far as it goes, with all the implications in terms of improved science and technological benefits, that seems like a steal.

Another impressive piece of prediction, this time in the field of biology, resulted in a spectacular validation of the theory of evolution (which despite being called a 'theory', is in fact one of the most well-substantiated ideas in science.) In the mid-1990s, palaeontologist Neil Shubin and his colleagues were searching for evidence of the elusive missing link between life in the sea and life on land, a change that the fossil record suggests took place over a relatively short period of 20 million years from about 385 to 365 million years ago, but for which no convincing transitional form had ever been found. They knew that to find one they'd need to target rocks of that exact age, but an exhaustive study of geology around the world showed that the only places where they could be found in locations that were conveniently exposed to the surface were in China, South America and Alaska – all of which presented problems of access.

But then they had a piece of luck. They discovered that one other potential location, the Canadian Arctic Islands, not only had the rock strata they were looking for but had been extensively surveyed in the 1970s by oil and gas companies, and detailed location reports were available. Using these as their guide, the team narrowed their search down to a promising spot on Ellesmere Island. And it was there, after four expeditions and five years of patient and painstaking work, that they found what they were looking for: the fossil of an amphibious tetrapod, part fish, part land animal. It had the scales of a fish on its back, but its head was attached to its body by a neck like a crocodile, and it had webbed fins with bones that were jointed like an arm – complete with a wrist joint. The found it in exactly the kind of location they had expected to find it – in a rock formation dated to 375 million years old that had once been the bed of an ancient stream, a spot that went on to yield several other specimens.

The discovery of what became known as *Tiktaalik* (an Inuktitut phrase meaning 'large freshwater fish') was quickly compared to the famous fossil *Archaeopteryx*, an intermediate stage between dinosaur and birds, of which only 12 specimens are known to exist. But there is a crucial difference. The *Archaeopteryx* fossils – the first of which was found in 1861 – were all discovered by chance, and it took some time for their significance to be realised. What Shubin and his team did was to predict the position of a needle in a haystack, go looking for it, and then find it precisely where theory said it should be. Neither the Bible, the Koran nor any holy scripture has anything on that.

Then there's the Rosetta mission, which in 2014 landed a small probe on a comet. The numbers involved are so extraordinary it's hard to take in. To say a device the size of a large fridge – filled with state-of-the-art technology – was launched 500 million miles across space for ten years to land on an object 4km long still sounds plausible, if astonishing enough. But scale it down to sizes we comprehend, and the task is quite staggering: it's the equivalent of launching a piece of dust from England and having it land, exactly as planned, on a particular grain of rice in India – some ten years later. Given that we've only been able to leave the surface of our planet in controlled flight for just over four generations, the fact that we can now do that is utterly mind-boggling.

Convergence

If you've been to Korea (or even just to a Korean restaurant) you'll know they are the only culture in the world to use metal chopsticks. If you're not used to using them, it's a bit like trying to eat noodles with knitting needles, but there is – or was – a method to the madness: according to legend, their kings ate with silver chopsticks because they believed silver discoloured in the presence of poisons. A fashion for using metal chopsticks then gradually spread through the general population, despite the fact that other metals do not react in that way (although most people don't live in fear of others trying to poison them, either). But though the Korean kings may have known the effect that certain poisons had on silver, they are unlikely to have known why – the only real possibility is that the silver might react with the sulphur in arsenic sulphide, a readily available poison often used in the 'inheritance powders' employed in seventeenth century France and elsewhere to dispose of wealthy relatives who were living too long.

But they wouldn't have known because at that time – and really until the late eighteenth century – no one else did either. They might have noticed that it happened, but without any understanding of the true nature of chemical reactions, any explanation they might have been given would have been based on Chinese philosophical ideas involving the 'Five Agents' – water, fire, wood, metal and earth. It took the careful observations and even more careful measurements of eighteenth-century chemists to slowly uncover the reasons why things react as they do, and to reveal the surprisingly simple structure that underlies all matter. One of the keys to unlocking this understanding was the realisation that there was a clear pattern to the relationships between the chemical elements, a pattern that became known as the periodic table.

The first clue that there was some regularity in the seemingly random character of the few elements that had been identified at the time came though the work of the English chemist William Prout. In two papers published in 1815 and 1816, he noted that the atomic weights of elements discovered thus far appeared to be whole multiples of the atomic weight of hydrogen – though he had no idea why. Although around a dozen pure elements such as gold, silver and iron had been known from antiquity, no new elements had been discovered – or even really suspected – in the fourteen centuries that elapsed between the 3rd century, when the Egyptian alchemist Zosimos purified arsenic, and 1669, when a bankrupt German merchant named Hennig Brand accidentally isolated phosphorus from distilled urine in a failed attempt to discover the Philosopher's Stone.

This led to a slow trickle of new discoveries, and by the early 1800s around 50 elements had been identified, enough for a pattern to start to emerge. The next few decades saw Döbereiner's Law of Triads, de Chancourtois' Telluric Helix (the first system to recognise periodicity) and Newland's Law of Octaves, but the final pieces of the jigsaw were put together by the Russian chemist Dimitri Mendeleyev in 1869 – just months ahead of the publication of a very similar idea by the German Lothar Meyer, who had been working on the same lines for several years. Mendeleyev's realisation that there was a fundamental 'periodicity' to the elements – that their properties and behaviour recurred in regular groupings – allowed him to predict that there must be several as yet unknown elements, which should exist in the blank spots in his table.

This soon proved to be the case when gallium, germanium and scandium were isolated over the next 15 years, proving that his idea was essentially correct: the mystery of the elements was solved, even though it took another 50 years for the reasons to be discovered. This convergence onto a single answer that can be accepted by all is the logical outcome of language when free from political and cultural factors. To the extent that the two most popular world religions have adopted monotheism, they too show a tendency to converge: but in being so bound to issues of culture and identity, there is more pressure on religion to maintain traditional beliefs rather than seek out a common solution – particularly as there is no practical application in which it could be tested.

We have seen how the evolution of writing passed through similar convergent steps, in quite different traditions, in its path from analog to digital representation – and the same convergent process is at work in biological evolution as well: it is not just the eye that has evolved separately in so many unrelated species. The ability to fly is so useful that it has emerged independently in animals as diverse as birds, bats and insects (and the pterodactyls before them) who have all evolved their own solutions to the problem of flight, and enjoy the advantages of being able to explore a third dimension. And in just the same way, nature has converged on the advantages of organising information digitally in several different yet crucial domains: atomic structure, DNA and language.

One of the most pleasing examples of convergence is provided by the development of equal temperament, the most widely adopted solution to the problem of tuning instruments to a common standard. We saw in the previous chapter how the notes of a scale are related to each other by simple ratios, but with simple instruments there is a slight variation in the frequencies of intervals tuned to different notes, as the ratios do not match exactly: this meant it was difficult to play naturally tuned instruments together without sounding out of tune. This became an issue in mediaeval times when harmony started being used in compositions for groups of instruments – and when keyboard instruments with their fixed tunings become more widely available, as the twelve notes of the chromatic scale had to be spaced equidistantly in order to sound in tune.

Musical theory in the West dates back to Pythagoras in Ancient Greece, who had recognised the small but significant discrepancy (the so-called Pythagorean comma) that occurred when using multiples of intervals, as the Chinese had already discovered by 122 BC (a 12-note scale was in use in China as far back as the 5th century BC, as we know from tuning bells that have been found in grave burials). But it was difficult to formulate the interval needed for 'equal temperament' as the notes of the scale have to be separated by the same ratio, based on a number that turned out to be the 12th root of 2 ($12\sqrt{2} \approx 1.05946$). Various systems were tried out in Europe before this was known (the Flemish mathematician Simon Stevin was the first to apply it to musical tuning, in an unpublished manuscript of 1580) but it was the Chinese prince and court astronomer Zhu Zaiyu in 1584 who first accurately – and independently – calculated the correct ratio. The same musical problem was found to have the same solution.

But perhaps the most famous example of two minds independently homing in on the same truth is the story of the theory of evolution. Like Copernicus before him, Darwin was nervous of publishing his radical theories – not least because he knew the opposition it would provoke: the notion that humans had gradually evolved from earlier life forms and had not been purpose-built in an act of divine creation was not just anathema to the Church – it threatened to fatally undermine humanity's sense of its special importance in the scheme of things. With the earth already displaced from what had always seemed its rightful place at the centre of the universe, the idea that man might not after all be the chosen handiwork of God, destined to rule over the rest of creation, was a blasphemy that challenged the Church's very reason to exist.

Darwin might have maintained his silence had a young man called Alfred Russel Wallace not sent him a letter which suggested that he too had grasped the secret of evolution, an insight which threatened to throw Darwin's life work into jeopardy should Wallace publish his ideas first. As it turned out they were able to agree a way of publishing a joint paper which allowed Darwin to acknowledge the younger man's contribution while taking the main credit for himself – but the truth was out. And that is the key point: if it hadn't been Darwin it would have been someone else, because sooner or later the answer would have been impossible to ignore. However much we might have wanted to believe that mankind had been created in the image of a god, specially designed to be different to all other animals, ultimately logic – and the evidence – tells us otherwise.

The simultaneous invention of calculus by Sir Isaac Newton and Gottfried Leibniz, the German mathematician, is another well-known example of a significant scientific advance made by two people independently. Calculus was important as it made it possible to calculate the rates of change of objects in motion – such as planets – something that Newton had worked out for himself at the age of 22 but had never got round to publishing. To the end of his life, he believed that Leibniz – who published his method first – had somehow stolen his ideas, but their methods, though equally effective, simply reflect different solutions to a problem that needed to be solved. During his lifetime Newton made sure he gained most of the credit, but ironically it is Leibniz' ideas and notation that are the basis for the standard calculus in use today.

Closer to our own time, the invention of the telephone – or "talking telegraph" – was also subject to bitter disputes about who had priority. At least three people were working on a practical prototype, if on slightly different principles, but it was Alexander Graham Bell who managed to register his patent application sooner than his main rival Elisha Gray. Gray's application was actually made on the same day as Bell's, on February 14th 1876, but his was the 39th to be received that day – whereas Bell's was the 5th, and thus took precedence. The third contender was Antonio Meucci, an Italian immigrant, who had been working since 1849 on a design which he first registered with the Patent Office in 1871 – but his claim had lapsed by the time of Bell's application because he had been unable to raise the $10 renewal fee. Just like the evolution of new species, the natural selection of ideas is also subject to luck and timing.

The transit of Venus

Religion tends to be jealous of its sacred sources, be they scriptures or relics, and does not easily share them – not even between closely related sects. Yet ever since 1187, the key to the door of the Church of the Holy Sepulchre in Jerusalem – believed to be the site of the tomb of Jesus – has been entrusted to the keeping of a Muslim family. Why? Because the monks of the various Christian factions who have custody of the site – primarily the Greek Orthodox, Armenian Apostolic and Roman Catholic churches, assisted by other orders from both east and west – cannot agree on who should be in charge, and would otherwise fight over it. There is so little agreement between them that a maintenance ladder left in place below one of the main windows in 1757 is still there because a consensus cannot be reached on whose responsibility it is to remove it. Science may not be immune to such petty rivalries, but once it bloomed beyond its secretive and magical roots, the ability – and indeed the necessity – to cooperate with and convince one's peers became a crucial component of scientific advances.

As the information project pushed forward, driven by language, the urge to understand the nature of the cosmos and the origin and history of our planet inevitably took on an international dimension. It was no longer a question of Renaissance gentlemen furtively pursuing an alchemic quest to turn mercury into gold in a private laboratory (a pursuit that even corrupted the brilliant mind of Sir Isaac Newton, who probably died from the effects of mercury poisoning): the observations and experiments that needed to be conducted to confirm the more audacious theories about the structure of the universe could only be carried out with the help of collaborators across the globe. The scientists themselves well understood that this was not a political or national undertaking, though there was political or national pride at stake for those able to reach the goal fastest: one of the things that most distinguishes science from religion is its essentially collaborative nature.

The efforts made to observe the transit of Venus across the sun in 1761 and 1769 are an early example of the international cooperation required to take science to the next level. This rather rare event (it only occurs twice a century, spaced eight years apart) had first been observed in 1639 after a prediction by Kepler, but it was Edmond Halley, Astronomer Royal to George I, who first realised that the distance to Venus could be calculated using accurate observations from different parts of the world – which would in turn allow the distance to the sun to be worked out. This was important, as with the technology of the time there was no other way of working out how far away the earth was from the sun; Kepler's equations allowed astronomers to calculate the relative distances between planets, but the all-important question was the absolute distance.

Of this we had only the vaguest of notions. Aristarchus, one of the first people to advocate a heliocentric theory, had used trigonometry back in 300 BC to show that the sun must be at least 40 times further away from the earth than the moon (it turned out to be nearly 400 times distant) but there was no way of making a direct measurement. Given that the moon and the sun appeared to be the same size in the sky, he reasoned that the sun must therefore be enormously larger than the earth. He also concluded that it was extremely unlikely for such a large object to be in orbit around a smaller one – but with no means of proving that he was right, his counter-intuitive suggestion found few takers. Even though it was eventually accepted that the earth was a sphere, for the next 2000 years the prevailing wisdom remained that the sun went around the earth.

Though the logic of Copernicus' theory and the evidence of Galileo's early observations had won out against the complex cosmological ideas of Ptolemy – whose geocentric model of the universe was the standard teaching in the Middle Ages – there was still no way of improving on the estimates obtained from the simple experiments the Greeks had done. We found ourselves sitting on a ball of rock in space, seemingly in orbit around the sun, but with no way of accurately knowing how far away – or even how big – the sun really was. The transit of Venus provided a key opportunity to find out. If the time taken for Venus to cross the disc of the sun could be observed from different points on the earth and measured accurately, it would be possible to work out the angle between them as seen from the different positions on earth, and then use trigonometric ratios to figure out the distance to Venus, and thus to the sun. It's not quite that simple, but that's the essence of the proposition worked out and specified by Halley as a task for his successors, since he knew he would not live to see the next transit.

His heirs and successors fully understood the significance of what he'd proposed, so come the day, some 20 years after Halley's death – and 45 years after he'd urged that the opportunity be taken – as many as 200 astronomers from various countries set off to different parts of the world to take measurements. Knowing what was at stake, these international scientists were determined not to miss the chance: but unfortunately the European powers were embroiled in the Seven Years' War, and some of the rivalry was not entirely friendly – the ship bearing the astronomers despatched by the Royal Society in 1761 was overtaken by a French frigate and forced to return to port after only two days, although the British more generously allowed safe passage to a French astronomer. But on the second opportunity for observation eight years later, the French government specifically issued orders not to attack Captain Cook's ship the *Endeavour* since it was "out on enterprises of service to all mankind' (generosity that Cook took full advantage of by annexing Australia for England while he was at it.)

The results of the second observation proved more successful than the first, despite the logistical difficulties, and the resulting calculation of 93,726,900 English miles was eventually found to be accurate to around 0.8% of the currently accepted figure of 92,955,807 miles (149,597,870 km) – although nearly two centuries would pass before it could finally be confirmed directly, using the radar technology developed during World War II. Given that they were using nothing but simple observation, basic geometry and technology little improved since the days of Galileo, the accuracy of the result was remarkable. But to mount and execute a global enterprise which resulted in observations from 76 points around the world was an unprecedented exercise in international cooperation – one requiring funding and support well beyond the means of any single individual or government: it was the Large Hadron Collider of its day.

The true significance of the endeavour, despite the arcane nature of its task, is that this genuinely international effort – cooperation that still took place despite the prevailing conditions of war – was driven principally by a quest for information: countries came together because their governments recognised that there was more at stake than mere national glory. There is only so much you can do on your own. The petty rivalries of nations, the competing pride of countries determined to prove their own greatness and enrich their own citizens, is ultimately eclipsed by the shared desire to know and understand the truth about what and where we are – the most fundamental questions that language throws up. It is unfortunate that only necessity seems to bring us together in this way; but perhaps there is a measure of poetic justice as well.

In similarly ironic fashion, the world's first international organisation – the International Telegraph Union – also came into being against a backdrop of military conflict. Formed after months of negotiation when 20 countries finally agreed to sign the International Telegraph Convention in Paris in May 1865, several of the signatory states had been at war with each other until the previous year. But the mutual benefits to be gained from sharing the new technology were too great to be ignored, as they continue to be: the International Space Station is the largest, most complex example of international cooperation in history – and the need for a coordinated global response to climate change may yet prove the catalyst to end the current stalemate in international politics.

Most of us, most of the time, take the answers that science offers for granted. The idea that the earth goes around the sun is not something that we usually have the time or interest to verify for ourselves – or even just the idea that the earth is round, not flat. Unless we have a special interest in the subject, we take it on trust that the scientists are right about what they tell us when it comes to understanding the periodic table, or the structure of DNA. But if we haven't made the effort to find out for ourselves, how is that any different to believing what a priest tells us about God, or what the Bible (or any other holy book) tells us about the world and how we should live in it?

Well, here's the difference. If some disaster were to result in the loss of the cumulative cultural heritage of the last 5000 years, at some point we or some other life form would find a way to start the great adventure of gathering useful information all over again. And we can be fairly sure – for all the reasons we have seen – that both religion and science would make a comeback. But however long it took, we can be certain that science would eventually reach the same conclusions. The earth would once again be found to be a sphere, and to be orbiting around the sun. The relationship between the elements in the periodic table would remain unchanged. The double helix of DNA, and the simple system of digital encoding at its heart, would be found to be the same.

Religion, however, would not. No one has rediscovered the lost religion of the Druids, or reproduced the rituals of the Maya, because religion relies on tradition and lore to maintain its continuity. Once that tradition is lost, there is no means of recovering it, because it was only ever a poetic metaphor, a figment of someone's imagination. No-one could ever write the Bible again, or the works of Shakespeare. But the laws revealed by Newton and Einstein would eventually be rediscovered because they are not made up – they are pages from the book of the universe, a story which can be read by anyone who pays enough attention to detail. Einstein's seductively simple equation, $e = mc^2$ – the astonishing truth that the relationship between matter and energy is the speed of light multiplied by itself – will remain true as long as the universe exists.

These are the true fruits of language: solid scientific understandings whose value is shown by the ways in which our lives are improved by their practical application – penicillin has done much more to alleviate the suffering of mankind than the theological musings of even the most enlightened Pope. What's more, these steps to knowledge will have to be taken on any planet, in any era and by any form of sentient being who uses language to embark on the path of self-discovery. However long it takes, it's an inevitable process. And as ever, cooperation is the name of the game.

Because shared understanding is what transmutes information into knowledge.

KNOWLEDGE: *Memes over Genes*

"The heart makes us fathers and sons, not flesh and blood."
— Johann Schiller

Shock and awe

Sometime around 550 million years ago, something extraordinary happened to the life that had hitherto existed on our planet. It was a small enough change in itself. It had been bubbling away on and off in various forms for 3 billion years or so before that – though as far as we can tell from the fossil record, it had never really taken off before. But suddenly, somehow, it did. Big time. Single-celled organisms, the amoeba-like microbes that had reigned supreme since life first emerged on earth, began to find new ways to thrive and evolve as multi-cellular organisms. It may have been about survival, and avoiding predators by becoming too big to be eaten. It may have been about increased oxygen levels in the atmosphere and oceans. But whatever it was, it set off an evolutionary arms race. At the start of what geologists call the Cambrian Period, the most complicated forms of life on earth were simple sponges: by the end, some 50 million years later, the basic forms of most of the plant and animal life we know today had appeared. A world of individual micro-organisms isolated from each other in a primeval soup was overtaken by a profusion of species of startling variety and size, as shown by the richness of the fossils in the famous Burgess Shale.

Of course, 50 million years is still an enormously long time; but in geological terms – in evolutionary terms – it's just a blink of the eye. We still don't really know what happened to trigger this 'Cambrian Explosion', but what we do know is that the ability of cells to cooperate and coexist was a pivotal event in the history of life – a step change in what it was possible for evolution to achieve. In learning to act as units of millions, billions and then trillions, cells were gradually able to differentiate and develop more complex coordinated structures that led to everything from duckweed to dinosaurs. Single-celled organisms are limited in what they can do: they cannot grow beyond a certain very small size, cannot specialise, and have limited ability to interact with their environment. But multi-cellularity allows an organism to develop tissues and distinct organs – mouths, eyes, ears and limbs – which function cooperatively, creating integrated wholes that are more efficient, both in terms of their internal structure and their ability to survive.

The key change was the ability to interact. With individual cells now able to work together as cooperative units, the difference was dramatic: no longer isolated in a microscopic cell-eat-cell world, organisms were free to grow as big as food supplies and gravity would allow – and the tree of life exploded into diversity. But despite their impressive new powers and abilities, the individuals swimming in this sea of new species were still trapped in their own worlds, living by their own wits, limited to their own experience – as they are to this day. To the extent that they live in communities, all animals benefit from the nurture of parents, the comfort of companionship and – to a certain degree – the lessons of survival. But beyond the clues to be gleaned from observing others, no animal without language can be sure of what its peers are thinking, nor can they ever hope to express anything more than a few basic emotions to each other. They may slowly evolve the ability to out-swim, out-run or out-fly their rivals, but without an effective way to communicate, meaningful cooperation is almost impossible: they have no choice but to learn from their own experience, endlessly repeating the same old trial-and-error process of every individual born before them..

The emergence of language is just as dramatic a shift in the story of life as the switch to multicellularity – and for much the same reason: it allows us to interact with others. Animals may have been communicating in simple ways since they first appeared, but – as we saw in Chapter 1 – the unstructured nature of their cries and calls places severe limits on their ability to exchange meaningful information. In paving the way for more precise dialogue, the switch to a digital mode was a radical departure. Life without language is a guessing game, a daily struggle to survive that depends on finding something to eat before you are eaten yourself – a relentless engagement with the present where the only advantage comes from the hard knocks of personal experience or the sheer luck of evolution. Against that, the ability to share awareness, experience and information is not just a useful advantage, it is utterly transformative: a gateway to a world of conscious thought, dynamic intelligence and freedom from fear – a ray of light on a mental darkness that those of us who use language can barely comprehend.

That's because like most things we learn as children, we adopt language so easily that we have no memory of not being able to speak – and few of us have any experience of people who can't. This has not stopped the curious and powerful from trying to find out what it would be like, however: James IV of Scotland is said to have had two new-born babies sent to a remote island to be raised by a deaf-mute woman, so that he could see whether they would talk, and what language they would speak. He wasn't the first to do so – Herodotus tells us that the Egyptian Pharaoh Psamtik I tried the same experiment with two children and a shepherd, and similar efforts were made by the Holy Roman Emperor Frederick II, and again by Akhbar the Great, the 3rd Mughal emperor.

But despite any hopes that these children might spontaneously speak the original language of God, their failure to do so only succeeded in showing that language is not innate. Without the intense daily exposure most of us grow up with, the patterns of speech prove impossible to master – as shown by the fortunately rare examples of feral children from the more recent historical record: Victor of Aveyron, the 'Wild Child' who wandered out of woods near a French village at the age of 12 in 1800; Kaspar Hauser, a German boy found on the streets of Nuremberg in 1828 after being kept alone in a basement all his life; and Genie, rescued from abusive parents in Los Angeles at the age of 13 in 1970. None of them ever seem to have learnt to speak more than a few words.

The extraordinary story of Helen Keller is a unique insight into just how lonely and isolating a world without language must feel. Born in 1880, Keller became blind and deaf as the result of an unknown illness when she was just 18 months old. Although by the age of seven she had developed around 60 'home signs' which she used to communicate with the family, she was becoming increasingly unruly and frustrated at her inability to make herself understood. The following year her parents employed a tutor, Anne Sullivan, hoping she might help her learn to communicate. Sullivan began by spelling words into her hand, trying to show how they were associated with objects – but because Keller had no idea that things had names, she struggled to understand, thinking it was just a game. That is hardly surprising: without the awareness that what you are being taught even exists, there's no place to start from – nothing to look for.

The breakthrough finally came when she realised the signs Sullivan was drawing on one hand referred to the sensation she was feeling on her other hand. This moment of understanding was like a shaft of light in a dark room. She immediately wanted to know the names of everything around her: *"I stood still, my whole attention fixed upon the motions of her fingers. Suddenly I felt a misty consciousness as of something forgotten – a thrill of returning thought; and somehow the mystery of language was revealed to me. I knew then that w-a-t-e-r meant the wonderful cool some-thing that was flowing over my hand. The living word awakened my soul, gave it light, hope, set it free!"*

What she was describing is the true magic of language, the simple yet compelling trick at its heart: the ability to name things. Communication is about shared understanding, and that means being able to recognise what the other person is referring to. Language allows you to pinpoint the object of your attention, and tag it with a simple yet easily remembered combination of sounds – or letters. As children we learn that skill without realising how precious it is: the remarkable thing about Helen Keller's account is that she was old enough to understand what it meant, and intelligent enough – and loved enough – to be able to explain it. And she was lucky. Her parents knew Alexander Graham Bell, and with his help were able to find a specialist tutor who could help her – a woman who had been through her own struggles with blindness and neglect – who remained her constant companion and interpreter for the rest of her life. It is mainly through her that we know something of the astonishingly vivid impressions that learning language made on Keller, who went on to become an inspirational speaker.

But there may also be significant group of people who are excluded from language not by abandonment, neglect or abuse, but simply by the fact that they cannot hear. Most deaf children are treated with care and kindness, and from ancient times have learnt to communicate using signs – as mentioned by Plato in one of his Socratic dialogues. But in poor rural communities, that is not always the case. In her book *A Man Without Words*, Susan Schaller, a teacher of sign language, movingly describes her work with a profoundly deaf Mexican man who she calls 'Ildefonso' – who had reached the age of twenty-seven with no understanding of human language whatsoever. He eventually led her to a community of similarly 'languageless' adults who had developed ways to communicate using simple gesture and mime, but had no symbolic signs common to the group, and no grasp of abstract concepts like the passage of time. Despite this, some were quite skilled, and had found work as mechanics – and were quite capable of taking a bicycle apart and reassembling it without any problems. But they lived in the present, and were deeply puzzled by the behaviour of most of those around them.

Schaller reports a similar shock of understanding with Ildefonso, whose breakthrough word was 'cat'. His sense of awe at what this meant was so strong that he burst into tears, and like Helen Keller, became intensely curious to learn more – and eventually managed to become fluent in sign language. And that's what it takes: a breakthrough moment. Until you grasp the idea that the otherwise apparently random sounds or signs actually refer to something, you won't make any progress, no matter how much exposure you have.

No wonder it's proved so difficult to teach language to our animal cousins: not only do they have no tradition of helping others to learn, or loving parents surrounding them with speech, they have no awareness that there is anything to learn.

Food for thought

An experiment carried out with capuchin monkeys in 2005 by researchers at Yale University gives a fascinating insight into the relationship between understanding and behaviour. The plan was to try to teach them the concept of money by getting them used to exchanging a plain metal token for different types of food – slices of apple, grapes and cubes of jello. After several months of patient training, the monkeys finally grasped the idea and researchers were able to test their ability to use this 'money'. To everyone's surprise and delight, they behaved as logic would predict – choosing to 'spend' money in ways that revealed a clear grasp of value, and even showing an interest in risk and gambling. Their evident understanding that money could be used to buy services as well as things was graphically demonstrated when a male monkey managed to steal some extra tokens – the first thing he did was to 'pay' a female monkey for sex, who promptly went and exchanged the token for a grape. The logic of that clearly needed no explanation.

This is important, because it shows that other species have the capacity to understand and apply 'human' concepts once they become aware of them. When shown how to, the bonobo Kanzi we met in Chapter 1 quickly learnt to how to light a fire and toast marshmallows on a stick, and more recent studies have shown that chimps possess all the cognitive skills needed to cook. In the 1980s a chimp called Cedo was even trained to work as a farmhand, driving a tractor, feeding livestock and mending fences. But it's not just primates who demonstrate human levels of intelligence. Animals as diverse as crows, rats, sheep and octopuses have shown the ability to solve complex problems. What they don't have is an effective means of sharing the ideas they come up with – but that may not be because they aren't smart enough, just because they don't know how.

The reason the group of profoundly deaf adults that Idelfonso lived with had so little knowledge about anything not immediately in front of them, and were effectively dysfunctional when it came to participating in human society, was not because they lacked the capability – they could easily copy things they had been shown to do, if they saw it was useful – but because without language they had been unable to learn.

The default assumption has always been that only a brain as complex as ours could handle language. Of all the millions of species on earth, the reason why only humans have learnt to speak must be – so the thinking goes – because our brains are bigger and better than the others. Our brains are certainly big: in terms of the 'encephalization quotient' (the size of an animal's brain relative to its body size) we clearly come out top. Though whale and elephant brains are far larger than our puny noggins – at 8kg and 5kg respectively, against mere 1.25 kg for us – they are still smaller than ours as a proportion of body size. But some birds and mice have bigger brain-to-body ratios than us, so the relationship between quantity and quality cannot be entirely straightforward (Einstein's brain was found to be about 18% smaller than the average) – and though we may be steadily improving our ability to monitor brain activity, we still don't know nearly enough to be able to say how brain size relates to intelligence.

Nonetheless, one thing is quite clear: our brains have expanded rapidly – and relatively recently. Around six million years ago, when the homo genus split from our nearest relatives the chimpanzees, our brains were roughly the same size as theirs – about one third of the size they are now. Nothing much changed in terms of brain size for the next three million years or so. But then, slowly but surely, it began to ratchet upwards. In fact our brain-cases tripled in size over the next three million years, an astonishing rate of change in evolutionary terms. Under normal circumstances most species evolve quite slowly, and some have hardly changed since they first appeared on earth: ants have been around for 120 million years, the 'living fossil' deep sea coelacanths have existed for 360 million years and jellyfish have been with us since the beginnings of multicellular life 550 million years ago – all happily filling their own little niche without

feeling much pressure to change. So something unusual must have happened for our species to have transformed itself so quickly.

Then there's another puzzling fact: large brains are a high-mainte-
nance organ – ours consume around 20% of the energy that we get from
food, compared to the 8% that chimpanzee brains get by on. Yet just as
we would have been needing more food for our burgeoning brains, we
seem to have started losing bulk and strength in our muscles, especially
in our jaws. This is odd, as the ability to survive in the wild depends on
the ability to catch and eat prey, and defend yourself against predators.
Not only would an individual human, unarmed and naked, not survive a
fight with a chimpanzee – without help we'd also struggle to catch most
of the animals we've traditionally relied on for food. And there's more:
our expanding skulls soon began to push up against the physical limit
for childbirth – yet far from stopping at that point, the pressure to deliver
bigger brains was such that we began to give birth prematurely, leaving
mother and child more vulnerable while the infant brain grew outside the
womb instead of in it.

One theory is that socialisation was the driver: we needed a larger
brain to keep up with the politics of living in larger groups. That may be
so, but it also applies to other animals known to live in large groups, such
as baboons – who clearly manage their affairs quite well with smaller
brains. Then there's the tool-use theory, which claims that when we first
started using tools, the advantages were such that it stimulated brain
growth. This is also fine as an idea, apart from the fact that other animals
also use tools, and they haven't grown bigger brains – and that during
the first million years in which our brains first doubled in size, tool use
hardly changed at all. A third idea commonly advanced is that we needed
to become more intelligent to adapt to rapid climate change – but again,
that applies to all other species as well, and they have managed just fine
as they are.

But there is another possibility. Language may not have just happened along one day because our brains got bigger, after all. In fact,
exactly the opposite could be true: our brains may have got bigger

because we started using language. If the first steps toward language were much simpler than we have previously assumed, then not only would it have required less brain power to get going, it would rapidly have become a powerful incentive for evolution to select for intelligence. As we have already seen, language offers a huge advantage over those that don't have it – an advantage that is not just comparative, but absolute: pooling group knowledge takes the game to a completely new level. On our own, we are dependent on our own brain-power, but with language we can harness the intelligence of our entire group. The ability to communicate, in however primitive a form, allows ideas to be shared and spread, whether it be creating new tools and weapons or cooperation and planning in hunting. However hench, an ape acting alone could never hope to best a hungry tiger – but a community of talking nerds armed with pointed sticks and a cunning plan could easily take down a mammoth. With language, for the first time it becomes more useful to be smart than strong.

For language is a simple trick with explosive consequences. Given the ability to share ideas, the otherwise inexplicably rapid expansion of our brains and the subsequent rise to dominance of our species starts to make sense. Being able to talk to one another meant we could afford to replace our canine teeth and strong muscles with cooperation: there would have been an enormous benefit in doing so. No longer would we have to rely on whatever we as individuals can learn and remember in the course of a short life – during which most of our attention would be taken by up either trying to find food or avoid becoming someone else's lunch. With language, ideas can be shared with the family, tribe and group. The best ideas – be they practical like how to fish, or social, like how to maintain order and authority – are passed on down the generations. Suddenly it is possible to free ourselves from the long, slow stumble of evolution – for language not only pushed us in the direction of bigger brains, it gave us the ability to store knowledge.

But this moment was a long, long time coming. To the extent that we can judge from the evidence it leaves behind, life on earth began at least 3.5 billion years ago. On that scale the rise and rise of *homo sapiens* presents an exponential trajectory: the history of our species is just a surface smear on the deep history of the planet, but our achievements have been extraordinary. Until as recently as 10,000 years ago, to all intents and purposes we were still living in the wild. All of us. We may have had a few tools, spears, bows and arrows, fire and some form of clothing, but otherwise we were living much like other animals, hunting and gathering whatever we could find and catch or harvest. Although we had managed to venture beyond the shores of Africa, our home continent, we had neither agriculture nor permanent homes. Yet just 400 generations later we live in vast cities with glittering skyscrapers, have secure food supplies, and can fly around the world with ease (over 4 billion plane journeys were made in 2017, a record-breaking year – which means as many as a million people worldwide could have been in the air at any one time). We have even built an artificial moon, the International Space Station, which is permanently occupied. And it will surely not be long before we start to colonise another planet.

Why? The answer is our vast store of shared knowledge. With language, we have found a way of encoding, transferring and storing information that now, with the internet, allows anyone with a computer to access almost everything that's ever been known – especially knowledge of anything useful or interesting that's been invented, created or simply been popular. We haven't got smarter. Our brains are much the same size as they were 250,000 years ago – if anything, they've actually got smaller as we domesticated ourselves. The only thing that has changed is the efficiency with which we share our knowledge. Just as language allowed us to break the profound silence of being, information technology (of which the invention of writing was the first step) has driven the rest. And the effects of that deliver compound interest. Even if only a few of us are ever interested in pushing the boundaries of knowledge beyond the limits of accepted wisdom, language allows the best ideas of such curious individuals to become the shared property of us all.

Going viral

The critical factor determining the growth of culture has always been how easily we have been able to access what's already known, and build on that. Spoken language may allow knowledge to be shared and passed on through tradition, but anything passed on through oral transmission is only as good as the memory of the person conveying it – and can so easily die with them. To that extent, writing was a great step forward in the preservation and spread of knowledge, as real history – records we can refer to long after the people that made them have gone – begins with the written word: though there is much we can learn from digging up what they left behind, without written records we have no way of knowing what people thought about what they were doing, or why they did it. Until and unless we invent a time machine, we will never know who built Stonehenge – or why. The culture of Britain before the Romans invaded and started keeping records will forever be lost to us, just as what we know about the pre-literate culture of the Incas is limited to what the Spanish *conquistadores* wrote down.

That doesn't mean that people at the time had no means of knowing the history of their culture. As with many living cultures around the world, there would have been a rich oral tradition of spoken poetry that preserved the great deeds and legends of the tribe through the generations. Often there would be a special class of people charged with remembering and passing on the tribe's accumulated wisdom. The Druids of ancient Britain are a notable example – as we are told by the Roman historians, the only source for the information we have about them. We also know that the Romans took that seriously enough to send out a crack force of troops to exterminate Druidism in the very heart of its stronghold, amid the holy groves of the Isle of Anglesey. They did so because they knew that by killing all those with knowledge of the traditions, the culture itself would die – for without written records, there would be no other means of passing it on. And without a common culture, resistance to Roman rule would effectively cease.

As far as we know, all prehistoric cultures had rich oral traditions.

Many have survived into the historical era, especially where literacy was never widespread. The storyteller plays an important role in cultures with no other form of popular entertainment, as in many rural parts of Africa, India and China, where these traditions remain strong – and we know that Homer's epic poems contain stories and language dating back hundreds of years before they were first written down. Like most innovations, the techniques of literacy were not always welcomed – there was often strong resistance to putting things in writing. The Druids banned written texts to prevent knowledge getting into the wrong hands: according to the Romans, their training was strictly oral, and could take twenty years to master. There are parallels elsewhere: the famous Pythagorean Brotherhood left no writings, in part to maintain the secrecy of their teachings, but perhaps also for the same reason that Socrates gave as his objection: *"The living word of knowledge... has a soul, of which the written word is properly no more than an image."*

We can be thankful his student Plato did not feel the same way, or we would have no record of one of the first philosophers whose actual words – or something close to them – come down to us through history. But though we know about Socrates from ancient texts, we mustn't forget how few copies of these precious manuscripts ever existed in antiquity: they were expensive to produce (especially when illustrated) and would only ever have been created in very small numbers for royalty, rich patrons, or possibly for early libraries – and were thus vulnerable to fire, looting and the many other dangers that beset life in those times.

Even as recently as 1424, the great library at Cambridge University had no more than 122 volumes in its collection: and although these would have been important works of scholarship, that's less than the number of books the average UK household has on its bookshelves at home, according to a recent survey – even if not all of them have been read. Books were once rare and precious objects – until the start of printing, there were probably no more books in existence than a single scholar with the freedom to do so could have read in his (and it would have been 'his') lifetime. That is if he could ever find them: no more than a few copies of all but the most precious titles were readily available. Petrach, 'the father of humanism' – one of the most educated and privileged men of his day – took a lifetime to build a private library of as few as 200 books. It has been estimated that there were no more than 30,000 books in existence in the whole of Europe before Johann Gutenberg printed his first Bible in 1455: but within a couple of generations more than 10 million books had been produced – and once printing became widespread, the line was quickly crossed between the amount of knowledge available and the ability of any one person to keep abreast of it.

For printing was a crucial step in the advance of knowledge. The Europeans came to it rather late: along with paper, gunpowder and the compass, printing had been one of the four great treasures of China, in use at least four centuries before Gutenberg's press began to roll (the Chinese had invented moveable type by the 12th century and were even printing in more than one colour as early as the 14th century). Until the invention of printing, all books were copied by hand, a process which not only introduced errors but was very labour-intensive: an illustrated vellum manuscript of the type produced for libraries in the Middle Ages would have cost thousands of pounds in today's money. Their value is demonstrated by the chained libraries still found in the oldest cathedrals in England, and even the most well-endowed of such institutions had very few volumes on their shelves – the majority of which would have been interpretations of the Bible and discourses on theology, the main subject of scholarly interest at the time.

The dramatic effect printing had in making a greater variety and quantity of books available and affordable is shown by the rapid subsequent emergence of the so-called 'scientific revolution'. This radical break-point in human history was not the result of suddenly discovering that we were ignorant: it was driven by a material change in the availability of information – the fact that, through printing, knowledge only previously accessible to an exclusive few could be shared with anyone who could read. This in turn stimulated a growth in and demand for literacy, creating a multiplier effect in human intelligence, a virtuous circle that meant the accumulated legacy of human thought could be accessed and worked on by an ever-increasing pool of brain-power.

Prominent among early printed books was Ptolemy's famous *Geographia*, the Latin translation of a text first produced around 150 AD. Ptolemy, a Roman citizen probably of Greek origin who lived and worked in Egypt, wrote several scientific books that were highly regarded during the Middle Ages (the Arabs were great admirers of his work and made many translations). As a record of the geographical knowledge of the world at the peak of the Roman Empire, the *Geographia* was an invaluable and unrivalled store of information to which little was added over the next thirteen centuries – despite depending on ideas developed by Greek mathematicians still hundreds of years earlier.

The Greeks had in turn inherited the experience and insights of the Egyptians, an ancient culture sophisticated enough to have built the pyramids, structures that still astonish us today. As we saw in the last chapter, simply by 'doing the math' – they had to invent much of it first – the ancient Greeks had not only already worked out that the earth was a sphere, but had correctly estimated its size, the distance to the moon and realised that the sun was enormously bigger than both. The great advances made by the mathematicians, philosophers, astronomers and geographers of ancient Greece were a short-cut to knowledge and understanding that amazed the thinkers of the Renaissance when they stumbled onto them some two millennia later. That they did so at all is quite remarkable – the threads that connect such precious books through the mediaeval period to the age of printing were incredibly fragile: only 46 manuscript copies of Ptolemy's *Geographia* survive, error-filled copies of translations of copies, and none from earlier than the 13th century – over 1000 years after it was first written.

The vulnerability of such texts was such that many of the most important works of antiquity only survive through the most tenuous of links. We know from references in works by other authors that Aristotle, one of the greatest minds of classical Greece, wrote around 200 books of which only 31 survive – many of them only as Latin translations of Arabic translations of Syriac translations of the original Greek. That they do so at all is testament to the dedication of the mostly unremembered ancient scribes and translators who laboured to preserve such precious knowledge for posterity.

But the emergence of electronic media means the importance of books as a store of knowledge is rapidly giving way to sources of information that no longer depend on the written word: as Marshall McLuhan predicted in the 1960s, the value of literacy is slowly receding – and with the invention of recording technology, we have even found a way to capture and store time itself. Writing and printing may have been radical step-jumps in the development of communication, connecting us with minds beyond our immediate circle of family and friends, but the extraordinary functionality of smart phones and the internet means we can now access virtually anything on any topic, at a time, at a place and in a medium of our choosing. There is no need to go to the library or even to your desk: knowledge is literally at your fingertips, in the palm of your hand – we've created a world that is constantly connected to the cumulative understanding of our past.

Thicker than blood

Around about the time that Francis Crick and James Watson were celebrating their discovery of the structure of DNA with a few pints down the Eagle pub in Cambridge, my parents were busy conducting a genetic experiment of their own – one that resulted in my arrival into the world some nine months later. There was very little in my family background to suggest that I would pursue the life I ended up leading. My immediate grandparents were all of solid yeoman stock with little interest in anything beyond making as good a life for themselves as circumstances would permit. And why not? Survival is the first priority of life. Certainly, my parents were never much interested in broadening my intellectual horizons; although they encouraged me to go to university, I was the first of my immediate family ever to have done so – and to the end of his life my father regarded me as a bit of an 'egg-head' because I liked to read books, and wouldn't sit quietly in front of the television of an evening.

But from my teenage years onward I slowly discovered that my real 'family' – the ones I felt closest to and respected as people who had something valuable to teach me – were mostly already dead or otherwise inaccessible to me. As I started to understand the value of science, literature, music and art, it was among the icons of the modern world that I found my early heroes – H.G. Wells, George Orwell, Igor Stravinsky, Salvador Dali, Frank Zappa. These were the people I related to, much more so than the people I was actually related to: they were people who spoke a language I understood, the language of intellectual enquiry, a refusal to take things for granted – and who delighted in crossing boundaries and finding connections in unexpected places. As things turned out I eventually got to know Frank Zappa personally, and was able to spend time with him over the last few years of his life – and in many ways he felt much more like a father to me than my own father ever did. I certainly grieved his death more intensely.

How could that be? How could someone not actually my father feel more like a father than my 'real' father? Perhaps it's not such an uncommon occurrence. Though the circumstances may be very different, there are many people who have been treated more kindly by strangers than by members of their own family, and there will be many more who wish they had. In the same way that language is the carrier wave of culture – our genetic inheritance is simply the 'carrier wave' of consciousness, the physical mechanism that allows us to function in this world. The equipment we are born with may be the luck of the genetic draw, but the way we use it is down to our ability to use our minds, an ability hugely affected by the tools we acquire after birth. And whereas genes only change once in a generation, memes change much more rapidly.

Ironically the word 'meme' has itself mutated since it first appeared (being used more these days to mean visual gags that spread like wildfire on social media before being equally rapidly forgotten), but it was originally coined by Richard Dawkins in his book *The Selfish Gene* to mean "units of cultural transmission." He was talking about ideas and concepts that reproduce through a population in the same way as our genes: he wanted to show how human culture had developed a trajectory of its own, and was no longer determined simply by 'selfish' genes, but was driven by memes. In this he was following TH Huxley, "Darwin's bulldog", who had already observed in 1880 that *"The struggle for exis-tence holds as much in the intellectual as in the physical world."*

And the memes we identify with are always going to be more pow-erful than the genes we inherit – which is why political differences cause such rifts in families, and why those in power and authority have always tried to suppress subversive or inconvenient information. Records of such deliberate destruction of knowledge go back at least as far as the 3rd century BC, when the first Qin emperor of China ordered the burning of all books that he had not personally approved – and had 460 unruly scholars buried alive to underline his point. The burning of books is an act of cultural vandalism that echoes down through history as least as far as the infamous *Säuberung* of Hitler's Reich, which targeted the work of Jewish intellectuals in an attempt to suppress any 'Un-German' ideology. But in vain: as Helen Keller wrote at the time in an open letter to those responsible, *"History has taught you nothing if you think you can kill ideas."*

For memes are the lifeblood of human society. It is our ideas that most distinguish us from our animal cousins, because language allows them to spread freely to other minds, irrespective of cultural and political taboos. Ideas are subject to evolution as much as physical characteristics: those that find favour are preserved by natural selection just as genes are passed on by organisms that survive long enough to reproduce. But though there is little we can yet do about our genes (even if gene therapy may soon become a reality) we can do a lot about our memes: that's why education has been so highly prized throughout history. Unlike a gene, the beauty of a meme is that it's not the property of any one individual: no one remem-bers who first invented the wheel, or discovered how to make fire. But we remember what they invented, and how to make use of them. And in terms of the human project, that's a far more significant legacy.

The genes that express themselves in us are no different to those in most of the animal kingdom; the difference between us and our closest cousins – the great apes – may be no more than a percentage point or two, but even the gap between us and much less obviously related species is far less than we might like to think – we have 85% the same genes as mice, and even 50% the same as worms, for example. What is not the same is our thoughts. Other animals clearly can think and communicate to some extent, as we have seen – but it's our ability to tag thoughts with organised sounds and use this trick to explain and exchange sophisticated ideas and understandings that gives us the exponential evolutionary advantage that we have developed. Language liberates us from the tyranny of our genes.

It's the ability to benefit from new memes which controls the success we will have in human society, as has long been recognised: knowledge is the key to power. And with the knowledge that such information gives us, we can imagine new ways of doing things. Without that, we default to our genetic norm – and the genetic norm is the tribe. As Darwin noted in his journal in 1838, *"He who understands the baboon would do more towards metaphysics than Locke"* – by which he meant that our instincts have evolved from the behaviour of primates, and as such the default mode of human behaviour is still that of the baboon. Baboons, like chimpanzees, live in hierarchical packs ruled by the violent bullying of a dominant male. This is the historical default mode of humans throughout history. It takes an effort of imagination to depart from this pattern. And if you are big, strong and stupid, you are unlikely to see why you should.

But in a world where memes matter more than genes, what you know can trump what you are. Blood may be thicker than water, but as Aldous Huxley once observed, water is wider than blood. Go into any stately home and you are likely to find a long family tree, a sinuous and often rather dubious link through time and the generations to the first person granted the title to the land that forms the source of the family's fortune. Many of the descendants will have been wastrels and scroungers – the family will be lucky if their inherited assets lasted more than three generations without having had to sell up, marry wealth or divest to some distant relative. That's because the talent and luck (often mostly the latter) that first led to the acquisition of the property do not usually come with the genes, but are more a matter of being hungry for success, or having a knack for being in the right place at the right time – and being born into wealth does little to encourage a drive to succeed.

Other forms of talent are rarely inherited, either. Most of us can name some of Shakespeare's plays, but how many of us can name his children? Even if his son and grandsons had not been taken by the plague, they are unlikely to have escaped the shadow of his fame; and however talented, his daughters were eclipsed by the chauvinism of his times. But though we can't necessarily say that there would have been another Shakespeare if Shakespeare hadn't lived, the contributions he made to the English language were accepted because the time was ready for them. Whether their survival is due to chance, their value as propaganda for the Tudor dynasty, or simply their popularity on the stage, the beauty of the meme of Shakespeare is that it doesn't matter whether his work was written by the man born in Stratford on Avon, by Edward de Vere, or by any of the other people who have been thought responsible for the writings. They're all dead anyway, so it doesn't matter to them.

But it matters to us that we have such a body of literature in the language. Of the 35,000 different words that 'Shakespeare' used in his work, an astonishing 40% of them – some 14,000 – are new coinages. Then there are the many expressions he appears to have invented, or at least recorded for the first time. In terms of the English language, British culture and even human civilisation, this is a quite extraordinary contribution. But it stands on its own, regardless of its author. His genes may have died with his grandchildren, but his genius is passed on to anyone who pays attention to his work. That's what remains, in people's hearts and minds, and still inspires respect.

The human project

Shelley's famous poem *Ozymandias* is supposed to remind us of the vanity of human ambition and the inevitable ruin of empire. And history largely is a tale of collapse and degradation: the mighty mostly end up fallen. But though their mortal remains may vanish and their grand buildings crumble, an echo of their ancient regimes survives through the records of their thoughts and deeds. Their names can even lurk in words we still use today: whether or not we realise it, *czar* goes back 2000 years to Julius Caesar – and the Tzars of Russia and Kaisers of Germany honour him in their titles. This is so despite the fact that the Latin word *caesar* did not originally mean a powerful person but was just a kind of nickname – the 'cognomen' of the man formally known as Gaius Julius – and lives on due simply to the personal force with which he invested it.

Knowledge is abstract, not material: whether transmitted through speech, writing or any other medium, the words we use to express it are symbolic – representative rather than real. Knowledge exists in the minds of those that understand it, and can be freely and easily reproduced in any medium: you can kill people who have an idea, but not the idea itself. To the extent that language (and especially writing) enables the collective experience and wisdom of previous generations to be passed on to their children, culture is a vast storehouse of knowledge – which is why teaching and centres of learning have been greatly valued in all societies since ancient times. And no wonder: if you know things that others don't, it gives you an enormous advantage. As the Chinese sage Mencius put it in 300 BC: *"Those who labour with their minds govern others; those who labour with their strength are governed by others."*

In most cultures, the first stirrings of education are associated with religion. Whether in ancient India or the monasteries of Europe, the emergence of a priestly class meant that the holy texts had to be studied and learnt, and that meant being able to read: the precepts of Pachomius, one of the fathers of early monasticism, state that if a novice is illiterate, *"he shall go at the first, third and sixth hours to someone who can teach and has been appointed for him... even if he does not want to he shall be compelled to read."* As far afield as China and the Aztec Empire, whose educational traditions had a more secular focus, teaching still centred on the rote learning of ancient texts. But this learning was rarely made widely available: though talented pupils from humble backgrounds might be lucky enough to gain some form of scholarship, it was the children of the nobility and the rich who were the primary beneficiaries, cementing the relationship between knowledge and power.

But the ability to read opened the door open to non-religious texts as well: the scribes and translators toiling through the Middle Ages in Christian cloisters and Muslim *madrasas* are the ones we must thank for much of what remains of the earliest writings of classical Greece and Rome. And it was a careful reading of the religious texts that eventually led to the Reformation, and the demand that individuals read the scripture for themselves and make their own judgments. This was bitterly opposed both by the Church and the governments whose power they supported, who were not slow to spot the challenge to their own authority: such was their concern about the loss of power that several early translators of the Bible were burnt at the stake for their trouble.

The urge to break from the stranglehold of religious thought eventually burst into the flowering of rational enquiry that became known as The Enlightenment – so named as its champions believed they were throwing light on the truth obscured by the religious ignorance of the Middle Ages. Though the origins of the movement go back to the first days of the 'scientific revolution' – kick-started by the heliocentric theory and the advent of printing technology – it came into its own in the 18th century, with writers and thinkers from Philadelphia to St Petersburg uniting in a self-styled "republic of letters". This republic was built on correspondence between public intellectuals known as *philosophes*, who – in the words of Immanuel Kant – "dared to know". They advocated science, secular thought, and the application of reason to the practical problems of the world, which lead directly to demands for political freedom of the type expressed in the American Declaration of Independence, and later the French Revolution.

Front and centre of the Enlightenment was the work of the *Encyclopédistes*, a group of some 150 members of the *philosophes* who from 1751 – under the leadership of Denis Diderot – started publishing a massive 20-million-word encyclopaedia with entries under 75,000 different subjects. If anything exemplified the desire to know what's ever been known, this was it. As Diderot confidently put it: *"The purpose of an encyclopaedia is to collect knowledge disseminated around the globe; to set forth its general system to the men with whom we live, and transmit it to those who will come after us, so that the work of preceding centuries will not become useless to the centuries to come; and so that our offspring, becoming better instructed, will at the same time become more virtuous and happy, and that we should not die without having rendered a service to the human race in the future years to come."* It is a stirring manifesto for the human project.

But for all their confidence in themselves, the Enlightenment scholars did not invent the idea of an encyclopaedia. The word itself seems to have been a misreading – or perhaps just a misunderstanding – of the phrase *enkýklios paideía*, which means 'complete instruction'. In Ancient Greece, this referred to the general course of study that a well-educated citizen was expected to have undergone (grammar, rhetoric, philosophy, arithmetic, music, geometry and astronomy). But during the Renaissance, scholars in Europe – inspired by the new spirit of humanism – took it to mean everything that could be learned, and from the late 16th century made various attempts to gather together the essence of human knowledge under the general title of 'encyclopaedia'. But in doing so, they were channelling a desire with roots much further back in time.

The earliest attempt that still survives is the *Naturalis Historia* of Pliny the Elder, a Roman statesman writing around 70 AD, which packed more than 20,000 subjects into its ten volumes, running to over a million words. In the early 7th century, the celebrated scholar St Isidore of Seville put together his *Etymologiae*, an enormous 20-volume work so comprehensive that some 1500 years later, the Vatican made him patron saint of the internet. Another monster was the *Suda Lexicon*, a 10th-century Byzantine work with 30,000 entries, but the grand-daddy of them all, outstripping even Diderot's *Encyclopédie*, was the giant 永樂大典 (*Yongle Dadian*) commissioned by the Ming dynasty's Yongle Emperor in 1403. Completed in just 5 years, its 11,095 volumes filled 40 cubic metres and ran to 370 million characters (the equivalent of some 250 million words), making it over five times longer than the *Encyclopaedia Britannica*.

But even with this cornucopia of knowledge available from antiquity, access was still limited by literacy. It's hard to estimate what the levels of literacy were in ancient times – guestimates put it at 5% for the population of Ancient Greece and 10% in the Roman Empire, but what's certain is that the ability to read was a luxury most people around the world could not afford until quite modern times – even in the most developed societies. And estimates of literacy in countries where better records exist are often simply based on the ability to write one's name on a marriage document, a yardstick that may wildly overestimate the ability to read, as many people who had learnt to write their name were in practice functionally illiterate. It is thought that even as late as 1820 only 12% of people around the world could read, and even in the UK – one of the most advanced societies of its day – it was barely more than 50%.

The 'rebirth' of learning ushered in by the Renaissance led to a gradual separation of schooling from religious training, but it wasn't until the 18th century that reading and the other two 'R's of 'Riting and 'Rithmetic – or 'Reckoning' as it was then known – came to be thought of as the basic skills required (although as religion was still a key part of education until the end of the 19th century, there were really four 'R's to contend with). Ironically religion did lead to a boom in reading, at least in Western Europe – but even so, those who could read were still in a tiny minority. Edmund Burke, the renowned 18th century politician and author, claimed in 1790 that the reading public numbered no more than 80,000 people – and though that may be a considerable underestimate, it's clear from the numbers of books sold in the Georgian period that the audience for books was small. The average print run for a book published in the 18th century was around 1500 copies; even Diderot only sold 4,250 copies of his *Encyclopédie*.

One reason for this was expense. Although printing substantially reduced the cost of books since there was no longer any need for hand-copying, printed books were still not cheap. In the early 19th century you could expect to pay nearly £100 in today's prices for a popular novel, and membership of a library could cost as much as gym membership does today: the annual fee was the equivalent of £400 – and you could still only borrow up to 20 books a year. The first wooden presses had only been able to produce about 25 pages an hour (still about ten times faster than the speediest scribe), but gradual improvements meant that speeds reached about 250 pages an hour by the time the first metal printing press appeared at the end of the 18th century. Ten years later the use of steam technology rapidly shot this rate up to 1000 pages an hour and the rotary presses introduced from the 1850s soon brought it to ten times that speed. This is reflected in the print runs of newspapers: the circulation of The Times rose from 5,000 in 1815 to 50,000 in the 1850's, and since then easier access to libraries and now the internet mean that the global illiteracy rate has dropped from 88% to 17%.

In the same way that your genome is a living record of the evolution of the human species, as well as what you are personally, so human history is a living record of what we know, and how we came to know it: welcome to the memome. Whether or not we choose to actively access it, this is a body of knowledge that represents an extraordinary wealth of detailed understanding about the nature of reality, a network of intelligence that exists independently of any individual. Wikipedia, the largest compendium of human knowledge to have ever existed, now has some 6 million articles in English alone, but publishes articles in over 300 other languages – taking the total to more than 55 million articles and nearly 30 billion words. No matter how much expertise a person might develop in a particular field, no single human could ever get close to knowing all of it.

A machine, however, perhaps could.

Soft machines

Somewhere in the late 1960s I became interested in a band called *The Soft Machine*. They were a hip jazz-fusion outfit with a progressive attitude and I liked their music. I bought several of their albums and even heard them play the Proms in the Albert Hall – when that was still a radical thing for a 'pop' group to do. But I never thought what the name meant, beyond the fact that it sounded cool. I didn't even know they'd named the band after an infamous book of the same name by William Burroughs. And it took even longer before I got round to thinking what he – and presumably they – had meant by the phrase: that along with every other form of life on our planet, the thing that we are – the form our bodies actually take – is in fact a 'soft machine'. We don't usually think like that because – even though we know our bodies are basically levers, wiring and plumbing – the idea that we might be a machine still seems intuitively wrong: our pliant softness, ability to have children and our sharp sense of consciousness appear completely at odds with the hard, mechanical stiffness we associate with machines. But are they?

The idea that humans might be no more than machines is not new, of course. Ahead of the game as ever, the Ancient Greeks were already onto the concept – even if they couldn't quite bring themselves to abandon the idea of a separate soul. But as the Epicureans taught it, the soul was still a material entity, made of atoms just like the rest of us – though they believed that the atoms of the soul were so fine and delicate that they permeated every part of the body. Descartes thought the soul was located in the pineal gland – but that apart, was convinced that the body was mechanical and that other animals were merely automata. This teaching did not go down well with his most famous pupil, the precocious Queen Christina of Sweden, who is said to have rebuffed him by pointing to a clock and regally demanding that he *"see to it that it produces offspring."* History does not record his response, perhaps because he died shortly afterwards – though it seems likely his death had more to do with having to rise each day at 5 am for the royal lessons than despair at her logic.

But without a soul, the puzzle has always been how to account for what Darwin called our 'god-like intellect'. Alfred Wallace, his younger collaborator, eventually gave up the struggle and plumped for the soul solution, writing that *"Nothing in evolution can account for the Soul of Man. The difference between Man and the other animals is unbridgeable... It is clear to me that the soul was a separate creation."* Despite the sophistication of modern scanning technology, however, we have yet to find one – and have no idea where we might even begin to look. But perhaps our total reliance on language is overcomplicating things for us. In his famous test of intelligence, the mathematician Alan Turing – the father of modern computer science – pointed out that our only hope of identifying intelligence would be through behaviour: we should consider a machine intelligent if it behaved in a way we would recognise as intelligent if we saw a 'natural' being behave that way – because the only way we make can judgments about people is through their behaviour.

An early experiment to test the evidence for Turing's assertion was carried out by Dr William Grey Walter. By the standards of the late 1940s, Dr Walter was a bit of an oddball. For one thing, he had a beard – something that definitely flagged you as a weirdo in those days. Left of centre, a jazz fan – even a bit of an anarchist – he was a trained neurophysiologist and a pioneer robotician whose professional interests also extended to medical diagnosis, forensic detection, marriage counselling, and even international diplomacy – and he had worked on automatic targeting technology during World War II. But despite sounding like a man who might have been partial to the odd reefer, he did more than almost anyone to show how surprisingly complex behaviour could emerge from a small number of brain cells, as long as they were provided with enough connections. And like the many other ways in which complexity can be shown to arise from simple origins, his elegant demonstration was a model of economy.

In part, this was because he had no choice: the technology of his time did not allow him to do anything more sophisticated. His prototypes consisted of two small battery-powered machines that he called *Machina Speculatrix* – affectionately known as Elmer and Elsie – that ran autonomously on three wheels and were programmed to move toward a bright light while avoiding any obstacles and returning back to their charging station when their battery power was running low. Due to their appearance and slow movement, they were soon also dubbed 'tortoises' – in part because of what Walter believed they "taught us" about our own behaviour. He was concerned to show that despite their apparent simplicity, these machines could exhibit complex behaviour that, were it an animal, would be recognised as self-awareness. This was particularly evident when the machines were presented with two or more lights to choose from – or a reflection in a mirror – when their movements would become erratic and indecisive in ways that, if seen in an animal, would be interpreted as hesitation.

We have come a long way from those early experiments now with neural networks and boid computer simulations, but the direction of travel has been clear for some time. In his 1990 book *The Age of Intelligent Machines*, Ray Kurzweil, Google's 'chief futurist', predicted a machine would be able to beat a human at chess by 2000, a prediction fulfilled in 1997 when Gary Kasparov, the reigning world chess champion, was beaten by IBM's Deep Blue computer – a feat that was trumped less than 20 years later when Google's DeepMind computer beat the reigning world Go champion Ke Jie, a much harder problem that experts had thought would take at least another decade. Even more impressive from the standpoint of an ordinary Joe, in 2011 IBM's Watson computer system beat two acknowledged champions of the quiz show *Jeopardy!* – winning the $1 million prize money in an open real-time competition that showed just how well AI could perform when connected to an unlimited data source.

Kurzweil argues that by 2045 the progress in artificial intelligence will be so great that humans will no longer be able to comprehend it, and that *"human life will be irreversibly transformed"* – an event he calls 'the singularity'. He takes this concept from the worlds of maths and physics, where it refers to a point where all previous rules and laws break down – at a point of infinite density, for example. The singularity that Kurzweil is talking about will be transformative for us in ways that we literally cannot – and will not – be able to imagine, as systems that are more intelligent than our own naturally-evolved mental processing capacities take over the running of almost everything around us.

But we humans have already witnessed a singularity. If we haven't noticed, it's because we've been part of it: but as far as the rest of the natural world was concerned, that point occurred when we acquired language – which was transformative for us and for everything else around us in ways that other life-forms cannot even imagine. For if you do not have language, by definition you cannot imagine what the ability to communicate as we humans do actually means. If it seems like anything at all other than extremely scary, the ability of humans to outsmart you at every step must seem little short of magical. No wonder other animals are so scared of us. They have absolutely no means of beating us at our own game, because they have no idea what that game is.

Language was humanity's Helen Keller moment, and the rest has just followed naturally. AI has been quietly working its way into all of our lives, almost without us noticing it. In many ways AI already runs our world, uncomplainingly performing complex tasks ranging from financial investment and medical decisions to driving vehicles and exploring space. Few achievements are more impressive than voice recognition, which is now so good that it comes as standard in your phone, in multiple languages, and really does work. Just 50 years ago, when the first voice recognition devices were being trialled, this would have seemed like science fiction. If anything clearly demonstrates the essentially digital nature of language, this is it. Machine translation may have a way to go before it reaches flawless human standards, but it is surely just a matter of time.

To the extent that it is not yet perfect, the argument can be made that what's 'human' about us is the bit that AI can't do. But, like the "God of the gaps" fallacy, that's to look at it the wrong way round. The question we should be asking is not *"What can humans do that AI cannot?"* but *"Why would we think that what AI can't yet do is not, ultimately, a calculation?"* If what our brain does – what our mind does – is to spot connections, see patterns and solve problems, what part of that process might not be amenable to 'artificial' intelligence? And how might 'natural' intelligence usefully be distinguished from it? It's not about 'reducing' human thought to a mechanical process: like the debate about the soul, there is nothing to reduce. Whether we have a soul or not, we remain the same. Whether our thinking is 'mechanical' or not, it doesn't change. The only thing that changes is how we understand it. And that changes everything.

In fact it has been doing so for a very long time: writing is the first form of artificial intelligence, a prosthetic memory that allows us to retain and recall information that might otherwise be lost to us – a prosthesis extended still further by printing and the internet. Education is artificial intelligence – allowing us to get up to speed with what's been discovered and thought through history instead of having to try and work it all out for ourselves. Whether you are a human, an octopus or a worm, the skill at the heart of intelligence is pattern recognition. That involves looking at the available data – whether directly sensory or 'artificial' in the form of records – and deciding what action to take based on particular needs (whether the need to find food, or the match for a particular face in a crowd). The fact that we have now invented logical steps to make these determinations for us – which is all an algorithm is – is the reason why machines can take decisions based on pattern-recognition. You are only as good as your algorithm.

But even if the idea of being a machine makes us uncomfortable, there's another sense in which we can think of ourselves as 'soft' machines. The vast body of knowledge of which each one of us is the beneficiary – just by virtue of speaking a language and learning about the culture we are born into – is much like the software that computers rely on to function: we may be born with the basic 'software' in the form of instincts that enable us to survive, but the education we obtain as we grow is a continual upgrade of the programmes that run us, providing the instructions we need to function in a particular human environment. As we absorb information every day in the form of new memes, we're downloading knowledge which affects our behaviour just as surely as a new version of an old operating system changes the behaviour of a computer. If sex is about downloading genetic data that fits the digital key of our gametes, education is about downloading memetic data that fits the digital key of our minds.

The World Brain

The writer HG Wells made a number of grim predictions that came true in his lifetime – among them the use of tanks on the battlefield, the development of biological and nuclear weapons, and the start of World War II. But in 1938 he published a book called The World Brain, which laid out his ideas for a new 'world encyclopaedia' which he hoped would allow all the available information in the world to be gathered together so that *"any student, in any part of the world, will be able to sit with his projector in his own study at his or her convenience to examine any book, any document, in an exact replica"*. He was less sure how this could be accomplished with the technology of the time (the computer had yet to be invented), but he could nonetheless see that this must be the next phase in the project to spread knowledge of everything that was known as widely as possible – a process which he saw as a vital step on the road to achieving world peace, the best guarantor of civilization.

Though with hindsight this can be read as a prediction of the internet and the World Wide Web, it was really just the latest version of the desire not just to catalogue and summarize all human knowledge, but to gather together its source material – a desire that dates back at least as far as the Great Library of Alexandria, built in Egypt during the third century BC. This was a unique collection of manuscript scrolls, estimated to have numbered as many as half a million texts at its peak – covering everything from mathematics, astronomy and physics to philosophy, history and poetry. Although large libraries and archives are known from previous cultures (the treasure-house of cuneiform tablets excavated from the Royal Library of Ashurbanipal is a notable early example), this was the first known attempt to consciously gather together all the books in the known world, with the express intention that the library should contain *"the writings of all men as far as they were worth serious attention."* According to one account, a legend inscribed above its doors read *"Place of the cure of the soul."*

It's an interesting phrase. Whether we think of the soul as an eternal entity that outlives the body or simply the sharp end of a complicated biological calculation, there's no doubt that a thirst for knowledge has united our more curious minds throughout history. Though curiosity may sometimes kill the cat (Pliny the Elder died in Pompei when his desire to see the effects of the eruption of Vesuvius in 70 AD got the better of him), the satisfaction that brings it back is the cure our wisest souls are constantly in search of. And the satisfaction they seek is the resolution of contradictions between pieces of information that do not seem to fit together – for as with the current conundrum over the theory of quantum gravity, the cognitive dissonance that stems from having to accept two apparently incompatible systems is otherwise uncomfortable to live with.

The Great Library of Alexandria was housed in two large buildings as part of what was known as the *Mouseion*, or 'House of the Muses' (from which our word 'museum' comes). It was in effect a university complex – a centre of knowledge which in addition to providing storage for all the manuscripts, was also home to a number of salaried scholars. Besides cataloguing and indexing the texts, it was the scholars' job to make copies of new books acquired from other sources (the originals were often kept and a copy returned to the owner) and the library was also able to make a useful income by copying its own books for other libraries and rich patrons.

But although reputed to contain the greatest store of knowledge in the ancient world – much visited by scholars and other intellectuals – we have very little detail about what the library actually contained, as it was completely destroyed in two separate incidents. Julius Caesar was the first culprit, burning down the main library building while trying to set fire to a besieging fleet in 48 BC, and what remained was finished off in 391AD when the surviving facilities were ransacked on the orders of Theophilus, bishop of Alexandria, in an attempt to root out all vestiges of pagan teachings. This wanton act of ignorance is often attributed to Muslims during the 7th century Arab invasion, but it seems certain that the Christians had already done their work for them.

The destruction of a library of manuscript documents is a much greater loss than any losses that have occurred since the age of printing: to the extent than there were no other copies of many of the texts, the knowledge that went up in flames in Alexandria was irreplaceable, and significantly set back the advancement of human understanding. The scale of the loss is clear from the many books mentioned in the writings of ancient authors that have not survived – and while the disappearance of literary texts like the much-praised poetry of Sappho is undoubtedly regrettable, the science was critical. Among the more important books of mathematical scholarship we know were lost include the works of Aristarchus of Samos: another 18 centuries were to pass before someone else was able to produce a work suggesting reasons why the sun was at the centre of the solar system – time that would have been much better spent building on that knowledge rather than recycling ancient ignorance.

But the story of a precious and hard-won store of knowledge being destroyed by fire, war or pillage has sadly been repeated many times through history – with most falling victim to some form of religious intolerance. Among the worst examples are the Mahavihara Library at Nalanda, India, a great centre of Buddhist learning destroyed by Turkic Muslim invaders in the 12th century; the Imperial Library of Constantinople, one of the last great storehouses of Greek and Roman knowledge, sacked by the gallant knights of the fourth crusade instead of going to Jerusalem; the *Bayt al-Hikma* or House of Wisdom in Bagdad, a major intellectual centre of the golden age of Islam destroyed by Mongol invaders in the mid-thirteenth century, and perhaps most painful of all, the unique Maya codices of the Yucatán, condemned to be burnt as 'works of the devil' by the Spanish conquistadors, who coolly noted that the surviving Maya people *"regretted their destruction to an amazing degree, which caused them much affliction."*

I have around 2000 books on the shelves of my study. Just think of what that means in terms of the time spent writing them alone. Leaving aside how long it took to have the experiences that enabled each book to be written (which might be anything up to a lifetime), we can conservatively say that each and every book represents at least a year of someone's life committed to writing it. That means my shelves are holding at least 2000 years of human consciousness, containing ideas that can I can benefit from in just the time it takes to read them.

That's still a long commitment – if it takes around 8 hours to read the average book, 2000 books is about 5 years' worth of solid reading. But it's still many thousand times more efficient than having to go through the experiences that went into them, even assuming you would ever reach the same conclusions.

Now consider that the British Library, a major copyright library, holds over 13 million books. Given that the most one person could hope to get through in a lifetime of non-stop reading would be around 30,000 books, that's a quite astonishing resource. But that's not all. Their archive also holds some 60 million patents for inventions that people may have spent a lifetime developing. If language allows us to talk to one another, written records turbocharge the process. Writing is an artificial medium we have been using for the last 5,000 years to enhance our memories – the practical limit for the size of human heads having been reached about 250,000 years ago. And the internet has now taken that process of artificial enhancement to a new frontier.

Even though printing was both a step change in the availability of knowledge and a guarantee that enough copies would survive any future destruction of libraries (there are long lists of books lost to us from the ancient world, but very few titles that have been lost since printing came onstream), the internet has now vastly extended the trick of language. These days people can share not just thoughts and ideas, but pictures, sounds and images of what they are doing, allowing them to be seen and experienced in real time anywhere on the planet. Whereas you were once limited to the information you could get from your immediate family and friends, now you can tap directly into everything that's ever been known. Instantaneously. HG Wells' vision of The World Brain is right here, right now, realised within the lifetimes of his grandchildren.

The quest to make knowledge more widely available has brought us to the point where anyone who has finished secondary education knows things that it took millennia for us to discover – even something as obvious to us now as the length of a year, so crucial for early agriculture. Then there's the more technical knowledge we've picked up since the industrial revolution, knowledge that's transforming our lives to the point that it's quite possible to claim that the first person to live to be two hundred years old may already have been born. What we have created is a body of knowledge that hugely exceeds the sum of its parts – even if no one individual can ever hope to know anything but a small fraction of what is known. It is no longer just our genes that we pass on to future generations – language has created a world where all of us can plug into the cumulative understanding of humanity, a world where that knowledge can be accessed and applied effortlessly.

Let us see where logic of that thought now takes us – and how knowledge might be turned into wisdom.

WISDOM: Raising the Game

"The dream is real... Failure to realize it is the only unreality."
— Toni Cade Bambara

Imagine Piece

It's an interesting quirk of the English language that the letters which form the word *'sword'* can be rearranged to spell *'words'*. There's nothing odd or deliberate about this (any more than the fact that the letters of the word *'sacred'* can be rearranged to spell *'scared'*) but it's a useful metaphor for one of the key functions of language: its ability to offer a route to peace that avoids violence. All animals compete over resources; it's the struggle at the heart of the process of evolution. And with no effective way to signal subtler meanings, that struggle is usually settled by physical force — or the threat of it. But language allows us to negotiate, to find a compromise that lets us satisfy competing demands and manage resources without having to come to blows. In giving us a way to tag and share awareness, it provides a means of endlessly refining our ability to put ourselves in the position of others, the crucial imaginative leap without which no true communication can ever take place.

As we have seen, language is at the heart of what makes us human. It's the one thing that allows us to penetrate the wall of incomprehension that would otherwise separate us, leaving us trapped in our own skulls, forever uncertain of the motives of others. Language is what allows us to become 'us' — to recognise that we are in it together, engaged in the same game and better off working with each other than suffering on our own. Just because we can talk doesn't mean we won't fight, of course. The strong are always tempted to bully the weak, just as the downtrodden and oppressed are always driven to seek redress. But the default mode of the group is peace, not war. We fight with those we consider enemies, not friends; whether it be family, tribe, village, town, county or country, we give our loyalty to 'us'. And the thing we most want for ourselves is peace – even if we've so often had to fight for it.

In 2007, I was asked to supervise the translation of the phrase 'Imagine Peace' into twenty-four different languages for inscription on the well of the Imagine Peace Tower in Reykjavik, Iceland. It was an unexpectedly challenging task. First of all, with over six thousand languages still in use around the world, there was the question of which ones to choose. With both a historical perspective and visual impact in mind, some early suggestions included ancient scripts such as Egyptian hieroglyphs (the British Museum even supplied a translation into Akkadian cuneiform, which looks like this: 𒂍𒍑𒁹𒊑 𒄩𒈦𒋾𒈨), but in the end it was felt best to stick with living languages to be sure that the translations reflected contemporary thinking. The final choice was based on the broadest possible selection of world languages and scripts.

That settled, you might think the translation work itself wouldn't be that time-consuming – after all, how difficult can it be to translate just two words? – but the reality was quite different. Just because an idea can be expressed by a single word in one language, that doesn't mean it can always be translated by a single word in another. Every language has its own way of representing ideas, and the choice of words will be greatly influenced by context. Both words 'imagine' and 'peace' can have different resonances and historical contexts in different cultures, and the concepts behind them reflect assumptions and expectations which can't necessarily be expressed in two words in another language. It turns out that they can't in most cases, in fact.

Wanting to 'double-source' the translations, my first thought was to play safe and ask both academics and diplomats to submit translations for each language, so that we could get both a scholarly and a pragmatic perspective as a basis for comparison. I approached university departments and embassies for help, but soon discovered that there were issues with both. The academics were generally too cautious, preferring 'explanatory' translations that tended to be stiff or wordy. On the other hand, it turned out that despite their other skills, diplomats are often not great linguists – though they may be good 'at' languages, their political allegiances usually mean that they are rarely good 'with' them. Ultimately I had to turn to poets and artists for more fluent translations that better reflected the nuances of the original.

It still wasn't an easy thing to do. Even in English, "Imagine Peace" is not an entirely transparent statement. What kind of peace are we talking about, and in what way are we to imagine it? It's not quite the same thing as asking someone to 'Imagine yellow' or even 'Imagine a unicorn'. Is it simply encouraging abstract speculation, or inviting more active consideration? The key to understanding it lies in the lyrics to the song *Imagine*, from which it derives. For the phrase "Imagine Peace" is not just some vague, wistful dream of an ideal future – it's an invocation, an instruction to positively visualize a world at peace, without countries, wars or religions. This is important, especially in translation, as the choice of words needs to reflect that.

It's also interesting that the phrase was originally coined by Yoko Ono, as English is not her native language. In fact, it's quite tricky to express the concept elegantly in Japanese. The standard translation in Japan, 「平和な世界を想像してごらん」, back-translates literally as "Try imagining a peaceful world." It's not the only language which has to add a word or two to clarify the meaning. Chinese also feels the need to specify that it is 'world' peace we are talking about, whereas Inuktitut back-translates as "Let us have peace amongst each other". With Russian, on the other hand, in the modern language the word МИР (Mir) conveniently means both 'world' and 'peace'. Then in French there's that subtle difference between 'paix' (tranquillity) and 'la paix' which refers to the absence of war – and in both Hebrew and Arabic, where the word commonly used for 'imagine' has a more abstract sense, the word 'dream' better expresses the meaning of actively wishing for peace. Let's not forget that even in English there's a distinction between the meaning of 'peace' in phrases such as 'peace of mind', 'keeping the peace' and 'war and peace'.

With some of the translations it took weeks to fix on a final version, with back and forth discussions between several parties. All this "just for two words!" So does that mean that it's an impossible concept to translate? Not at all. It just reinforces the point that all languages say things in different ways, and are only ever one way of expressing the thought that lies behind them. As we saw in the first chapter, it's important to keep in mind that there's no 'original' language. Any expression of anything in any language is already a translation of a thought that existed as an idea before it was put into words. That thought will be expressed in the context of a particular language and culture in a way that makes sense to the people who are part of that community – and though a way can always be found to translate the meaning into another language, the exact phrasing will not necessarily match at the level of words. It all depends.

What doesn't depend is the concept itself. Whether or not we can yet see how it could work out in practice, it's an idea we can all recognize as desirable. It's no accident that the song *Imagine* touches people right around the world. When John Lennon wrote the lyrics, he was aware he was going to be labelled a dreamer. *A world without countries and religion? Nothing to live or die for??* How crazy is that? Pretty crazy, when you sit down to think exactly how that could come to pass in the world we actually live in. But not crazy enough to stop many people thinking about it. So much so, in fact, that *Imagine* is consistently voted one of the most popular songs on the planet – and as President Jimmy Carter once pointed out, in many countries it's played at significant national ceremonies almost as much as the local national anthem. That makes it a world anthem, of sorts.

Because the whole point is that Lennon is *not* the only one. He is not the only one who dreams of such things, though there may be some who still don't, or can't yet bring themselves to do so. Many of the biggest changes in the way we live and organize ourselves have been kick-started by dreamers, people who dared to say and believe that things could be better, and were ready to argue their case, protest, fight and even die for their cause. Think of the abolition of slavery. Think of the emancipation of women. Think of Gandhi. Think of Martin Luther King. Such dreams take time to come into being – the world has to be ready for them. But when the time is right, it is words that provide the impetus: and world peace is an idea whose time is upon us.

As we look at the ongoing regional violence around the globe, the terrorism threatening the heart of Europe and growing tension between the global superpowers, that may still seem an impossible, even a naïve dream. But every idea can sound crazy until it actually comes about – at which point it can suddenly seem entirely obvious. It took centuries for the idea of democracy to take root in Europe, and many more for full emancipation to be achieved. Until the middle of the 18th century, the idea of abolishing slavery would have seemed impractical, unworkable and slightly mad – but today we are astonished that it was ever tolerated. Even just a century ago, the idea that women should be given the vote was still considered unthinkable. But these things came to be. Progress does happen, however slowly – and what drives it is the power of language to persuade us by giving voice to our thoughts.

Though life is still difficult for many people – even in our most advanced societies – things are greatly improved for most of us alive today compared to almost any other time in history. Thanks largely to the political freedoms our forefathers achieved, almost everyone in the 'free' world enjoys a standard of living only kings would have known just a few generations ago. We may not all live in palaces, but in other ways our lives are more comfortable, richer and safer than even our grandparents could have imagined – whether in terms of the variety of food we eat, the ease of travel both at home and abroad, the quality and quantity of entertainment and information available to us, access to effective medical treatment, or our ability to communicate instantly across the world. Not only that: unlike previous generations, most people in democratic societies today have never had to go to war, or even felt the threat of it.

All that remains is to extend those advantages to all the other people we share our planet with. As trade and technology slowly allow us to expand the circle of 'us' from family to tribe, from village to town, and from county to country, we are now pushing up against the last remaining barrier. In reality, we already function like a global community, with supplies of goods and services connecting us around the world as if we were a single country. We just need to acknowledge that reality, end the ancient enmities between nation states, and find a way for the whole world to live together in peace – as we have done within our own communities.

And since we've already agreed to do it, how hard can that be?

Cashing the cheque

Martin Luther King remains one of the more famous dreamers of recent history. But few people seem to remember that when he arrived in Washington 50 years ago to make his famous "I have a dream" speech, it wasn't just a dream he'd come to talk about. As he explained in the preamble, he had a far more practical goal in mind. He'd come "to cash a cheque" – to demand that the government and the country make good on a promissory note they'd signed off on when the nation was founded, in the form of the US Constitution. Far from being merely an impassioned plea, his words were actually a legal challenge. It's a powerful speech, addressing America's clear failure to extend to all of its citizens – black and white – the rights to life, liberty and the pursuit of happiness that its great contract with its own people explicitly promises.

He was able to make this challenge because, despite the horrors of its formative years, America still holds a unique place in human history as the first – and as yet the only – country founded for a principle rather than a prince. And the principle the Americans fought for, later enshrined in their Constitution, is the principle of the equality of all before the law: the idea that all citizens should be free to follow whatever path they choose, regardless of creed, breed or birth – and not just because they were born into the right skin, the right family or the right place. It is this principle, however imperfectly it may function, that is the true essence of the American Dream – not some non-negotiable notion of a particular lifestyle. It's about potential and opportunity: America's enduring appeal and strength is based on that. It's that potential and opportunity which is symbolized by the Statue of Liberty, given to America by the people of France in 1876 to mark the 100th anniversary of US Independence and to celebrate the ongoing history of their own imperfect revolution, inspired in so many ways by America.

But here's the thing: this is not an aspiration that's unique to America. It may be unique in the sense that no other country has succeeded in realizing it, but it's not unique in terms of what people all round the world aspire to and want. We'd all like to live lives in which we were free to pursue our own notion of happiness, but that's not yet an option for most of the members of our species around the planet. For those of us living comfortable democratic lives in the West that may be easy to forget: but for so many of those for whom this isn't the case, America still can still seem to offer a beacon of hope, something to be emulated and admired.

To get a sense of how close that American Dream is to all of us, try substituting "the world" for the patriotic phrases like "our nation" often used by US Presidents in their best speeches about their aspirations for America: you'll soon discover this applies to all humans living in all societies everywhere. That this is so is recognized in the 1948 Universal Declaration of Human Rights, one of the very first documents signed into law by the United Nations. Raising the achievement of the United States' own constitution to a global level, this is a document drawn up and agreed on by all the nations of the world as a benchmark for human society, the minimum set of standards that we have all agreed should be guaranteed for everyone living on our planet. Given how little attention is paid to it, that's worth restating: *by virtue of their membership of the United Nations, every government of every country in the world has publicly agreed on a set of rights that are guaranteed for everyone living on our planet.* That's not just an aspiration – it's a legal commitment. We've all signed off on it.

And yet, over half a century later, we are little closer to honouring this commitment than America was to honouring its constitutional cheque when Dr King called them on it in 1963. Why is that? Well, we have explored some of those reasons in this book. The seductive traps of culture, religion and identity, and the sheer dragweight of tradition are still powerful barriers to acknowledging that we are all the same people trying to solve the same problems in the same limited space. Recognizing that fact requires a fundamental change in the way the world has seen itself through most of its history, and such fundamental changes don't always come quickly, or easily.

Let's not forget it took over a century from the foundation of America for slavery to be abolished, and for the principle of equality for all to be enacted. It took another century before people began to take racial equality seriously, and two more generations before they could bring themselves to elect a black President – even if he is, as he once endearingly described himself, just a 'mutt'. Nor can anyone pretend, especially with the resurgence of white supremacists and ongoing incidents of police violence against African Americans, that this marks the end of racial discrimination in America. You can't eradicate a culture that evolved over centuries in just a few decades.

But that doesn't mean that the struggle is not worth the effort, or that defeats along the way will not pay off in the end. It's never a question of just changing the culture: there are real 'interests' at stake, and their beneficiaries do not usually give them up without a fight. History is littered with the bodies of those who dared to oppose them, even if their name and fame live on. It's almost as if the best we can do is to take two steps forward, one step back. Even the famous Magna Carta, the first attempt to legally constrain the power of an English monarch, was soon set aside – King John reneged on the deal almost before the wax had dried on his royal seal, and the abuses of power that had sparked the revolt rumbled on.

Fifty years later, the rebel baron Simon de Montfort may have finally succeeded in calling a parliament based on the Magna Carta's principles – a much more significant event in determining the future course of democracy – but his dream was brutally cut short. Within a matter of months de Montfort was killed by conservative forces loyal to the king, his body cut into pieces, and his head presented to the wife of Lord Mortimer, a leading supporter of the king, with – in a gruesome mediaeval touch – his severed testicles either slung over his nose, or, in another account, stuffed into his mouth.

We should perhaps not be so surprised at that: wanton brutality meted out to those who lose out in the power struggle of a hierarchy is not an activity restricted to humans. Frans de Waal, a careful long-term observer of the behaviour of our closest cousins the great apes, has described how feuding chimps will 'emasculate' their rivals for the position of alpha male by biting into their scrotums and squeezing out the contents. You don't need language to work out the symbolic force of such an action; and to that extent it is all the more remarkable that we have managed to restrain our biological instincts to the point where such behaviour now revolts us, even if it is still only a few short generations behind us. For that, we also have to thank the power of words.

But despite de Montfort's grisly fate, within a generation a representative parliament was finally appointed by Edward I, son of the king in whose name de Montfort had been killed, establishing a model for all those that followed. That's important, because it set a recognised standard, an officially sanctioned forum for debating and deciding laws. Laws may not always be followed or enforced, but they encode an agreement about acceptable behaviour, and form a benchmark against which actions can later be judged. Records of such legal codes go back almost to the beginning of writing – and the establishment of laws to limit the power of kings and emperors, though not as explicit as in the recent history of Europe and America, is a theme that runs through history.

Even as far back as the 6th century BC, the Akkadian King Cyrus the Great proclaimed the "Charter of Freedom of Mankind" which laid out laws for the fair treatment of other races and cultures, freeing slaves and others held against their will. The Romans made the law the basis of their Republic, which did away with kings. In China, the edicts of Confucius laid down the principles for moral behaviour which all were bound to follow – even the emperor. All societies at all times have found it necessary to use laws to limit the ability of the strong and powerful to take advantage of the weak. Like democracy itself, the development of a system of laws that all members of a group agree to follow is what biologists call an 'evolutionarily stable' strategy, enabling us to codify and refine the arrangements we have agreed without descending once more into chaos.

For all its faults, the great strength of democracy over any other political system is that it allows us to have open discussions about contentious issues, and reach a majority decision about the best course of action based on reasoned argument rather than physical violence. It's the process in which we most clearly see the power of language at work, the power of words over the sword. That's why it is so important that laws exist which, at least on paper, prevent people from doing things we have agreed should no longer be allowed – even if we are slower to actually stop doing them. It was the force of law which fuelled Martin Luther King's argument, and in the end it was unanswerable. No, you won't always be able to enforce laws immediately, and perhaps never enforce them perfectly. But it is a much better situation than having no laws at all, or being subject to arbitrary edicts by an unaccountable tyrant.

This is the ladder we have been slowly climbing up. Nothing has changed except that we have now come to the top rung. The history of every part of the world echoes with the din of struggles between groups with interests they wish to protect. And mostly that struggle has been resolved through war. Every region of the globe is stained with the blood of its 'warring states' period. Because there are only two ways to resolve a conflict of interest – to use physical violence until one side yields through fear, pain or both; or to talk it out until one side prevails through persuasion before a jury of their peers, be it in parliament, court or simply by winning over public opinion. The former process favours strength over intelligence, because strength always thinks it can do what it likes, and will usually try that option first. But ultimately, that only causes intelligence to get smarter – and we are now getting close to the point where we can finally cash the cheque that's been issued in our names both by the UN Charter and the Declaration of Human Rights. Because above and beyond the fact that we've promised to do it, there's actually not much choice left out there.

War is over

Whether we're ready to acknowledge it or not, we are now witnessing the end game of the 'warring states' era of the planet. Almost every country with a long enough history – and many with much shorter ones – has fought brutal and lengthy internal wars between smaller local states until one eventually prevailed. America itself had to endure a bloody civil war less than a hundred years after achieving independence. And even once established, nation states have fought for centuries over their territorial ambitions.

During the last century there were two ruinously expensive 'world' wars conducted on a global scale – even if Mao Zedong was more accurate when he referred to them as the European Civil Wars, colonial disputes over territory that were mainly fought at home. But post World War II, things are different. It is no longer possible for modern nation states to have another all-out military struggle for control of the planet and its resources. There are three main reasons for that, one conceptual and two that are practical. And we need to face up to them, understand the implications, and act accordingly.

The conceptual reason is that the world is no longer the same size it once was. Back in 1600, when the first British seafarer made it to Japan, the journey had taken him 18 months – and he was lucky to have survived. But within the foreseeable future we will be able to travel 50 million miles to Mars and back in the same time or less – and with a much better prospect of survival. For most of us living in the 'developed' world it is now possible to travel to almost anywhere on our planet within the space of twenty-four hours – and for no more than the price of a few weeks' work. Even as recently as sixty years ago – within the lifetimes of many people – that would have been quite unthinkable for an ordinary person, for whom the only opportunity to travel abroad would have been in times of war.

Not much more than a century before that, and for the rest of human history, most people's ability to travel was limited by how far they could walk. In 1788, when George III left Windsor Castle to take the fashionable waters of the spa at Cheltenham, it took as long as 10 hours to travel the 100 miles – in the best and most comfortable form of transport available at the time. For commoners wanting to travel that distance, the journey would have taken up to three days. The evolution of transport technology has literally shrunk the world to the size of a day's travel, a span well within the traditional boundaries of a single tribe – and with nearly half the population of the world now potentially connected via social media, we can be aware of events happening all round the globe almost as they happen. In terms of our conceptual understanding, the planet has effectively become one place. To the current generation living in this wired-up global village, the idea of going to war in your own backyard increasingly makes no sense.

But even if it did, two practical reasons make it impossible. First of all, nations with nuclear weapons can no longer settle things by war: to do so would be to risk total annihilation. In terms of direct conflict, war between them is now over. They may talk the talk, but they aren't walking the walk, and never will. 'Wars' still go on, of course, but despite their desperate horror they are essentially side-shows, internal disputes and regional conflicts with the character of asymmetric police operations. They are not wars in the conventional sense, because they are not conflicts in which the full military might of the major powers is committed; no significant geo-political interests are at stake. Through history, war has generally been waged between adversaries who are evenly-matched (at least in their own eyes), who believe they have a reasonable chance of winning, and who will use every and all means at their disposal to defeat their opponents. But we have reached the end of that road. The force that science has now made available to us is so deadly that we would destroy ourselves utterly and devastate the planet if we were to use it to its full extent.

And we've been to the brink of that. 50 years ago in Cuba, there was a real possibility that the situation would spill into nuclear war, and we blinked. We blinked because both sides calculated that the damage the other party would be able to inflict was not worth the potential gain. The odds involved in that calculus of risk have only worsened in the inter-vening decades, and remain an unanswerable argument for retaining nuclear weapons. Atomic bombs are the big sticks that allow us to speak softly – the threat that any use of nuclear weapons would be swiftly coun-tered by an equal or more deadly force stays the hand of those who might otherwise not hesitate to use them. And when you add to that the vast escalation in the size of nuclear payloads since Cuba – modern weapons have warheads with an explosive force many hundreds of times greater than the two bombs dropped on Japan in 1945, and both the US and Russia have developed weapons several thousand times larger – the stark reality of Mutually Assured Destruction becomes all too obvious. We cannot go to war in any meaningful sense any more. The risks are just too great.

This is the reality of the situation we find ourselves in. It may not be the best solution to the problem of world peace, or the one we might wish for – but like the flawed structure of the human eyeball, it is the one that we actually have. And just like our inefficient eyeball, it has worked out quite well for us. Though horrific proxy wars are still conducted by 'conventional' means, we have had no substantial or unrestrained use of force between the 'great powers' since Hiroshima and Nagasaki, and there are unlikely to be any going forward. It is very hard to imagine a scenario where nuclear disarmament would actually lead to a better situ-ation – its advocates have yet to explain why a nuclear-free world would not immediately revert to a 'conventional' state of war over territory and resources. Not only that: if it were ever possible to get an agreement to eliminate nukes, the genie is out of the bottle. You cannot uninvent nuclear weapons. Sooner or later, someone would make one again.

This is a new situation for humanity, which has always settled its scores in blood. Whether the Wars of the Roses, the American Civil War, the Warring States periods in Japan and China or the two 'World' wars in the 20th century, the resolution of conflict and the unification of territories under a new ruler has usually taken place by force, with one side com-pelled to surrender and accept terms. Where that has not eventually led to further conflict, the resultant peace has generally enabled – and required – disputes to be settled by other means. Laws are enacted and then applied by a professional judiciary, and enforced as necessary by a civilian militia (which we call 'the police') acting on behalf of the ruling authority. And the more democratically accountable that ruling authority becomes, the easier that system is to live with. Once established within any given society, it's proved to be a stable arrangement: democracies rarely go to war with each other. And as the Mexican standoff between countries with nuclear weapons means the 'great powers' have no choice but to remain at peace, we now have a unique opportunity – even an obligation and a necessity – to ratchet that principle up a notch and apply it to the whole world.

The other practical reason why war is no longer feasible is this: the main problems that now confront us are global issues which can only be dealt with effectively at the planetary level – so we are going to have to find a way to settle our differences in order to resolve them. Even without considering pandemics, the looming crises around climate change, energy and resource management, and imbalances in the global economy affect us all, and will not respond to piecemeal action by individual nations. Global warming cannot be tackled by one country acting alone; nor can we adequately regulate transnational financial institutions or manage dwindling natural resources at the national level.

This is especially true for the environment, which has no natural borders. Pollution in one country affects the whole world, and whether or not climate change is mainly driven by human activity, it seems certain that dramatic steps will need to be taken in the near future to deal with its effects. And if we get to the stage where decisions have to be made to radically curtail the use of fossil fuels or – more likely – adopt global engineering solutions because we have left things too late, we will need an efficient mechanism that allows us to act decisively as a species. You cannot save the planet in your own backyard.

The economy is also something that now needs to be considered and managed globally – as it already is by the institutions that manipulate it. If we are to prevent or at least mitigate the excesses that brought world markets to their knees in recent years, we cannot rely on limited action at the national level. Unless the appropriate controls are formulated and applied internationally, investors and corporations will once again find ways to exploit the loopholes between jurisdictions that allow them to avoid paying their fair share. Energy sources, too, will have to be radically rethought. Though fracking technology may offer the opportunity to extend our dependence on fossil fuels for a few decades, even at the most optimistic estimates it can deliver just another 100 years of energy supply, and only at the risk of a terrible cost to the environment. That may be long enough to see out those of us alive at the moment, but are we really going to be that short-sighted? When we factor in the likely increase in demand from emerging economies, we will eventually have no choice but to look at the problem from a sustainable global perspective.

This reality is in effect recognized by the existence of the various global 'G' groups that have been slowly proliferating since the mid-1970s, but apart from the difficulty that they are not properly representative – even if the numbers are slowly creeping upwards – they cannot take decisions which are binding on their members, let alone the rest of the world, because there are no voting powers. And as a self-appointed group with common interests and no motivation to consider the needs of the wider world, they are increasingly out of tune with the times. Accountability is the watchword of our social-media-savvy era, and in a world that cannot go to war – one in which we have no choice but to learn to live with each other – we need a global forum that can both demand and deliver it.

Coming together

The idea of uniting the world under a single umbrella is not a new one, of course: every aspiring empire from the Akkadians onward has tried to extend its rule to the boundaries of the known world – even Hitler was hopeful that his Reich would one day span the globe. Genghis Khan's Mongol Empire was probably the largest land empire in history, though in more modern times the prize for occupying other people's territory must surely go to the British, who managed to invade or establish a military presence in all but 22 countries of the world – if not quite all at the same time. But any empire won by force is bound to fail when its grip on power eventually (and inevitably) slackens, and a new generation fights their way to the top – either the children of those who have suffered under the yoke of empire, or simply those that spot an opportunity. This has been the human way throughout history, and probably through most of prehistory as well. Rival groups, be they villages, towns, provinces or states only usually come together when the alternative is worse; despite the best efforts of philosophers, union is generally born more of necessity than idealism.

And it is necessity that knocks at our door now. As a species we may have usually preferred to give war a chance, but even if we still wanted to, war is no longer able to take us any further. There are no military solutions when the outcome is Mutually Assured Destruction – and the consequences of a nuclear confrontation would certainly be mutual, assured and very destructive. But the world no longer has to be 'won' to become as one. In fact, it's much more likely to become and stay 'one' when we are persuaded by words, not the sword. Most of the major countries in the world have now come to at least recognise the principle of democracy, even if its citizens are not always fully enfranchised. Within democratic nations it is taken for granted that decisions should be made by representatives chosen by vote, people who can be removed from office if they ignore the will of the electorate. Democracies reject the notion that any single person or organization should have absolute control over their people while ignoring their wishes: and the evidence from the Arab Spring and elsewhere is that people do not willingly accept tyranny in countries where they feel their rights are being denied. So the stage is already set for taking the democratic principle to the next stage.

Given how the world actually is, it's the boundaries of our perceptions that are out of kilter. We're happy enough living in countries where what once were small fiefdoms and provinces are now governed by a single, central, elected administration, so why would we not be willing to scale that natural process up a level and accept the same idea for a world body – a form of global government – which could use the power of language rather than force to raise, discuss and decide on issues that affect us all? Such a body would function much as governments do within any other democracy. A chamber of representatives would debate and then vote on issues that concern the whole world, just as national parliaments debate and vote on issues that concern their countries.

Would this be a perfect system of governing the world and organizing human life on the planet? No – it would be as messy and frustrating as democratic processes are at any level of government around the world. Would it be better than the current system of covert threats, dodgy alliances, military posturing and proxy wars? There can be no doubt about that. It may yet be a long and tricky road before we reach that point – but unless we want to destroy ourselves, we no longer have any alternative but to go there.

Some people worry that talk of a world government is part of a sinister conspiracy, a plot to take over the world on behalf of rapacious global capitalists who will manipulate the global economy for their own ends. But here's the bad news: we're already there. The operations of international businesses now span the globe and exploit local conditions to their advantage without the need for any help from a world government. Many of them already control funds that exceed the budgets of all but the largest nation states. The ten most profitable corporations in the world – among them Walmart, Shell, Apple, JP Morgan and Toyota – collectively enjoy an income stream that exceeds the tax revenues of the 'poorest' 180 of the 195 countries in the world combined; yes – really. And more than two thirds of the largest 100 economic entities on our planet are now in fact corporations. If we're worried about their accountability, we need to strengthen the idea of world government, not weaken it.

No individual national government can do anything to limit the power and reach of such corporations, because even if something is done in one jurisdiction, operations can simply be switched to another. Large global corporations are adept at avoiding taxes and other regulations by shifting their base of operations to countries with more favourable policies, and there is currently no international legislation which can pre-vent them doing so. Global markets need global regulation. It's exactly the same principle that applies within a country, or a federation of states like the US: without a central body that can apply laws across the board, you get chaos, conflict and cronyism. Free markets may bring the vir-tues of competition, innovation and efficiency to inert economies; but without proper oversight and control, the inequalities they foment can become a dangerously destabilising force – and only a government with global reach can effectively regulate global businesses and capital.

Another potential worry is political freedom. If we had a single world government with a global army or police force to back it up, what would be able to stop it from turning into a fascist state with complete control over the world population? In theory, nothing. But in practice, almost everything. First of all, the same concern is present for sovereign demo-cratic states at the moment. There is nothing to stop the British Army from launching a coup and taking over the Government of the UK. The same is true for the United States and other democratic countries. But it hasn't happened. Why? Because there is no motivation for it to happen. As the recent history of the world shows, a military regime is not the best way to run a country. It is neither efficient nor stable, from a game theory point of view. It might make sense where there are limited resources and a poor, uneducated population – and that is where you find them. But for developed economies that rely on cooperation and at least the illusion of civil freedom, a military take-over would be a complete disaster, and not just for the people on the street.

And there's a further reassurance: in practice any such global army or international police force would be divided into smaller national group-ings that would naturally monitor each other in their own self-interest. Just as a police force is required to 'maintain the peace' in democratic countries that accept the rule of law, in a united world a police force will still be required to deal with those who do not respect it – but no one country or single force could be tasked with policing the entire globe. Even in a world where war was over, where local conflict was merely a question of policing, each country would require its own military force to deal with local issues – and at least some of them would remain armed, as they are now, at a level sufficient to maintain the military stalemate that is the current guarantee of international peace.

But given that any global government would have to be democratic to be fully legitimate, how could the voting arrangements be made to work? If all the countries of the world are to be represented, should their voting power reflect their population or economic status, or should each country have just a single vote? On the face of it, it would seem unreasonable that a country the size of China, with 1.5 billion people, should have no more voting power than Monaco, with only 33,000. But the reverse proposition is just as absurd: if countries were to be assigned voting power proportional to their populations, China and India between them could effectively out-vote the rest of the world. And besides, as a properly proportional system would require the average size of an electoral district to be based on the population of the smallest country (currently Tuvalu, at around 10,000), the number of delegates to a world government needed for a full quorum would exceed half a million – a quite unmanageable number.

Things are no better if we use GDP as a comparative measure; the gap between the richest and poorest nations balloons to a ratio of over 400,000, and even if ranked on a per capita basis, it's still around 250 to 1. And then there's the question of self-interest: if rich nations were given more votes there would be little incentive to consider the interests of smaller nations. So is it impossible to create a fair voting system, then? Far from it. We just have to return to first principles. What is it that we are attempting to achieve? In exactly the same way as for the institutions we have developed after centuries of political struggle in the so-called free world, the goal to which we aspire should be a democratic forum where decisions are made by debating issues and winning them by force of argument. Policy could be formulated by an executive group which might consist of an inner cabinet of more influential countries, but any proposals would have to be passed democratically, with each country casting an equal vote.

Never work? Well, actually, that's exactly how the countries of the world do vote in the General Assembly of the United Nations. The principle that's been accepted since its foundation is 'one country, one vote' – no matter how big or small. So why doesn't the UN already take all the big political decisions on behalf of the world? If we need some form of world government, what's wrong with the organisation we've already got? To answer that, we'll need to take a look at the UN's dirty little secret.

Resolution 377

The UN was set up with the best of intentions. In the immediate aftermath of World War II, the victors of the struggle felt the need to do something to prevent another world war from ever happening. The UN Charter, the founding document of the United Nations, was created for that sole purpose, and 193 countries of the world are now signatories to a legal agreement, in which they pledge to *"maintain international peace and security, and to that end: to take effective collective measures for the prevention and removal of threats to the peace, and for the suppression of acts of aggression or other breaches of the peace."* That's pretty clear. The primary mandate of the UN, which we have all signed off on, is to *"bring about by peaceful means, and in conformity with the principles of justice and international law, adjustment or settlement of international disputes or situations which might lead to a breach of the peace."*

And yet, since that document was signed, there have been over 200 major wars and conflicts in which over 20 million people have died, some 90% of whom have been civilians. Global military expenditure is now nearing an eye-watering $2 trillion per year, an amount equivalent to the combined GDP of over 60% of the world's poorest countries. Just think about that for a moment. The amount of money spent on making weapons of war exceeds the total income of more than half of the poorest people on the planet – not that ordinary citizens get a great deal out of it, with nearly half of all federal tax revenues in the US, for example, going towards current or past military costs. It's hard to see what part of the UN's mission to bring about the settlement of international disputes by peaceful means is served by this reality.

Given the UN's founding commitment to maintain peace, why has this been allowed to happen? Though the reasons behind it may be complex, the grubby answer at the heart of the rhetoric is quite simple: because there is a veto. In theory, the UN is a democratic organisation where resolutions about how to deal with world affairs are proposed, debated and decided by democratic vote – except that any of the five so-called 'permanent members' of the Security Council have the right to veto any resolution, even one passed unanimously by all the other members.

Since 1945, this power of veto has been exercised more than 250 times. Let's remind ourselves what a veto is. It comes from a Latin word meaning "I forbid" and grants its user the right to prevent any proposed change to the status quo, without having to give a reason. This is essentially the same power that an absolute monarch or a despot uses to exercise control over their country – and we know how harshly history has tended to deal with such people. How could the UN, the finest flowering of humanity's desire to live at peace with itself, have fallen foul of such an elementary error?

To understand that, a little history is required. The League of Nations was the first attempt to establish an international organisation that could maintain world peace. It was set up in 1920 just after the First World War – a conflict which had resulted in utterly devastating losses, including some 38 million civilian and military casualties worldwide. At the outset the League consisted of 44 states in a General Assembly, of which eight (four 'permanent' members and four 'non-permanent') made up the League Council – a smaller group comprising the 'great powers' with a similar function to the UN Security Council today. Though it eventually expanded to as many as 58 states and 15 Council members, the League of Nations was never a fully inclusive organisation – and the veto situation was even worse than in the United Nations: a unanimous vote of all members was required for any measure to pass.

This set an almost impossible bar to effective decision-making, and the League of Nations eventually dissolved in a puddle of inaction that allowed member states to flout resolutions with impunity – a situation that ultimately lead to World War II. The post-war establishment of the United Nations was intended to fix the flaws of its predecessor, but though its founders saw the need to reform the unanimous vote requirement, they could not bring themselves to go all the way and make the decision-making process fully democratic. So resolutions passed by majority vote in the General Assembly are only 'advisory' and are not considered binding on any of the members.

Any 'substantive' decisions with enforceable consequences in the real world still have to be taken by the Security Council, which comprises just 15 of the 193 UN member countries. 10 of these council members are elected by the General Assembly on a rolling 2-year basis, which does at least allow other countries to take a turn at the wheel, but although the principle of majority voting is accepted (a resolution passes if nine of the fifteen members vote for it) there is a sneaky catch: the five permanent members – the victorious allies of World War II – must all concur, i.e. not oppose the vote. That means that if any one of them votes against it, the deal's off.

This ability to block a positive vote is not actually called a veto (it's considered a 'failure to concur'), but in practice a veto is what it is. And that was the price of entry to the club: at the initial conference in San Francisco in 1945 the US delegate dramatically tore up a draft copy of the Charter as a reminder to other countries that they must agree to the veto or have no Charter at all. But times have changed. Though the 'great powers' still have interests and client states they wish to protect, the idea that a small group of powerful nations could unilaterally prevent the resolution of substantive issues affecting world peace increasingly goes against the grain of the times – all the more so given the conflict of interest arising from the fact that the five permanent members of the Security Council are among the top ten weapons-exporting countries, together responsible for over two-thirds of reported global conventional arms exports. Once again, it's hard to see how this veto power can be made to square with the terms of the UN's core mission – let alone with

Article 2.1 of the UN Charter, which states that *"the Organization is based on the principle of the sovereign equality of all its Members."*

On the 800th anniversary of Magna Carta in 2015, much was made of its significance as the first formal legal restraint on the absolute power of kings, thus acting as a beacon for the establishment of human rights more broadly. And indeed, for eight centuries the Magna Carta has been the foundation for a progressive series of provisions that have effectively abolished political tyranny in the West – striking a fatal blow not just against English sovereigns acting from a sense of Divine Right, but against the legitimacy of undemocratic state power anywhere. Such milestones as the Petition of Right, the Bill of Rights and the Act of Settlement paved the way for the Declaration of Independence and all that followed from it, from the French Revolution to the Russian Revolution.

Though this might seem a very European tradition, it is a mistake to see this as part of an exclusively Western culture that is of little relevance to the rest of the world. As we have seen, the establishment of laws to limit the power of kings and emperors, though not perhaps as explicitly developed as in Europe and America, is a theme that runs through history. This is the sense in which the pen is mightier than the sword – because to animals who have discovered language, logic is ultimately more important than strength. Indeed, that is arguably what language is essentially for, to persuade others that there is a better way to do something than what they were otherwise going to do. That is the essence of civilization, wherever it is found.

It just so happens that this particular process has been taken furthest in the West. That does not endow the West with any moral or cultural superiority: it's just that for a number of technical and practical reasons, the West has been in a position to work things through further than in other countries. We have had the meetings. We have done the math. In the so-called 'developed' nations, the freedoms that have been won by minorities and other disadvantaged groups, be they religious, sexual or social, are undeniable and now irreversible. The fight against slavery and racial and religious discrimination, and for equal rights for women,

LGBT and disabled people are hard-fought struggles that were ultimately won by the force of logic and persuasion.

Like the wheel, democracy is an idea that cannot be ignored without taking a giant step backwards. Just as almost every machine depends on the concept of a wheel in some form – a simple engineering solution that took our ancestors nearly as long to invent as writing – so the successes of our modern societies depend upon freedom of speech and democratic process. And although not all societies developed the wheel at the same time, the obvious advantages it conferred meant that it was universally adopted wherever it was introduced. And the logic of this process tells us that democracy must now take its seat at the UN Security Council.

In fact, there's not much more that needs to be done. There's a mechanism already in place: the veto can be overcome. Though it's generally only known to international lawyers (and even they often need reminding) the United Nations has a provision on its books that allows a Security Council veto to be circumvented. It dates back over 65 years, but on November 3, 1950, after fourteen days of deliberations, the United Nations General Assembly finally voted through Resolution 377A(V) – an agreement which became known as the 'Uniting for Peace' resolution. The purpose of this resolution, passed by an overwhelming majority vote of 52 to 5 – with two abstentions – was to ensure that a deadlock in the Security Council could be resolved by a vote in the General Assembly should the circumstances warrant it.

The resolution was carefully designed to address the Security Council's fatal flaw. The relevant clause states that where there is disagreement between the permanent members, meaning that the Security Council is unable to approve action to prevent war – or, as the resolution puts it, *"fails to exercise its primary responsibility for the maintenance of international peace and security in any case where there appears to be a threat to the peace, breach of the peace, or act of aggression"* – then the decision may pass to the General Assembly, which is thereby empowered to make recommendations for collective measures, *"including... the use of armed force when necessary, to maintain or restore international peace and security."*

Though lawyers may argue about the nuances, what that essentially means is that a veto exercised by any of the permanent members of the Security Council can be bypassed if necessary by the General Assembly. Let me restate that, because it is not well-enough known or understood. *If a Security Council resolution is blocked by the veto of a permanent member, then – according to international law – it can be referred to the General Assembly for a democratic decision.* All that's required is that a majority of the member states request an emergency session to debate the matter, with a two-thirds majority being needed to pass the resolution. Resolution 377A(V) is still valid and has previously been used to dramatic effect, most notably during the Suez Crisis. For even if recommendations made under this 'Uniting for Peace' resolution are not legally binding, they have a moral force on the international stage that will become increasingly difficult to ignore. We need to dust it down again.

The Great Stink

Winston Churchill is often credited with saying that *"America will always do the right thing – but only when they have exhausted all the other options."* As an observation it's amusing enough, but America has no monopoly on this frustratingly widespread form of social and political madness. Any effort to improve things usually involves a challenge to the status quo, and – given the pressure to conform that language and culture so dramatically reinforce – a bad situation generally only gets sorted out when it becomes really unbearable. No one wants to be the first to break the mould, because it goes against the balance of accepted wisdom, the way things have always been done. That takes real courage, and again and again we see the conservative bias that tradition brings to bear on our most vital decisions, with the collective voices of the past drowning out the voice of common sense.

For centuries, the River Thames was little more than an open drain into which all the sewage from London's ever-growing population flowed. That's the way it had always been, but with the city's population doubling in size every 50 years since Tudor times, by the mid-19th century things had begun to reach a natural limit. Various public bodies were formed to deal with the health problems that this caused, but each one was only concerned with its own district – and as the end of the line for an endless flow, the Thames gradually became overwhelmed.

Finally, in the hot summer of 1858, the terrible smell from the untreated sewage flowing past Sir Charles Barry's stylish new Parliament buildings became so overpowering that MPs were at last compelled to do something. With the press baying about the "Great Stink" (especially after the smell had forced Queen Victoria and her husband Albert to abandon a planned pleasure trip on the Thames), a bill was drawn up within the space of eighteen days and quickly voted through to fund a comprehensive reconstruction programme for London's sewers – bringing an end to the political bickering that had frustrated all attempts to solve the problem over the previous half-century.

We are in the midst of our own Great Stink right now. Though tyrants have been slaughtering their own people with scant regard for world opinion since the beginning of time, it has often been because the world has known little about it until too late, and could do nothing about it when they did. But with rolling news coverage now able to rush fresh images of atrocities from the latest regional conflict straight to our laptops and living rooms, these modern-day horrors are happening right in front of our eyes.

And we naturally react to it. We can't just watch innocent people being shot, gassed, bombed and burnt without wanting to stop it. Pleas for donations in the media regularly attract large sums of money from horrified viewers, and online petitions register huge support from concerned citizens who believe their governments should live up to their international responsibilities. But frustratingly, our creaking 20th century institutions – themselves the product of 19th century mind-sets – are seemingly unable to match or even reflect this spontaneous generosity of spirit.

Instead of decisive action by the Security Council to authorize an international intervention to stop the fighting and enforce a ceasefire, laying the ground for a political solution to be negotiated, we are treated to the ignominious spectacle of the permanent members continuing to veto each other's resolutions. This predictably leaves a vacuum into which individual nations and ad-hoc coalitions of third parties step – but without any wider consensus, this only results in further illegal and partisan action from the safety of drones or high-tech aircraft, while civilians keep dying on the ground.

Like the stench from the putrid waters of the Thames, the smell is becoming unbearable. The existence of the veto contradicts the very principle for which so many people around the world have been risking their lives to confront the autocratic regimes that oppress them. Just as the four letters of the word 'veto' can be rearranged to spell the word 'vote', so the autocratic structure of the only international forum capable of legitimately dealing with matters of world peace and security needs to be rearranged and reformed to allow it to act. It's time to do the right thing.

We are teetering towards that possibility. The Earth Summit held under the auspices of the UN in 2005 produced a document which for the first time formulated agreed ideas on the 'responsibility to protect' or R2P, which would enable the UN to intervene in the affairs of a sovereign country (something expressly forbidden under the UN Charter) in the case where a civilian population requires protection from its government, stating *"In this context, we are prepared to take collective action... should peaceful means be inadequate and national authorities manifestly fail to protect their populations from genocide, war crimes, ethnic cleansing and crimes against humanity."* Significantly, this was then endorsed by the Security Council under Resolution 1674. That means that, should we be able to agree on a course of action, we have the legal means to do it. And if it means invoking the 'Uniting for Peace' Resolution to get things going, so be it.

Because these ongoing humanitarian crises are a joint international responsibility. This may not have seemed so obvious in the immediate aftermath of World War II, when divided and competing nations had just ended yet another monstrous military struggle for dominance of the planet. But we are no longer in that situation. No stick is now big enough in the hands of one person, one tribe. There are no powers on the planet able to control or dominate another by force, both because of the risk of mutual annihilation, and because even with conventional weapons, it has become impossible to settle conflicts in that way. If nothing else, the interventions in Iraq and Afghanistan have proven that. It is time for the UN to take on its true role in human affairs, to become the parliament and policeman of the world. We have reached the point where we should all finally acknowledge to ourselves – as we have already promised – that unilateral violence is neither acceptable nor effective.

And there's another problem. Even if the principle and sheer inhumanity of the situation does not move us, we should be concerned by the wider dangers it poses to ourselves. For terrorism is moving with the times, even if we are not. 9/11 showed the devastation that can be brought to the heart of our own cities by people who feel frustrated enough – and angry enough – to die for their cause. Are we going to sit back and watch a new generation of young people grow so resentful at the inability of the international community to act that they will take their revenge with some terrible weapon of mass destruction? If we do nothing to answer the frantic cries for help from those caught in the agonising chaos and desperation that envelops them, it is not hard to imagine that some abandoned chemical, biological or even nuclear device may one day fall into the hands of those bitter enough to use it on a large civilian population. If only for reasons of self-defence, we must find a way to defuse the situation.

The thing about language is that it allows us to make a reasoned case. Only in an environment free from violence can I effectively explain why I feel so aggrieved, why I feel my neighbour has no right to my land, for example – and vice versa. It's a question of law, logic, and justice. Of course these things can be influenced by a clever lawyer, but ultimately it's about rights: who has the right to do such things. In the court of natural human justice – let alone in international law – the French had no right to be in Vietnam. The Afrikaans government had no right to impose apartheid. The British had no right to annex India or Ireland, just as the Israelis have no right to remain in control of the West Bank. The list goes on and on. But until the UN starts to properly exercise its intended function, there is no global forum where such injustices can be brought before a court, allowing the issues to be heard – and decided – in the context of the Human Rights legislation that we have all signed up to. And so we have terrorism, and will continue to do so until we create such a forum.

But the strongest argument for doing so is the fact that this is what all our most stable and successful societies have slowly learnt and now choose to do. We do not go to war within our own countries, because we have mechanisms to prevent it: due process, courts and police to stop violence between arguing parties and enforce judgments, so that might does not prevail over right. The principle is accepted, however much the practice may fall short, and the results are clear – violence is rare and rapidly suppressed. This took a long time to establish, and required strong central government to enforce, but very few who benefit from living in such societies would want to return to a world where violence take precedence over the law. And the law is no more than the codification of an agreement on how best to do things.

Not everyone always agrees with the law, of course. People have different views, and always will. That's what politics is about. But any system other than democracy ends up with a minority imposing their will on a majority – an unstable situation that eventually results in that majority finding a way to overthrow them, usually violently. In a democracy, power is held by elected representatives, who are chosen for the persuasiveness and popularity of their ideas. Those who lose the argument have to accept that their ideas weren't good enough, and that – however tempting – violence is ultimately a loser's game. In the end, it's a matter of logic.

Walking the talk

The word 'logic' comes from the Greek word *logos*, long translated in English versions of the Bible as 'the word', though it also has the wider meaning of 'reason' or 'plan'. It's not the word normally used in Greek for a 'word' in the grammatical sense (for which they use *lexis*), but both ultimately derive from an older word *lego*, which means, among other things, "to lay out, gather, select and count." That echoes Hobbes' thought that the true function of speech is simply to 'reckon' things, whether using reason to work things out, or simply keeping track of what we own – as with the later emergence of writing, which seems to have first developed as a means of keeping track of possessions. What we can certainly say though, is that one of the most useful aspects of language is that it enables us to describe and explain our ideas, and use them to influence others through the power of argument.

This ability to persuade others is the cornerstone of human society and civilization, because in allowing us to share ideas and spread knowledge, it offers the chance to change minds, and cause people to act differently than they might have done without the extra information that language makes available. This is why freedom of speech is so important: in allowing as many ideas as possible to be brought to the table, it lets us choose the ones that make the most sense, or offer the best solution to a problem. And it's for just that reason that freedom of speech has been so bitterly opposed throughout history by controlling interests with power, prestige and property to lose if the ideas that support their position in society are shown to be wrong.

The struggle for life that Darwin identified as the driver of evolution is essentially about competition for limited resources. In a world without language, where the life of an individual is inevitably limited to the business of staying alive and reproducing, the only way to ensure survival is to fight for what you need – because if you lose that battle, your genes die with you. Nature is still fundamentally red in tooth and claw, and the language of the survival game is violence: without words there is no means of negotiating a more reasonable solution. Language is so crucial because it allows us to share consciousness, to be aware of what our fellow creatures feel and want. It opens up the possibility of being able to discuss better ways of exploiting resources without having to physically fight for them, allowing ideas to lead the way.

That doesn't mean it's the first route we're going to take, however. Our brains evolved to fight long before we could talk, and that's still the default position when the going gets tough. We're happy enough to talk as long as we don't have to give anything up, but those lucky enough to have more than others are often reluctant to surrender their advantage. In common with all other animals, the real issue that human society has to deal with is how to resolve the consequent struggle for power, which in one form or another lies behind most of the conflict that exists in the world.

The struggle may be political, economic, or personal. A dictator in the form of a king or other unelected leader can impose arbitrary decisions that affect the well-being and opportunities of other members of society; a large corporation can use its monopoly power to ignore the rights of both its employees and its consumers; and a family member can exercise psychological or physical control over a spouse or children. But the result is the same in each case. People do not like to be suppressed, ignored, slighted and belittled. They do not like feeling powerless in the face of someone who will not listen to their concerns, and in the end, they will not stand for it.

However much they may have been suppressed through history, the voices of the downtrodden cannot be silenced forever. Individuals may die or be killed, but language lets their ideas live on and spread through entire populations, reproduced by word of mouth. That's why education is so important, and why tyrannies have discouraged literacy and banned books. Because once an idea attains critical mass, society as a whole starts to change. This is the power of democracy, which allows the majority to oppose a ruling minority – a much more stable political arrangement than an exclusive elite can hope to offer, no matter how well-intentioned. It offers the political and social equivalent of biological evolution, as the ideas and opinions that survive are the ones that fit most closely with the times and conditions that give rise to them.

Back in the 1960's, at the dawn of space travel, the Russian astronomer Nikolai Kardashev started thinking about what an extra-terrestrial civilization might look like if ever we were to find one. No one can be sure what kind of life might evolve in other parts of the universe, but insofar as the laws of physics still operate, any advanced civilization will certainly need to harness the energy available to it as efficiently as possible. He proposed three levels at which such a civilization might have mastered the use of energy, which he named Type I, Type II and Type III. A Type I civilization would be one which has managed to harness all the available energy sources on its home planet. A Type II civilization will have been able to harness all the energy of its nearest star. A Type III civilization will have found a way to harness the energy of its galaxy.

Purely theoretical, of course, as no evidence of any such civilizations has yet been detected: unfortunately, here on Planet Earth we are still a Type 0 civilization. This means that our world has yet to evolve to the point where we have truly started thinking of the planet as a single unit – managed to put aside the factional, religious, sectarian and nationalistic struggles that have characterized the majority of human history to date, and begun to focus on working together on what is best for the planet as a whole. The good news is that by most calculations we could be only a century or so away from making it to Type I status. Why? Because not only will we have to get along if we want to survive, but the accompanying and accelerating growth in technological development will eventually allow us to effectively harvest sustainable solar, geothermal and fusion energy sources on an industrial scale.

But the odds on our surviving that long may not be so good. The physicist Enrico Fermi, the man responsible – amongst other things – for developing the world's first nuclear reactor, once suggested that according to calculations about the probability of intelligent life existing in other parts of the universe, the earth should have been visited by aliens many times over. The fact that we appear not to have been so visited – and that we have also failed to find any evidence of alien civilizations, despite our increasing ability to peer deep into the universe – leads to the disturbing possibility that once a life-form has evolved to the point that it is able to unravel the secrets of atomic power and DNA, the greed and stupidity of powerful individuals inevitably leads to the destruction of the civilization before it can develop beyond a fledgling Type I status.

That is the risk we run now, and is another compelling reason why we should focus our minds on how to escape that fate. We already know enough about our ecosphere to realise that war is no longer the only way in which we could destroy ourselves – as we push up against the limits of our planet, we have to find a way to take collective responsibility for the climate and the natural environment, and learn to husband our resources, together. The only way we can do this is to raise our game to the next level. We have to get wise to the traps of language, culture, religion and identity, and accept that we are a single species, struggling to survive in a limited space. There is no 'them': we are all 'us'. The UN must become democratically accountable. The veto has to go. Nothing else will do. That is the only way forward for our planet, the only way we can avoid further pointless rounds of self-destructive violence.

That's easily enough said, of course. But how do we persuade the existing powers to do anything about it? Well, like every other change that takes place, we have to start by talking about it. Without that, nothing happens – and no one is talking about it. Like all ideas, it's about creating a momentum, a momentum that eventually becomes unstoppable. How did slavery become abolished? How did democracy take hold? How did women win the right to vote? All of these things needed the groundswell of public support before they became a reality, regardless of the economic factors that helped drive them. Politicians are rarely leaders. They are usually opportunists who catch the mood of the public and run with it. And in a democracy, the public is always right.

And democracy works. It may not be perfect, but without question it is the least bad system available to organize people without conflict. It's not rocket science. It works because people do not like to be told what to do. With democracy, you at least have the opportunity to change things, however hard that may be, without resorting to violence. Under no other system is that the case. Feudal monarchies can only be maintained by force of arms and institutionalised ignorance. Single party states, whether based on religious or political ideology, struggle to suppress dissent. Tribal and family groupings are notoriously fractious. It's taken us long enough to work it out. We've had the meetings as a species, and the best technology available to us is democracy. We just need to take it all the way. We need to begin a conversation that will change the world, because that is the only alternative to violence: the ultimate logic of language is peace.

The thing is, this is no longer a pipe dream. Back in 1970 when the song *Imagine* was written, the world was still in the throes of the Vietnam War, and memories of World War II remained vivid for those of Lennon's generation. But for those of us alive today in the so-called developed world, peace is all we have ever known. Ours is a completely different world to that of our grandparents and great-grandparents, and looks set to remain so. And we now have it within our means to extend the benefits of that peace to all those who live on our planet. Not only do we have it within our means: we have actually promised to do it. It's a simple question: Are we going to admit that we are hypocrites, that the bank of international justice is bankrupt? Or are we going to insist that the cheque already issued in our name should finally be cashed? It's down to us.

Which means it's down to you, too. The anthropologist Margaret Mead once said *"Never doubt that a small group of thoughtful, committed citizens can change the world. In fact, it's the only thing that ever has."* World peace is an idea whose time has come. You don't have to fight for it. You don't even have to give anything up for it. All you have to do is spread the meme, and help get the conversation going. We know what needs to be done; all that's required now is to stand up and say so. If a journey of a thousand miles begins with a single step, our very first step as humans was to learn to speak. And as we stand on the brink of a world free from war, the step we must now take is to speak out about how it can and must be done.

Because, as it always has, language changes everything.

Appendix

I have attached no notes to the pages or chapters of this book because most of the content I refer to in the text is widely known: I have simply joined up the dots. If you want to know more about anything I cite, an online search will quickly furnish you with further details. The only exception to this is the argument in Chapter 1, which is my own – although here too, I have merely made the connections. These, however, are slightly harder to discern as they are only to be found in more specialist areas – so for those who are interested, I attach a paper originally written for *Science*, though it was turned down as being 'too specialized'. This is extensively noted with references to academic journals and other publications that will allow you to check my sources should you wish to do so.

ON THE ORIGIN OF SPEECH: A New Perspective

by Simon R Prentis MA (Oxon), Dip RSA, Simul Acad., MITI

Abstract The transformation of meaningful analog signals into combinations of arbitrary signs with unrelated composite meanings is an effective strategy for digital communication seen in the evolution both of writing and mathematical notation – a duality of patterning also present more fundamentally in the organization of DNA and atomic structure. Here I show how the functional redundancy of phonemes and their progressive depletion with the diversification of language suggest that, long before the emergence of grammar, the crucial step enabling speech was the digitization of an existing repertoire of analog calls. This hypothesis is supported by the incipient use of combinatory signs in the communicative strategies of other species, placing language on an evolutionary spectrum. The limitless opportunities for communication enabled by this simple switch from analog to digital and their consequences for group survival also plausibly account for the otherwise inexplicably rapid encephalization observed in the fossil record of the homo genus.

Introduction Despite its vital importance to everything that distinguishes us from other animals, the origin of speech is still shrouded in mystery[1]. Believed by many cultures throughout history to have been a divine gift to humanity, early attempts at more scientific explanations of language in the 19th century were hampered by the apparent absence of physical evidence, a frustration that eventually led learned societies to ban discussion of the subject[2]. Almost a century later, Noam Chomsky breathed life back into the debate by proposing that humans are uniquely endowed with an innate faculty for language[3], but although theories based on this idea still tend to dominate the academic literature, more recent research is now beginning to cast significant doubt on the notion of a biologically constrained Universal Grammar[4]. Field studies of less familiar languages unequivocally reveal that there is very little systematic correlation between the highly diverse grammatical strategies adopted by unrelated linguistic families[5], and cognitive neuroscience has yet to identify any mechanisms in the brain that are dedicated solely to language[6].

However, we have perhaps been misled by the historical focus on grammar as the key to language. For grammar is not the first pre-requisite of speech – and there has long been doubt as to how a faculty supposedly dependent on a genetic trait unique to our species could have spread without a selective advantage independent of language[7]. As if mesmerized by the apparent complexity of syntactic structures, we appear to have forgotten that before everything else, language begins with words: it should not be surprising that other species do not demonstrate syntactic skills when they have insufficient utterances at their disposal to necessitate the use of grammar. For the question of the origin of words is not trivial; without an adequate lexical base to operate on, there can be nothing for grammar to work with. This paper focuses on the importance of the fact that what fundamentally differentiates words from other forms of animal communication is that their core structure is digital[8].

Whereas the calls and cries used by other species to communicate are essentially analog and holistic in nature, words involve the systematic use of a limited set of discrete sounds to create composite digital constructs that are mnemonically efficient. This simple yet crucial mechanism is what first unleashes the power of 'digital infinity', enabling the creation of a potentially unlimited lexicon of words that can be easily recognised and reproduced. Grammar, though a vital component of language as we know it, is a second-order phenomenon which could only emerge as an organising principle once a certain critical mass of words was available[9]. It is thus not necessary to postulate the serendipitous emergence of some new cognitive capacity to explain the origin of speech – the switch from analog to digital at the level of words is the essential starting point. Indeed, far from being a side-effect of fortuitous brain growth, it is more plausible that the development of words was a critical factor in driving it.

Argument Though traditionally dismissed by humans as 'dumb animals', it is clear that other species are also able to communicate with each other – albeit not with the same degree of sophistication as our own. As we apply better analytical tools to the study of the communicative strategies used by animals in the wild, we increasingly see the use of precise and distinct utterances that convey warnings and other meaningful signals[10]. Such communicative calls appear to be both arbitrary and species-specific, yet function as effective survival strategies for members of groups that use them. Animals evidently understand the idea of danger, an abstract notion contingent on the ability to read the potential of a situation in the light of previous experience. Their lives depend on being able to recognise it and take evasive action when they see it, and this ability to associate meaning with an acoustic signal that is symbolic rather than iconic or indicative is thus a phenomenon that appears not to be unique to humans[11]. However, the unstructured analog signals typically used by other species to convey meaning have limited utility. Holistic calls that cannot be broken down into constituent parts are difficult to categorize and remember, even for humans – as noted by Miller in his classic paper on memory and chunking[12].

In contrast, it is much easier to retain and recall signals that are combinations of other elements – whether acoustic or otherwise – organised as a fixed system of 'digits' that can be easily interchanged to construct a unique mnemonic. Take the example of numbers: the decimal counting system has ten digits that symbolise the quantities 0-9, combining two or more of these digits for quantities greater than nine – enabling larger numbers to be represented precisely according to a system that is sensitive to position. The number 1348, for example, is a precise and easy way of specifying an amount that would be almost impossible to represent if each separate quantity were assigned a unique analog symbol. The historical record shows the struggle our forebears went through to develop an effective system of counting that enabled calculations to be done efficiently, but their earliest solutions inevitably involved chunking into units, be they of base five, ten, twelve, twenty or sixty[13].

A similar process is seen in the evolution of writing[14]. The earliest records we have date back 5000 years, but each time a writing system developed independently – whether in Sumer, Egypt, China or Meso-America – the evolution followed the same route from analog to digital. In every tradition, the first writing was pictorial, with figurative images representing an object or idea. But as the number of symbols proliferate, a limit is eventually reached. This limit is determined by at least two factors – the inability to effectively differentiate between more than a certain number of symbols that are unsystematic in character, and the inability to represent abstract ideas that have no obvious visual analog. In each case a solution was found independently through the gradual use of rebus, in which combinations or adaptions of existing images are used to represent other words by chunking them phonetically (we see this process even with Chinese characters)[15]. This eventually led to the creation of syllabaries to enable systematic phonetic spelling, and then to a true alphabet in which individual phonemes are more effectively and efficiently represented, in the same way as with numbers, by unique visual digits known as letters.

Nor is it just humans who employ such strategies. At the most fundamental level, the nature of all matter is digital[16,17]. The apparently limitless complexity of the world around us is founded on particulate combinations of some 90 elements differing only in atomic number, a quantity that increases as a multiple of discrete units – and are themselves composites of a smaller number of more fundamental particles. All chemical reactions are interactions between molecules that are digital combinations of these elements, and the chemistry of life depends on the ability of certain of such combinations to reproduce themselves according to a system that is ordered and encoded digitally with several different layers of patterning. It should thus not be surprising that language employs a similar method, as this is the most efficient way of employing finite means to generate an effectively infinite number of possibilities. Indeed, the complex layering of proteins, ultimately encoded by a simple quaternary code in the DNA double helix, is remarkably analogous to the structure of language[18].

Method The way in which a limited set of phonemes are used in combination to generate an unlimited lexicon of words can be illustrated as follows: although it is of course possible to isolate the functionally discrete elements of words that linguists know as phonemes (in simple terms, the vowels and consonants of a language) the fundamental working unit of any spoken language is the syllable[19]. Consonants can for the most part only be used to convey meaning in combination with a vowel, and although it is possible for vowels to be used independently as a meaningful utterance, this too is the exception rather than the rule. Although the precise definition of a syllable and the rules that govern them vary widely across languages, as a first approximation a syllable can be defined as a combination of a consonant and a vowel, which (with the exception of words consisting of singly articulated vowels) is the minimum productive unit of spoken language. Using this as a basis for calculation, a very rough number for the potential syllables available to any given language is given by (the number of consonants x the number of vowels). In practice syllables are much more complex, on the one hand frequently comprising more than two phonemes, and on the other being constrained by language-specific phonotactic rules that eliminate certain combinations. However, as this calculation only gives a minimum theoretical number, it will serve as an adequate first-order approximation.

Words are in turn formed by the combination of syllables, so the number of potential words available to a language is given (in this crude reckoning) by the number of potential syllables raised to the power of the number of syllables used. Thus for the English language, with 20 vowels and 24 consonants, the potential minimum number of distinctive words per syllable would be 20 x 24 = 480. This means that with just two syllables, the potential number of words available would be 480 x 480 = 230,400 – an order of magnitude greater than the size of the ordinary person's active vocabulary. It is thus unsurprising that the average number of syllables used in English words is around 1.6, which when factored against the theoretical number of syllables available gives a potential of $(480^{1.6}) = 19,497$ – a number commensurate with the average estimated vocabulary of an adult speaker[20]. On the other hand, with only 5 vowels and 15 consonants, Japanese would have the potential of generating 5 x 15 = 75 words with a single syllable, $75^2 = 5,625$ words with two syllables and $75^3 = 421,875$ words and with three syllables. Again, it is no surprise that the average number of syllables used in Japanese words is higher at around 2.3, yielding a potential $75^{2.3} = 20,541$ words, a number again commensurate with average adult vocabulary sizes[21].

As noted, these numbers merely give a crude comparative measure, and in practice will vary with dialect, context and corpora, but despite any scholarly disagreement on detail[22], they unambiguously illustrate the point that the exponential character of the combinatory maths means that a reduction in phonemes need not affect the ability of a language to generate a lexicon sufficient to meet the needs of its speakers, and is constrained only by the trade-off between a smaller number of phonemes and a larger number of syllables, and the potential time lost in articulation. And as most languages suffer no disadvantage in having words of three, four or more syllables, in principle there is no reason why a language cannot function adequately with a much smaller number of phonemes than the worldwide average, at around 35. Thus from a mathematical perspective there exists a substantial redundancy in the base number of phonemes comprising the digital units that constitute all known languages, which range from as high as 141 with !Xũ to as low as 11 in Rotokas and Pirahã.

Indeed, in purely theoretical terms, language could be reduced to just two distinctive phonemes, with all words created using a binary phonetic code, but in order to create a vocabulary commensurate with the lexicon found in other human languages, this would require words with at least 14 syllables ($2^{14} = 16,384$) and the resultant speech would sound like the exchange protocol of a fax machine. The limitations of articulation in the human vocal tract would also reduce the speed of transmission (Morse code, an early binary system, was slow due to the inherent limitations of human operators and in practice at best could be sent at 20 wpm[23], less than 15% of the average speed of speech), and without a system of channel coding would leave such a minimally distinctive and non-redundant medium highly vulnerable to noise. Thus in practice there is a lower limit to the number of phonemes necessary for communication to be viable.

However, though there may be a practical limit to the minimum number of phonemes in human languages, the key point to note is that, beyond accretional accidents of fashion and cultural assimilation, there is no evolutionary pressure to increase them in ergonomic terms – Japanese, a language with half the number of phonemes used in English, certainly suffers no disadvantage in terms of its expressive potential, and as we have seen, there is no efficiency to be gained by increasing their number. Rather, the reverse is the case; the loss of contrastive phonemes can be readily compensated for by contextual clues. The voiced and voiceless dental non-sibilant fricatives (the initial consonants of word like 'thing' and 'this') so characteristic of English and yet relatively rare worldwide – present in only 4% of known languages – are under pressure to disappear in international usage, and are known to have vanished from most other Indo-European and Semitic languages[24]. That this should be so is not surprising: most native speakers of other languages find them difficult to pronounce, and their omission is rarely problematic for understanding in context.

Discussion The knack of combining discrete sounds in this way results in the ability to generate huge numbers of words; the exponent nature of polysyllabic speech means that with just three vowels and eight consonants – the smallest known repertoire of phonemes in any human language[25] – it is theoretically possible to create as many words as the average speaker knows within the space of just three syllables (24^3 = 13,824). This is the fundamental trick of language, and if we are to understand it as a process that has evolved from what other animals do, we should expect to see this combinatory behaviour, at least in embryo, in the communication of other species – as field studies have been increasingly finding[26]. Though further targeted research may show this strategy to be a more widespread practice, certain species (among them the putty-nosed monkey and Campbell's monkeys) have been found to use specific calls as warnings when uttered in isolation which mean other, unrelated things when used in combination[27]. This phenomenon has been cited as potential evidence of the prior emergence of syntactic structure[28] – but it is equally plausible that in the absence of arbitrary signs, the lexicoding of meaningful calls is just a staging post to the emergence of true phonocoding, a necessary first step to the isolation and digitization of analog sounds essential for the formation of words.

More recently, more obviously phonological behaviour has been noted in the babbler bird[29], which has been found to use contextually meaningless acoustic elements in different combinations to distinguish meaningful calls. Here is further evidence that the capacity to combine sounds digitally in communication exists in other species, placing the emergence of human language on an evolutionary spectrum. This is important, as one of the key barriers to unlocking the origin of speech has been that it has hitherto been understood as an isolate, a unique phenomenon with no known biological cognates. This behaviour enhances the likelihood that such combinatory phonetic constructs, the key to a large lexicon, initially arise from a vocabulary of analog calls used both holistically and in combination – a process eventually driven in the digital direction by the logic of efficiency as explored by Nowak et al[30].

Is there any evidence that this might have happened? Records of human language date back no further than 5000 years, and attempts to reconstruct proto-languages from the known trajectory of historical changes peter out at about 15,000 years ago[31]; yet it turns out that the phonologies of existing languages yield a vital clue to the deep history of speech, just as genomic analysis has thrown light on our evolutionary past. In a 2011 paper[32], Atkinson showed that the number of phonemes used in languages around the world is clinal, decreasing with distance from Africa, the site of our oldest linguistic lineages. Despite criticism of his methodology and conclusions, the crucial point about depletion of phonemes still stands[33], and has been substantially confirmed in a more thoroughgoing study of the sources[34]. Regardless of any serial founder effect in terms of process, the gradual elimination of phonemic redundancy over time is entirely consistent with the hypothesis that all existing languages evolved from earlier languages with larger numbers of phonemes that were slowly isolated from a prior inventory of meaningful sounds – as this paper argues. Indeed, it is the most likely scenario given the fingerprints they leave behind.

For analog forms of communication remain embedded in language today. Not all our utterances sit neatly within the digital structure of words. Every language has numerous ideophones that, while tagged phonetically for convenience, are refractive to grammar and do not conform to type[35]; the difficulty of standardising expressive sounds like *shh!*, *tsk* or *woah!* could well account for the popularity of emoticons. Pulling in the opposite direction, the more refined articulation of academic discourse may provide a useful precision, but often strips language of its emotive power, quite apart from rendering it virtually opaque to all but specialists. And speech contains a deeper connection to the analog past of language. We can only talk at all because of vowels, the 'original sound' (as the Chinese formulation 元音 has it) – the resonant vocal flow that provides the stage for the complex choreography of our consonants. Speech is possible precisely because this stream of sound acts as a wave on which digital signals can be carried as mnemonic bytes of phonemes.

And we still use this analog carrier wave to calibrate the emotional tone of the meaning our words express, adding colour and affect to the communication that other species can only convey with unmodulated lowing, mooing or hooting – as we ourselves must once have done.

But there is another, bigger picture to explore. Once language is viewed more simply as a technique rather than a trait – a trick, not a lucky treat bestowed by benevolent providence – we can start to look for earlier traces of its emergence. It has long been assumed that the complexity of human language is such that it can only be explained by some unique cognitive ability not possessed by other species. This is the essence of Chomsky's claim, no matter how attenuated in his Minimalist Program. Even Everett, who recognises that language is a 'tool', still sees the key to its development as a more nebulous capacity to use symbols[36] – a thesis for which the evidence is circumstantial at best, and lacks a convincing theoretical basis. Pagel claims that the secret to language is that we are somehow 'wired for culture'[37], but this too is circular reasoning. For it is at least as likely that rather than being a concomitant result – or simply a chance side-effect – of the extraordinarily rapid growth in hominid brains over the last three million years, language was actually the cause of it.

Speech represents a decisive turning point in the growth of awareness. Even at the simplest level, long before grammar became necessary, the ability to share insights and ideas would have been transformative. And once language took hold, its evolution was bound to become exponential[38]. Just as there was an explosion of new life once multi-cellular organisms evolved from the single-celled microbes that had dominated the first three billion years of life, enabling previously isolated cells to communicate and diversify into complex forms, so the ability to communicate with language empowers individuals with horizons hitherto limited to their own awareness and lifetime experience to start cooperating and thinking in ways that species without language cannot even begin to imagine. If pattern recognition is the core skill of the brain[39] – any brain – then a way of linking brains together represents a radical change, even without any increase in individual intelligence. The ability to share information would pay huge dividends, as the best ideas quickly became the common property of the entire group, their collective value multiplied by the size of the community. Looked at in this light, the emergence of language is nothing less than a singularity in the evolution of consciousness – the more so as it inevitably becomes a medium for thought as well as communication.

This would also create a strong evolutionary pressure for brains to become larger, the phenomenon we actually observe in the fossil record. The rapid encephalization of early hominins is otherwise puzzling[40], as not only is it not seen in any other species, it occurs in tandem with a reduction in muscle mass. Just at the time when our expanding brains would have required more energy to sustain them, our physical strength appears to have been decreasing[41]. This makes little sense in the absence of a better strategy to obtain food. In contrast to other theories, which rely on factors not exclusive to our species, language offers a persuasive scenario for a virtuous evolutionary circle that would have put a premium on cooperation and reduced the need for individual strength. No matter how big their brain, an unarmed human would be lucky to survive a solo encounter with a hungry predator: but a well-organised group armed with pointed sticks and language could take down a mammoth.

If this hypothesis is correct, we also have to ask why only humans have taken advantage of the trick of speech. After all, as we have seen, the first steps towards combinatory utterances are already present in other species. But the switch from analog to digital is not an incremental change, it is a paradigm shift. It may have taken time to achieve critical mass – early humans were roughly shaping stone tools in the Oldowan style for a million years before Acheulean handaxes appear, and took another million years to develop pressure flaking – so even after the use of words became widespread, complex grammar may have emerged gradually, hand in hand with enhanced cortical processing power. But once established, its effects would have rapidly outstripped the pace of mere biological evolution. For the results are incontrovertible: in the space of just a few thousand generations since we first ventured beyond our ancestral continent, our species is at the point where it may soon be possible to colonise other planets – an exponential pace of change.

Conclusion: The known depletion of phonemes in spoken languages over time coupled with the evident redundancy of phonemes in most known languages relative to their lexical needs is consistent with the hypothesis that speech first evolved by extending the limited communicative capacity of meaningful analog calls through a combinatory process – a process that is both simple in essence and far-reaching in its consequences. This technique would soon have given rise to an unlimited vocabulary of digitally structured mnemonics composed from a limited set of arbitrary sounds, with grammar only emerging later as a secondary ordering principle once a critical mass of words had been attained. This hypothesis, which does not require assumptions about the development of symbolic thinking or other such prerequisite advances in cognitive capacity, has the advantage of offering a more plausible explanation for the uniquely rapid increase in encephalization seen in the homo genus over the last three million years, due to the evident advantages of the exponential increase in communicative capacity and conscious thinking conferred on any species adopting it.

References:
1. Hauser MD, Yang C, Berwick RC, Tattersall I, Ryan MJ, Watumull J, Chomsky N and Lewontin RC, *The mystery of language evolution*. Front. Psychol. 5:401 (2014)
2. Société de Linguistique de Paris, *Statuts de 1866*, Art.2
3. Chomsky N, *Aspects of the theory of syntax*. MIT Press (1965)
4. Ibbotson P and Tomasello M, *Evidence rebuts Chomsky's theory of language learning*. Scientific American (2016)
5. Evans N and Levinson, S *The myth of language universals*. Behavioral and Brain Sciences, 32(5), pp 429-448. (2009)
6. Hamrick P et al, *Child first language and adult second language are both tied to general-purpose learning system*. PNAS 115 (7) pp. 1487-1492 (2018)

7. Smith K et al, *The brain plus the cultural transmission mechanism determine the nature of language.* Behavioural and Brain Sciences, vol. 31(5), pp. 533+ (2008)

8. Oudeyer P, *From analog to digital speech sounds.* National Institute for Research in Computer Science and Control, France (2008)

9. Bates E and Goodman J, *On the emergence of grammar from the lexicon* In: B. MacWhinney (ed.). *The Emergence of Language*, pp. 29-79 (1999)

10. Kershenbaum A et al, *Acoustic sequences in non-human animals.* Biological Review, Cambridge Philosophical Society 91(1): pp.13–52 (2016)

11. Price T et al, *Vervets revisited: A quantitative analysis of alarm call structure and context specificity.* Scientific Reports Volume 5, Article number 13220 (2015)

12. Miller GA, *The magical number seven.* Psychological Review, vol. 63 (1956)

13. McLeish J, *How mathematics has shaped civilization.* Ballantine (1991)

14. Schmandt-Besserat D, *Evolution of writing.* University of Texas at Austin (2014)

15. Prentis S, *A fish called 「魚」 : Characters and the myth of difficulty.* International Japanese-English Translation Conference 26 (2015)

16. Travers A et al, *DNA information: from digital code to analog structure.* Phil. Trans. R. Soc. A 370, 2960–2986 (2012)

17. Abler WL, *On the particulate principle of self-diversifying systems.* Journal of Social and Biological Structures Vol 12, Issue 1, (1989)

18. Ganapathiraju M et al, *Computational Biology and Language.* Lecture Notes, Computer Science, (2004)

19. Cholin J, Schiller NO, Levelt WJM, *The preparation of syllables in speech production.* Journal of Memory and Language, Vol 50, (2004)

20. Cervatiuc A, *ESL vocabulary acquisition: Target and approach.* The Internet TESL Journal, vol. 14, no. 1, (2008).

21. Author's unpublished research on Japanese and English syllable length, (2018)

22. Pellegrino F, Coupé C and Marsico E, *A cross-language perspective on speech information rate.* Language Vol. 87, No. 3 (2011)

23. Milestone Technologies, *What were the Morse requirements?* FAQ, (2009)

24. Ladefoged P and Maddieson I, *Sounds of the World's Language.* Blackwell (1996)

25. Maddieson I, *Updating UPSID.* UCLA Working Papers in Phonetics 74,(1990).

26. Schlenker P et al, *Formal monkey linguistics.* Theoretical Linguistics, Vol. 42, No. 1-2, pp. 173-201 (2016)

27. Ouattara, K et al, *Campbell's monkeys concatenate vocalizations into context-specific call sequences.* PNAS 106 (51) 22026-22031 (2009)

28. Collier K, Bickel B, van Schaik CP, Manser MB and Townsend SW. *Language evolution: syntax before phonology?* Proc Biol Sci. 281(1788):20140263 (2014)

29. Engesser S et al, *Experimental Evidence for Phonemic Contrasts in a Nonhuman Vocal System.* PLOS Biology (2015)

30. Nowak M et al, *An error limit for the evolution of language.* 266 Proceedings of the Royal Society of London. Series B: Biological Sciences (1999)

31. Ehret C, *Reconstructing Proto-Afroasiatic (Proto-Afrasian): vowels, tone, consonants, and vocabulary.* University of California Press (1995)

32. Atkinson Q, *Phonemic Diversity Supports a Serial Founder Effect Model of Language Expansion from Africa.* Science (New York, N.Y.) 332. pp. 346-9 (2011)

33. Fleming L, *Phoneme inventory size and the transition from monoplanar to dually patterned speech.* Journal of Language Evolution, Vol 2(1) pp 52–66 (2017)

34. Wichmann S et al, *Phonological diversity, word length, and population sizes across languages: The ASJP evidence.* Linguistic Typology 15: pp. 177–197 (2011)

35. Haiman J, *Ideophones and the Evolution of Language.* Cambridge: CUP (2018)

36. Everett D, *How language began: The story of humanity's greatest invention* New York: W. W. Norton (2017)
37. Pagel M, *Wired for Culture: The Natural History of Human Cooperation* Allen Lane (2012)
38. Kurzweil R, *The Law of Accelerating Returns* Essay (2001)
39. Mattson MP, *Superior pattern processing is the essence of the evolved human brain.* Front Neuroscience. 2014;8:265. (2014)
40. Shultz S et al, *Hominin cognitive evolution.* Philosophical Transactions of Royal Society of London. Series B, Biological Sciences 367 (1599): 2130–40. (2012)
41. Bozek K et al, *Evolutionary divergence of human muscle and brain metabolomes parallels human cognitive and physical uniqueness.* PLoS Biology (2014)

Further Reading

During the course of writing this book, I have turned to many authors for information, inspiration, consolation and confirmation. The following is a short selection of some of the works I have found useful – both in shaping the overall arc of my argument and in helping me feel the project was worth persevering with. If you're interested in exploring the background to my thinking, take your pick. They're all good.

Attenborough, Sir David: *Life on Earth*
Aurelius, Marcus: *Meditations*
Balcombe, Jonathan: *What a Fish Knows*
Ball, Philip: *Critical Mass*
Blackmore, Susan: *The Meme Machine*
Burling, Robbins: *The Talking Ape*
Boyer, Pascal: *Religion Explained*
Bryson, Bill: *A Short History of Everything*
Caitlin, George: *North American Indians*
Campbell, Joseph: *The Hero with A Thousand Faces*
Carnie, Jamie: *Blue Sky Thoughts*
Cheney & Seyfarth: *Baboon Metaphysics*
Cohn, Norman: *In Search of The Millennium*
Confucius: *The Analects*
Dali, Salvador: *The Secret Life of Salvador Dali*
Darwin, Charles: *The Descent of Man*
Dawkins, Richard: *The Blind Watchmaker*
Dennett, Daniel: *Breaking the Spell*
De Wall, Frans: *Our Inner Ape*
Diamond, Jared: *Guns, Germs and Steel*
Dickens, Charles: *A Tale of Two Cities*
Dostoevsky, Fyodor: *Notes From The Underground*
Eagleman, David: *Incognito*
Eames, Charles & Ray: *Powers of Ten*

Evans, Vyvyan: *The Language Myth*
Everett, Dan: *Don't Sleep There Are Snakes*
Feiling, Tom: *The Candy Machine*
Frazer, Sir James: *The Golden Bough*
Freud, Sigmund: *Civilisation and Its Discontents*
Gibran, Khalil: *The Prophet*
Gladwell, Malcolm: *Blink*
Godfrey-Smith, Peter: *Other Minds*
Gribbin, John: *Deep Simplicity*
Harari, Yuval: *Sapiens*
Herodotus: *The Histories*
Herrigel, Eugen: *Zen in the Art of Archery*
Hesse, Herman: *The Glass Bead Game*
Hicks, Bill: *Love All The People*
Horowitz & Bowers: *Zoobiquity*
Huxley, Aldous: *Island*
James, William: *The Varieties of Religious Experience*
Kaku, Michio: *Einstein's Cosmos*
Keller, Helen: *The World I Live In*
Kline, Morris: *Mathematics in Western Culture*
Koestler, Arthur: *The Yogi and The Commissar*
Keeley, Lawrence: *War Before Civilization*
Kurzweil, Ray: *How to Create a Mind*
Lane, Nick: *The Vital Question*
Lao Tsu: *Tao Te Ching*
Leary, Timothy: *The Politics of Ecstasy*
Levitin, Daniel: *This is Your Brain on Music*
Mandelbrot, Benoit: *The Fractal Geometry of Nature*
Marx & Engels: *The Communist Manifesto*
McLuhan, Marshall: *The Gutenberg Galaxy*
Montgomery, Sy: *The Soul of an Octopus*
Morgan, Elaine: *The Descent of Woman*
Morris, Desmond: *The Naked Ape*
Morris, Jan: *Conundrum*

Nietzsche, Friedrich: *Beyond Good and Evil*
Ono, Yoko: *Grapefruit*
Orwell, George: *Keep the Aspidistra Flying*
Pagel, Mark: *Wired for Culture*
Pearson, Karl: *The Grammar of Science*
Pinker, Steven: *Enlightenment Now*
Plato: *The Republic*
Reich, Wilhelm: *The Sexual Revolution*
Reps, Paul: *Zen Flesh, Zen Bones*
Ridley, Matt: *The Origins of Virtue*
Ronson, Jon: *Them*
Said, Edward: *Orientalism*
Savage-Rumbaugh, Sue: *Kanzi*
Sacks, Oliver: *Musicophilia*
Sagan, Carl: *Cosmos*
Schaller, Susan: *A Man Without Words*
Schrödinger, Erwin: *What Is Life?*
Shubin, Neil: *Your Inner Fish*
Sterne, Laurence: *Tristam Shandy*
Stevens, Jay: *Storming Heaven*
Stravinsky, Igor: *Themes and Conclusions*
Surowiecki, James: *The Wisdom of Crowds*
Swift, Jonathan: *The Tale of a Tub*
Thompson, Hunter: *Fear and Loathing in Las Vegas*
Vincent, Nora: *Self Made Man*
Watson, Ben: *Art, Class and Cleavage*
Wells, H.G.: *The World Brain*
Wilhelm, Richard: *The I Ching*
Wilkinson & Pickett: *The Spirit Level*
Wolfe, Tom: *The Kingdom of Speech*
Wrangham, Richard: *Demonic Males*
Yü, Li: *Jou Pu Tuan*
Zappa, Frank: *The Output Macrostructure*

About the Author

Author photo by Tina Prentis

Simon Prentis was born in England in 1953. Initially accepted to study Chemistry at Oxford University, he graduated in 1978 with an MA in English Language and Literature before travelling to Japan to study Aikido. There he taught English and began studying Japanese while training for his black belt – gaining an RSA Diploma in TEFL along the way, and completing a course at Simul Academy, Japan's premier interpreting school. After returning to the UK in 1986 he was recruited to present a Japanese-language satellite news service for NHK, Japan's national broadcaster – but left after two years in front of the camera to set up his own bilingual production company. Over the next 25 years he travelled the world working on more than 250 programmes for Japanese television, while continuing to work as a freelance translator and interpreter for a select clientele – about which you can discover more on his website: www.simonprentis.net

He has three children and lives with his wife in West London.

Manufactured by Amazon.ca
Bolton, ON